BESTSELLING
BOOK SERIES

Active Server Pages For Dummies, 2nd Edition

Cheat Sheet

Server Objects

Created automatically and exists throughout the life of your applica...

Server Object

CreateObject method: Used to create server components like the A...... ....
Not to be confused with VBScript command, also named CreateObject. VBScript CreateObject is used to create scripting objects like the Dictionary and the FileSystemObject.

Request Object

Cookie collection: Access the value of a cookie.

```
UserName = Request.Cookie("UserInfo")("UserName")
```

Form collection: Access information submitted from a form.

```
Email = Request.Form("Email")
```

QueryString collection: Access information passed on the URL line from another page. Works like Form collection.

Shortcut: Access Form or QueryString collections directly:

```
ItemNum = Request("ItemNum")
```

Response Object

Cookie collection: Create and change user's cookie.

```
Response.Cookie("UserInfo")("UserName") = "Fred Smith"
```

Redirect method: Automatically changes the page to the passed URL. **Write** method: Passed HTML string is written to the page. **Buffer** property: Determines whether the page is sent as it is created (false, the default) or if the page must be completely created before it is sent out (true).

Dictionary

Holds paired values as *Keys* and *Items*; both are strings. See "What's a Dictionary? Look It Up!" in Chapter 6.

Add method: Pass Key and Item. Adds the new pair to the dictionary. **Item** property: Returns or sets the Item associated with the Key you pass. **Remove** method: Removes a Key/Item pair from the Dictionary.

For Dummies®: Bestselling Book Series for Beginners

Active Server Pages For Dummies, 2nd Edition

Important Scripting Objects

Create using VBScript's `CreateObject` function or JScript's `new` function. See Chapter 6.

FileSystemObject

Provides access to the drives, folders, and files on the web server. See "The FileSystemObject and Its Drives, Folders and Files" in Chapter 6.

CopyFile, MoveFile, CopyFolder, MoveFolder methods: Copy or move a file or folder from one location to another. **CreateFolder** method: Creates a new folder. **DeleteFile, DeleteFolder** methods: Delete the file or folder you specify. **DriveExists, FolderExists, FileExists** methods: Allows you to check to see if item specified exists. **GetDrive, GetFolder, GetFile** methods: Get Drive, Folder, and File objects specified.

TextStream

Used to create, access, modify, and append information to text files. See "Islands in the TextStream" in Chapter 6.

CreateTextFile method: Creates and opens a text file. **OpenTextFile** method: Opens existing text file to read or append. **Write/WriteLine** method: Writes string to a file. **Read/ReadLine:** Reads string from a file. **ReadAll:** Reads the entire file into a string. **AtEndOfStream** property: Contains true at the end of the file. **AtEndOfLine** property: Contains true at the end of a line. **Close** method: Closes file.

Application and Session Objects

Session variables: Created when it is first assigned a value. Exists for as long as the user is on your site. Can hold data between pages.

Application variables: Created when it is first assigned a value. One Application variable exists for the entire application — across all sessions. Holds application-level information, such as page hits. Can also pass or share information between sessions.

Application **Lock** and **Unlock** methods: Whenever an Application variable is modified, call Lock before and Unlock after. Assures that only one session changes the information at a time.

IDG BOOKS WORLDWIDE

For Dummies®: Bestselling Book Series for Beginners

TM

References for the Rest of Us!®

BESTSELLING BOOK SERIES

Are you intimidated and confused by computers? Do you find that traditional manuals are overloaded with technical details you'll never use? Do your friends and family always call you to fix simple problems on their PCs? Then the *...For Dummies®* computer book series from IDG Books Worldwide is for you.

...For Dummies books are written for those frustrated computer users who know they aren't really dumb but find that PC hardware, software, and indeed the unique vocabulary of computing make them feel helpless. *...For Dummies* books use a lighthearted approach, a down-to-earth style, and even cartoons and humorous icons to dispel computer novices' fears and build their confidence. Lighthearted but not lightweight, these books are a perfect survival guide for anyone forced to use a computer.

> *"I like my copy so much I told friends; now they bought copies."*
>
> — *Irene C., Orwell, Ohio*

> *"Quick, concise, nontechnical, and humorous."*
>
> — *Jay A., Elburn, Illinois*

> *"Thanks, I needed this book. Now I can sleep at night."*
>
> — *Robin F., British Columbia, Canada*

Already, millions of satisfied readers agree. They have made *...For Dummies* books the #1 introductory level computer book series and have written asking for more. So, if you're looking for the most fun and easy way to learn about computers, look to *...For Dummies* books to give you a helping hand.

IDG
BOOKS
WORLDWIDE

Active Server Pages

FOR

DUMMIES®

2ND EDITION

Active Server Pages

FOR DUMMIES®

2ND EDITION

by Bill Hatfield

IDG Books Worldwide, Inc.
An International Data Group Company

Foster City, CA ◆ Chicago, IL ◆ Indianapolis, IN ◆ New York, NY

Active Server Pages For Dummies®, 2nd Edition

Published by
IDG Books Worldwide, Inc.
An International Data Group Company
919 E. Hillsdale Blvd.
Suite 400
Foster City, CA 94404
www.idgbooks.com (IDG Books Worldwide Web site)
www.dummies.com (Dummies Press Web site)

Library of Congress Catalog Card No.: 99-65842

ISBN: 0-7645-0603-X

Printed in the United States of America

10 9 8 7 6 5

2B/RY/RQ/QQ/IN

Distributed in the United States by IDG Books Worldwide, Inc.

Distributed by CDG Books Canada Inc. for Canada; by Transworld Publishers Limited in the United Kingdom; by IDG Norge Books for Norway; by IDG Sweden Books for Sweden; by IDG Books Australia Publishing Corporation Pty. Ltd. for Australia and New Zealand; by TransQuest Publishers Pte Ltd. for Singapore, Malaysia, Thailand, Indonesia, and Hong Kong; by Gotop Information Inc. for Taiwan; by ICG Muse, Inc. for Japan; by Norma Comunicaciones S.A. for Colombia; by Intersoft for South Africa; by Eyrolles for France; by International Thomson Publishing for Germany, Austria and Switzerland; by Distribuidora Cuspide for Argentina; by LR International for Brazil; by Galileo Libros for Chile; by Ediciones ZETA S.C.R. Ltda. for Peru; by WS Computer Publishing Corporation, Inc., for the Philippines; by Contemporanea de Ediciones for Venezuela; by Express Computer Distributors for the Caribbean and West Indies; by Micronesia Media Distributor, Inc. for Micronesia; by Grupo Editorial Norma S.A. for Guatemala; by Chips Computadoras S.A. de C.V. for Mexico; by Editorial Norma de Panama S.A. for Panama; by American Bookshops for Finland. Authorized Sales Agent: Anthony Rudkin Associates for the Middle East and North Africa.

For general information on IDG Books Worldwide's books in the U.S., please call our Consumer Customer Service department at 800-762-2974. For reseller information, including discounts and premium sales, please call our Reseller Customer Service department at 800-434-3422.

For information on where to purchase IDG Books Worldwide's books outside the U.S., please contact our International Sales department at 317-572-3993 or fax 317-572-4002.

For consumer information on foreign language translations, please contact our Customer Service department at 1-800-434-3422, fax 317-572-4002, or e-mail rights@idgbooks.com.

For information on licensing foreign or domestic rights, please phone +1-650-653-7098.

For sales inquiries and special prices for bulk quantities, please contact our Order Services department at 800-434-3422 or write to the address above.

For information on using IDG Books Worldwide's books in the classroom or for ordering examination copies, please contact our Educational Sales department at 800-434-2086 or fax 317-572-4005.

For press review copies, author interviews, or other publicity information, please contact our Public Relations department at 650-653-7000 or fax 650-653-7500.

For authorization to photocopy items for corporate, personal, or educational use, please contact Copyright Clearance Center, 222 Rosewood Drive, Danvers, MA 01923, or fax 978-750-4470.

About the Author

Bill Hatfield is the bestselling author of several computer books, including IDG Books Worldwides' *Visual InterDev For Dummies* and *Creating Cool VBScript Web Pages*. He is also the editor of *ActiveWeb Developer,* a technical journal for professional Web developers using Microsoft technologies. He works as the Internet Practice Manager for InfoTech Consulting in Indianapolis, Indiana.

ABOUT IDG BOOKS WORLDWIDE

Welcome to the world of IDG Books Worldwide.

IDG Books Worldwide, Inc., is a subsidiary of International Data Group, the world's largest publisher of computer-related information and the leading global provider of information services on information technology. IDG was founded more than 30 years ago by Patrick J. McGovern and now employs more than 9,000 people worldwide. IDG publishes more than 290 computer publications in over 75 countries. More than 90 million people read one or more IDG publications each month.

Launched in 1990, IDG Books Worldwide is today the #1 publisher of best-selling computer books in the United States. We are proud to have received eight awards from the Computer Press Association in recognition of editorial excellence and three from Computer Currents' First Annual Readers' Choice Awards. Our best-selling ...*For Dummies*® series has more than 50 million copies in print with translations in 31 languages. IDG Books Worldwide, through a joint venture with IDG's Hi-Tech Beijing, became the first U.S. publisher to publish a computer book in the People's Republic of China. In record time, IDG Books Worldwide has become the first choice for millions of readers around the world who want to learn how to better manage their businesses.

Our mission is simple: Every one of our books is designed to bring extra value and skill-building instructions to the reader. Our books are written by experts who understand and care about our readers. The knowledge base of our editorial staff comes from years of experience in publishing, education, and journalism — experience we use to produce books to carry us into the new millennium. In short, we care about books, so we attract the best people. We devote special attention to details such as audience, interior design, use of icons, and illustrations. And because we use an efficient process of authoring, editing, and desktop publishing our books electronically, we can spend more time ensuring superior content and less time on the technicalities of making books.

You can count on our commitment to deliver high-quality books at competitive prices on topics you want to read about. At IDG Books Worldwide, we continue in the IDG tradition of delivering quality for more than 30 years. You'll find no better book on a subject than one from IDG Books Worldwide.

John Kilcullen
Chairman and CEO
IDG Books Worldwide, Inc.

Eighth Annual
Computer Press
Awards ≥1992

Ninth Annual
Computer Press
Awards ≥1993

Tenth Annual
Computer Press
Awards ≥1994

Eleventh Annual
Computer Press
Awards ≥1995

IDG is the world's leading IT media, research and exposition company. Founded in 1964, IDG had 1997 revenues of $2.05 billion and has more than 9,000 employees worldwide. IDG offers the widest range of media options that reach IT buyers in 75 countries representing 95% of worldwide IT spending. IDG's diverse product and services portfolio spans six key areas including print publishing, online publishing, expositions and conferences, market research, education and training, and global marketing services. More than 90 million people read one or more of IDG's 290 magazines and newspapers, including IDG's leading global brands — Computerworld, PC World, Network World, Macworld and the Channel World family of publications. IDG Books Worldwide is one of the fastest-growing computer book publishers in the world, with more than 700 titles in 36 languages. The "...For Dummies®" series alone has more than 50 million copies in print. IDG offers online users the largest network of technology-specific Web sites around the world through IDG.net (http://www.idg.net), which comprises more than 225 targeted Web sites in 55 countries worldwide. International Data Corporation (IDC) is the world's largest provider of information technology data, analysis and consulting, with research centers in over 41 countries and more than 400 research analysts worldwide. IDG World Expo is a leading producer of more than 168 globally branded conferences and expositions in 35 countries including E3 (Electronic Entertainment Expo), Macworld Expo, ComNet, Windows World Expo, ICE (Internet Commerce Expo), Agenda, DEMO, and Spotlight. IDG's training subsidiary, ExecuTrain, is the world's largest computer training company, with more than 230 locations worldwide and 785 training courses. IDG Marketing Services helps industry-leading IT companies build international brand recognition by developing global integrated marketing programs via IDG's print, online and exposition products worldwide. Further information about the company can be found at www.idg.com.

1/26/00

Dedication

This book is dedicated to those who took time out of their busy schedule several times each day to come up to my room and visit. To Tiger, Frisky, and Coco. Your distractions are what kept me sane.

Acknowledgments

Many thanks to Greg Croy, acquisitions editor; Nicole Haims, project editor; Jerelind Charles, copy editor; and all the rest of the IDG staff that helped make this book possible. Thanks also to my technical editor, Greg Guntle, for his thoroughness and thoughtful suggestions.

Thanks to my wife whose patience with me as I dove into this project has been beyond the call of duty. I work well under deadlines, but I'm pretty sure I'm not much fun to be around. I love you, Melanie. . . .

Thanks to my parents for being there to talk to and share my excitement and to act as both a pressure valve and a reality check.

Thanks to my friends: Brad, Mike, Curtis, Dee, Elizabeth and Stephanie. Time with friends like these are what make it all worthwhile!

And to my new friends and mentors at InfoTech (or whatever its name is now . . . Doug, Tom and Tim. Thanks for fun times and lots of new experiences.

Publisher's Acknowledgments

We're proud of this book; please register your comments through our IDG Books Worldwide Online Registration Form located at http://my2cents.dummies.com.

Some of the people who helped bring this book to market include the following:

Acquisitions, Editorial, and Media Development

Project Editor: Nicole Haims
(Previous Edition: Bill Helling)

Acquisitions Editor: Greg Croy

Copy Editor: Jerelind Charles
(Previous Edition: Elizabeth Netedu Kuball)

Technical Editor: Greg Guntle

Media Development Editor: Marita Ellixson

Permissions Editor: Carmen Krikorian

Editorial Manager: Rev Mengle

Media Development Manager: Megan Roney, Heather Heath Dismore

Editorial Assistant: Jamila Pree

Production

Project Coordinator: Maridee V. Ennis

Layout and Graphics: Amy M. Adrian, Angela F. Hunckler, Kate Jenkins, Barry Offringa, Douglas L. Rollison, Brent Savage, Jacque Schneider, Janet Seib, Michael A. Sullivan, Brian Torwelle, Mary Jo Weis

Proofreaders: Christine Pingleton, Nancy Price

Indexer: Rebecca Plunkett

General and Administrative

IDG Books Worldwide, Inc.: John Kilcullen, CEO; Bill Barry, President and COO; John Ball, Executive VP, Operations & Administration; John Harris, CFO

IDG Books Technology Publishing Group: Richard Swadley, Senior Vice President and Publisher; Mary Bednarek, Vice President and Publisher; Walter R. Bruce III, Vice President and Publisher; Joseph Wikert, Vice President and Publisher; Mary C. Corder, Editorial Director; Andy Cummings, Publishing Director, General User Group; Barry Pruett, Publishing Director

IDG Books Manufacturing: Ivor Parker, Vice President, Manufacturing

IDG Books Marketing: John Helmus, Assistant Vice President, Director of Marketing

IDG Books Online Management: Brenda McLaughlin, Executive Vice President, Chief Internet Officer; Gary Millrood, Executive Vice President of Business Development, Sales and Marketing

IDG Books Packaging: Marc J. Mikulich, Vice President, Brand Strategy and Research

IDG Books Production for Branded Press: Debbie Stailey, Production Director

IDG Books Sales: Roland Elgey, Senior Vice President, Sales and Marketing; Michael Violano, Vice President, International Sales and Sub Rights

◆

The publisher would like to give special thanks to Patrick J. McGovern, without whom this book would not have been possible.

◆

Contents at a Glance

Cartoons at a Glance

By Rich Tennant

The 5th Wave — By Rich Tennant

"Hold on, that's not a problem with the ASP scripting, it's just a booger on the screen."

page 105

The 5th Wave — By Rich Tennant

"We're researching Active Server Page applications that move massive amounts of information across binary pathways that interact with free-agent programs capable of making decisions and performing logical tasks. We see applications in really high-end doorbells."

page 313

The 5th Wave — By Rich Tennant

"Do you want me to help you name your Open Database Connectivity DSN, or do you have your own idea of what to call it?"

page 207

The 5th Wave — By Rich Tennant

ROOM 101

"I failed her in algebra but was impressed with the way she used Boolean variables with If...Then conditions on her Active Server Pages."

page 31

The 5th Wave — By Rich Tennant

"I'll tell you this—retraining them away from static HTML pages isn't going to be easy. Do you know how old some of these dogs are?"

page 9

The 5th Wave — By Rich Tennant

"It happened around the time we started creating that real-time chat room using ASP."

page 241

The 5th Wave — By Rich Tennant

IF BOB DYLAN HAD PURSUED A CAREER IN COMPUTERS

"He's a genius integrating databases into his Active Server Pages, but don't ask him to explain it, you won't understand a word he says."

page 291

Fax: 978-546-7747
E-mail: richtennant@the5thwave.com
World Wide Web: www.the5thwave.com

Table of Contents

. . . .

Introduction

● ●

*W*elcome to *Active Server Pages For Dummies,* 2nd Edition! This book shows you how to make your Web pages come alive and interact with the people that visit your Web site. And the best news is that you can do it all without having to learn mysterious and complex computer languages or dedicating a large portion of your life to your Web site!

If you are developing a Web site on Windows NT, using Internet Information Server (IIS), then you discover how to use one of IIS's most exciting features to create truly outstanding Web sites.

But even if you're running Windows 95 and Personal Web Server (PWS) for a small Web or intranet site, you can still take advantage of all the features Active Server Pages has to offer.

I Know Who You Are. . . .

If you've picked this book up off the shelf and are flipping through it, I can make some pretty good guesses about the kind of person you may be.

- ✔ You may be a Web site or intranet developer for a company.
- ✔ You may be an individual who has a personal or small business Web site.
- ✔ You may be a programmer who wants to get in on all the hot new technologies.

In any case, you're probably looking for ways to make your job easier and your Web site a lot cooler. I'd guess that

- ✔ You know how to use Windows NT or Windows 95/98 and you know how to use your web server software — either Internet Information Server (IIS) or Personal Web Server (PWS), at least well enough to get around.
- ✔ You're familiar with HTML and have played around with some advanced tags and maybe even other technologies like CGI or ISAPI.
- ✔ You've had at least a little exposure to a scripting language like VBScript, JavaScript, Perl, or REXX.

- ✔ You may have worked with a macro language such as you'd find in a spreadsheet or other application.
- ✔ You may have actually done some programming in Java, Visual Basic, C, or COBOL.

Don't worry. To get the most out of this book, you certainly don't have to be a programmer, and you don't even have to be an HTML guru. In fact, Active Server Pages makes activating your Web site easy.

Why Active Server Pages?

Active Server Pages makes it possible to use all the power of a real computer language right in your Web page. You don't have to write complicated C code to interface with the web server and then compile it into an executable or DLL file. All you have to do is create your HTML page, just like you normally would, but then put your programming code right alongside the HTML so that they work *together*. And that's it! No compiling, no complex interfacing, nothing!

This makes it easier for programmers and non-programmers alike to update a Web site as things change. Just bring up the page in your favorite HTML editor, make changes to the HTML and the code, and then save it out again. It's ready to go.

ASP backwards

You may think it's odd that I keep saying things like "Active Server Pages *makes* it possible. . . ." Shouldn't it be "Active Server Pages *make* it possible. . . ."? It certainly sounds better.

I wondered too, so I made a pilgrimage to the English Gurus and this is what they told me: Because the phrase "Active Server Pages" refers to a single technology, it is singular and takes a singular verb.

I've noticed that it doesn't sound so weird if I say something like "ASP makes it possible. . . .", so I often use the abbreviation when I'm referring to the technology.

By the way, ASP can be pronounced by saying each of the three letters (like FBI or CIA), or simply by saying *asp* (like the snake).

How This Book Is Organized

This book is divided into seven parts and each part is divided into several different chapters. Each chapter is further broken down into individual sections. The book explores the basics first and then moves on to the tougher stuff. But that doesn't mean you have to read it in order. Feel free to skip around or jump right to a section that has the answer to your specific question. But if you get confused when reading, that may be a sign that you need to go back and pick up some of the topics discussed earlier in the book.

Here's a list of the seven major parts and what is discussed in each.

Part I: Getting Started

Part I describes what Active Server Pages is and shows you how it fits into the world of CGI, ISAPI, ActiveX controls, and all the other Internet stuff that promises to make your Web site newer, better, and more exciting.

In this part, you also figure out how to set up your computer so that you can start creating your own Active Server Pages. You even create your very first ASP page.

Part II: Speaking Like a Native

Before you can use a programming language to enhance your HTML pages, you have to know a programming language. That's what Part II is all about. Here you're introduced to VBScript, Visual Basic's little brother. Never written a full-blown computer program before? Don't worry! VBScript is probably the easiest programming language in the world. It won't bite. I promise.

On the other hand, if you're already familiar with programming using C, C++, Java, JavaScript, or Perl, you'll probably find JScript (the Microsoft implementation of JavaScript) an easier language to learn than VBScript. For you, I have written a special chapter that gives you the quick once-over you'll need to begin writing ASP pages with JScript. Both VBScript and JScript have exactly the same capabilities and are completely interchangeable when creating ASP pages. So either way, you'll be ready to jump right in.

However, when I show examples throughout the rest of this book, I don't really want to show two listings every single time, so this is what I do:

If you already know C, C++, Java, or JavaScript, chances are you have some programming experience under your belt. And I'd be willing to bet that if I showed you an example of code in VBScript, you'd probably be able to figure out what the corresponding JScript code would be.

With that in mind, I do all of my examples in VBScript. This strategy works for all those who are new to programming and using VBScript. Those of you with more programming experience can translate. In fairness, though, if any code is significantly different in JScript, I make note of it and show you the code both ways. Fair enough?

Part III: Getting to Know Your Objects

The ability to use If..Then statements and loops in your HTML is nice, but if you can't get information about the server, the browser, or the person using the browser, then most of that power is going to waste! Part III shows you how to use objects that are a part of your web server to get all sorts of information and to change the way things work. It also shows you how to take server components that you or others create and integrate them with your ASP pages. Ah, the sweet taste of power!

You also begin to discover how all of this power can be put to use in the real world. In Chapter 8, I show you how to create a Guest Book, user-selected background music for your Web site, a personalized Welcome page, and more.

Part IV: Accessing the Database

One of the hottest topics today is accessing database information from a Web page. From corporate intranets to home shopping, everyone wants to know how to do it. In Part IV, you discover how to retrieve information and display it in a table, as well as how to add, update, and delete records in a database from your own ASP pages.

Part V: Really Cool ASP Applications

All of these new capabilities are interesting by themselves. But what's really interesting is what happens after you start to pull together the capabilities to create real Web applications. In Part V, I demonstrate two complete applications that I've written and included on the CD-ROM in the back of the book: a chat room and a classified ads site. I show you all the cool stuff I did to make these applications work so that you can take them and customize them to use in your own Web site.

Part VI: The Part of Tens

The ...*For Dummies* series of books always includes several chapters at the end that provide lists of ten items each, on all sorts of useful topics. Flipping back to The Part of Tens before you read the rest of the book is a little like eating dessert before the main course. I highly recommend it.

Part VII: Appendixes

Here you discover a development environment for Web site creation that could make your ASP development life a lot easier — Microsoft Visual InterDev. In addition, you can find a primer on relational database basics as well as step-by-step instructions on using Microsoft Access. You'll also be happy to find troubleshooting information, which can help you figure out some of the common problems people run into when they begin working with ASP. Finally, you discover all the cool stuff on the CD-ROM, how to install it, and how to use it.

ASP Me (No) Questions. . . .

If you want to send me feedback about the book, I'd love to hear from you! My e-mail address is

```
billhatfield@edgequest.com
```

My Web site is at

```
www.edgequest.com
```

And for a Web site completely dedicated to this book, check out

```
www.edgequest.com/ASPDummies
```

Here you find cool ASP applications, the latest book corrections, news, and links to other great ASP sites.

Help! It Doesn't Work!

If you run into any problems while reading this book, I've included Appendix D for all your troubleshooting needs. It answers many of the common problems folks run into when they get started with ASP.

But I can't address everything in one appendix. And I'm discovering new gotcha's all the time. So if you don't find the answer to your problems in Appendix D, go to the Frequently Asked ASP/Visual InterDev Questions section of my Web site:

```
www.edgequest.com/VIDFD/QnA.htm
```

At the site, you find additional questions and answers that have come up since this edition of the book was published.

Finally, if you still need more help, Chapter 14 lists the Ten Best Places to Look When You Have a Question. From books and magazines to newsgroups, user groups and ASP nerds, you have lots of options out there!

On the CD

The CD located in the back of this book includes all the big example pages throughout this book. It also has several other interesting things that will help you develop ASP pages more effectively.

Go ahead and install the CD on your computer so that you are ready to go. You can read all about the CD's contents, the system requirements, and the installation instructions in Appendix D.

Margin Icons

Sometimes I get carried away and go off on a tangent about some technical bit of trivia that is completely unessential to the topic at hand. But don't worry. If I do, I label it with this icon so that you know you can safely skip over it, if you want.

A quick idea or technique that will make your life a little better.

If you see this icon, always read and follow the accompanying directions. These important bits of information can keep you from having a very bad day.

If I'm exploring a new topic, I always enjoy it more if I can actually try it out while I'm reading. So I've included lots and lots of little examples throughout the book for you to try. When you see this icon, don't just read it — do it!

Sometimes things just don't work the way any normal, rational person would expect them to work. And it's those goofy things that trip you up every time. When you see this icon, watch for weirdness ahead.

This icon points to features you can find on the companion CD.

Part I
Getting Started

In this part . . .

To get you off on the right foot, these two chapters introduce Active Server Pages, describe how they work, and what kinds of problems they solve. After you've gotten your bearings, you are ready to dig in and try creating an ASP page of your own. This first project creates a small but interesting page and, most importantly, it shows you a process that you can use to create and test your own pages as you continue through the rest of this book.

Chapter 1

So What's an Active Server Page?

*W*hat's the big deal about ASP? It doesn't really let you do anything you couldn't already do before, right? So why bother learning yet another new thing? There are way too many new things to figure out already!

To answer these questions, in this chapter I show you what your non-ASP options are for creating interactive Web pages. Then I show you exactly what ASP is all about and how it works.

Boring, Dumb, Static HTML

Think about how a simple Web page works.

1. You click your favorite site's name under the Favorites menu in Internet Explorer — perhaps it's called "Lots Of Fun." (No, this isn't a real one. I just made it up.) The URL associated with "Lots Of Fun" is

   ```
   www.lotsoffun.com/default.htm
   ```

2. The browser looks for `lotsoffun.com` and finds the actual server machine on the Internet.

3. After it finds that machine, it requests that the machine send over the page named `default.htm`.

4. The server finds that page and sends it to the browser.

5. After the browser gets the page, it looks at what's inside. The browser reads all the HTML tags and then converts them into a beautiful (or ugly, as the case may be) formatted page.

This is how the World Wide Web was originally conceived. A pretty simple idea. But it provided for a very easy way to access information and gave the page designer quite a bit of flexibility in laying out a page.

Forms and CGI

But the communication for static HTML works only one way. There is no way to send information back to a web server. To fix this problem, *forms* and *CGI* were created. Forms are HTML tags that allow Web page creators to include controls like edits, check boxes, and radio buttons in their Web pages. That way, the user can enter information. Forms also provide a Submit button that sends the information off to the server.

But now the server has to be smarter, too. It can't just get requests for pages and send out pages. The server has to know what to do with this form information when it gets it. That's where CGI comes in.

CGI stands for *Common Gateway Interface*. CGI makes it possible for the web server to talk to another application that can handle the form information when it's sent back. Often these CGI applications are written in a language called Perl. When the CGI application receives the form information, it can save it to a text file, store it in a database, or do whatever else the Web site administrator wants it to do.

This system works great for simple guest books and the like. But if you want to make your Web pages really interactive, you may start running into trouble.

The problem with CGI is that if five people are submitting form information at the same time, five different copies of the CGI application have to be running on the server to handle them. If a hundred people are submitting form information at once — you guessed it! — a hundred copies of the application run at the same time. This is a great way to make a popular web server fall to its knees and crawl.

Server APIs

Because of the problems with CGI forms slowing everything down, *server APIs* were born. API stands for *Application Programming Interface*. The Microsoft server API is called *ISAPI*, which stands for the *Internet Server Application Programming Interface* (clever, no?).

Like CGI, ISAPI allows the web server to communicate with other applications running on the server machine. But ISAPI is much more efficient than CGI. It doesn't launch a separate program each time someone sends back information from a form. And ISAPI allows the application developer a lot more flexibility in how the server responds to the browser.

But ISAPI doesn't solve all the problems. You still have to write separate computer programs that have complex interfaces to your web server and that work closely with your Web pages. ISAPI isn't very intuitive, and it's difficult to create and maintain. Because of these problems, few businesses go to the trouble of creating truly engaging, interactive Web sites. Creating great Web sites with ISAPI just takes too much time, and most companies can't afford to dedicate a group of expensive programmers to the task of making their Web sites really, really cool.

Lofty ASPirations

Active Server Pages (ASP) solves all the problems associated with CGI and server APIs. In addition to being just as efficient as ISAPI applications, ASP is simple to learn and easy to use.

With CGI or ISAPI, you had to write a computer program in a language like Perl or C that had complex interface code connecting it to the server. Then you had to compile the application and associate it with the appropriate Web pages.

With ASP, you simply write your code in the HTML page itself. The HTML tags and the code are side by side. You write the code in a simple scripting language that is easy to learn and easy to use. Then you save the page to your Web site and it's ready to go. No compiling and no complex interfacing!

As you can imagine, ASP makes it much quicker and easier to create highly interactive Web sites. ASP also makes your pages easier to maintain and update in the future.

ASP as Easy as 1, 2, 3

So what happens when an ASP page is requested by the browser? It works like this:

1. You choose a Favorite or click a link in your browser to go to an ASP page (you can tell you're going to an ASP page because ASPs have an `.asp` extension, instead of an `.htm` or `.html` extension).

2. The web server locates the page and looks at it.

Say it again, with redundancy

You may notice that I occasionally refer to an "ASP page." You're probably saying to yourself, "Now wait a minute. Isn't that an Active Server Pages page?" My response: "Yup. It shore is."

You see, when I was on my pilgrimage to the English Gurus I asked them about the redundancy of "ASP page." This is what they said:

Because ASP refers to a technology, the phrase "Active Server Pages page" is, in fact, correct, and not redundant at all. The first "Page" is part of the phrase which describes the technology. The second "page" is the actual noun you're talking about. The Gurus never lie.

3. Because it is an ASP page, the web server executes the page. In other words, the server goes through the page looking for any code you have written and runs that code.

4. After the code runs, all the ASP code is stripped out of the page. A pure HTML page is all that is left.

5. The HTML page is sent to the browser.

This arrangement has lots of advantages:

✔ It is easy to write and maintain because the code and the page are together.

✔ The code is executed on the server, so that you have a lot of power and flexibility.

✔ The code is stripped out before it is sent to the browser, so that your proprietary applications can't be easily stolen.

✔ Because only pure HTML is sent back, it works with any browser running on any computer.

What Does an ASP Page Look Like?

If you're like me, you can only hear someone describe something for so long before you want to see it yourself. The code below shows you what a real, live ASP page looks like.

```
<html>
<head>
<title>My Home Page</title>
</head>
<body>
<h1>My Home Page</h1><p>
<% If Time >=  #12:00:00 AM# And _
     Time < #12:00:00 PM# Then %>
<h2>Good Morning! </h2><p>
<% ElseIf Time >= #12:00:00 PM# And _
     Time < #6:00:00 PM# Then %>
<h2>Good Afternoon! </h2><p>
<% Else %>
<h2>Good Evening! </h2><p>
<% End If %>
<h2>I'm happy you could stop by...</h2><p>
</body>
</html>
```

Most of this should look familiar. I identify a title for the page and use a first level head to display My Home Page at the top. But then comes the weird part. What are <% and %>? In ASP these are called *delimiters*. They set off the code from the rest of the HTML tags. That way you always know which is which. If it is inside the delimiters, you know it's code. Otherwise, it's got to be HTML.

It's not too hard to guess how this page works, even if you haven't done much computer programming. This code is written in VBScript and is very English-like. Time is a VBScript function that returns the current time (on the server's system clock).

So first I check to see if the time is between 12:00 a.m. and 12:00 p.m. If it is, the HTML after the Then is sent back to the browser:

```
<h2>Good Morning! </h2><p>
```

The next line is a continuation of the If..Then statement. It begins ElseIf. In other words, "If that didn't work, try this." The line checks to see if the time is after 12:00 p.m. and before 6:00 p.m. If it is, this HTML is sent back to the browser:

```
<h2>Good Afternoon! </h2><p>
```

Finally, Else is a catch-all. If none of the other conditions worked, send this HTML back to the browser:

```
<h2>Good Evening! </h2><p>
```

A note for client-side scripters

If you've written client-side scripts in VBScript or JavaScript, you're used to seeing code in a Web page that looks like this:

```
<HTML>
<SCRIPT LANGUAGE="VBScript">
<!--
Dim Net, Gross, Tax  ' Create
    three variables
Gross = 30000      ' Gross income
Tax = 4000          ' Taxes owed
Net = Gross - Tax  ' What's
    left...?
```

```
-->
</SCRIPT>
</HTML>
```

The SCRIPT tag isn't generally used when you create server-side scripts. The <% and %> delimiters are much more convenient.

Also note that you don't need to use the HTML comments (<!-- and -->) around the scripting code. ASP code is processed on the server and is stripped out before it is sent to the browser.

The End If lets you know that the If..Then statement is over. The next line of HTML is displayed, no matter how the If..Then condition worked out:

```
<h2>I'm happy you could stop by...</h2><p>
```

Notice that five lines of HTML are in the page. The first and last are always displayed. But only one of the middle three is displayed, depending on the time. Suppose the time is 7:00 p.m. and you go to this page. Your screen would look like Figure 1-1.

If you chose View⇨Source from the Internet Explorer menu, you'd see the HTML below.

```
<html>
<head>
<title>My Home Page</title>
</head>
<body>
<h1>My Home Page</h1><p>

<h2>Good Evening! </h2><p>

<h2>I'm happy you could stop by...</h2><p>

</body>
</html>
```

Figure 1-1:
The page at
7:00 p.m.

As you can see, all the VBScript code has been stripped out. And only the appropriate HTML line in the If..Then statement was sent. From looking at this, you'd have no idea that this was anything more than a simple HTML page that always says Good Evening!

For more information on If..Then and all the other VBScript commands, see Chapters 3 and 4.

How Is ASP Different from Client-Side Scripting?

You've probably seen all the books on the market teaching JavaScript and VBScript. How are these different from ASP?

Before ASP, you could use JavaScript and VBScript in your Web pages to do *client-side* scripting. Client-side refers to the browser and the machine running the browser, as opposed to *server-side* where the web server is running. ASP is a way of doing server-side scripting.

Client-side scripting works a little differently:

1. You choose a Favorite or click a link in your browser to go to an HTML page that includes client-side scripting code.

2. The web server locates the page and sends it back to the browser.

3. The browser interprets the HTML tags and, at the same time, executes any client-side scripting code that it comes upon.

4. Some code isn't executed immediately — it waits until the user does something like clicking a button before it runs.

Client-side scripting and server-side scripting are similar in that they both allow you to write code right alongside your HTML and have that code executed when the page is requested. And often you can do the same thing using either client-side scripts or server-side scripts. There are some important differences, though.

- ✔ The browser executes client-side scripts after the page has been received from the server. The web server executes server-side scripts before the page is sent.

- ✔ Client-side script code is downloaded as part of the page and can be seen from the browser by simply viewing the source for the page. This means that it is easy to steal others' scripting code.

- ✔ Client-side script can only run on browsers that support scripting and specifically support the scripting language that you use. For instance, if you use client-side VBScript in your Web page and someone accesses it using Netscape Navigator (which only supports JavaScript), the script will not execute at all. With server-side scripting you don't have to worry about the browser's capabilities because only pure HTML is finally sent to the browser.

The good news is that you don't have to pick between client-side scripting and server-side scripting. You can use both! Even in the same page. In fact there are some techniques for using them together that are very effective.

For instance, imagine you are selling music CDs from your Web site. The user fills out a form to order three CDs. He has to give his name, address, phone number, social security number, and so forth. When the user clicks the button to submit the form, you use a client-side script to check to make sure that he's filled in all the information. You can even check the phone number and social security number to make sure the number of digits is correct. If everything looks good, then you can send it off to the server. After it gets to the server, you can use an ASP page to save the order in your database.

Of course, you could check to make sure everything was filled in and looked good in your ASP page. But that means the user would have to wait for the bad data to be sent to the server, evaluated, and a message returned to the browser. Doing all that stuff on the client-side, before the data is sent, is much quicker and makes a lot more sense.

How Is ASP Different from ActiveX Controls and Java Applets?

You don't have to read much about the Internet before you see the words Java and ActiveX kicked around. They are two of the hottest topics in the Web development world. How is ASP different?

The concept of Java applets was created by Sun Microsystems. ActiveX controls were created by Microsoft. Both are small programs that are downloaded as part of a page, just as a graphic would be. But when they are received by a client machine, they are executed in the browser and the result is displayed on the Web page. Simple ActiveX controls or Java applets may provide a control that the user can use to enter information, such as a listbox. More complex controls or applets may allow you to explore three-dimensional VRML worlds, or view an animation, or see live video as it is broadcast from a Web site.

Client-side scripts are often used to coordinate several controls or applets on the page so that they work together. Using these technologies together, you can create something that works like a multimedia application or a game.

Java applets are written in Java and ActiveX controls can be written using Visual Basic, C/C++, Java, or other languages. They allow the site developer to create complex programs that couldn't be created using scripting alone.

You may wonder, if there are controls and applets that supplement scripts on the client-side, are there also controls or applets on the server-side that supplement ASP? The answer is yes. Server components are the topic of Chapter 9.

The World of Internet Development

The Internet is still a very young platform for application development. The growth of interest in the Internet, both for personal and professional use, has been staggering. This interest is bound to make the Internet a central focus of almost all major new development in the future.

But today we're still in the early stages, and the standards and development environments and tools aren't nearly as well-defined as they are for stand-alone application software such as word processors and spreadsheets. This is both good news and bad news. The pioneers always have the biggest opportunity to leave their mark on the future. But they also often have to work with very crude tools.

ASP, Java, and ActiveX are the forerunners of the tools of the future, and they are the tools that will begin to turn the promise of a truly exciting, interactive Internet into a reality.

Chapter 2

Just How Easy Is ASP?

● ●

In This Chapter

▶ Figuring out what you need to create Active Server Pages

▶ Understanding which scripting languages are available

▶ Creating a framework for developing and testing Active Server Pages

▶ Walking through a detailed step-by-step plan to create a simple page

▶ Exploring some simple and commonly used VBScript commands

▶ Executing your page and testing it

● ●

*A*SP is easy. I know you've heard this before, only to be overwhelmed with enough confusing gibberish to choke a camel. But this time, you can believe it. And by the end of this chapter, I bet you will.

In this chapter you set up your environment so that you can create ASP pages and immediately test them to make sure they work like you want them to. As soon as you have your environment set up, I walk you through the process of creating and testing your first page. After that you'll be ready to experiment all you like!

Everything You Need to Get Started

ASP isn't a software package you can just go to the store and buy. And that's too bad because it would make getting started with it a lot easier.

ASP is a *technology*, which is a fancy way of saying it's a cool feature that's built into some *other* piece of software. That *other* piece of software, in this case, is Internet Information Server (IIS) or Personal Web Server (PWS), depending on which operating system you are using. Let me explain.

Windows 2000 Server/Advanced Server and Windows NT Server come bundled with their copy of the Internet Information Server Web server. This is a full-sized, blow-your-doors-off, industrial strength web server that will handle pretty much anything you throw at it. If you own your own Windows NT Web server, or you rent space on one, or you're developing on one for your company, then this is the web server you'll be working with.

On the other hand, if you are working on a smaller scale, running on Windows 95/98, Windows 2000 Professional, or Windows NT Workstation, then you'll be using IIS's little brother — the Microsoft Personal Web Server. But don't be fooled — PWS is no slouch. In fact, it has most of the features IIS has. The biggest difference is that IIS is designed for high volumes, lots of hits, and heavy-duty file transfers. And PWS is designed for small- to medium-scale Web sites and intranets.

The important thing, though, is that both IIS and PWS do ASP. Any pages you create work just as well on either one. That means that if you are setting up a site for the first time, you can go with the easier-to-use PWS. Then if your site really takes off, you can upgrade to Windows 2000 Server or Windows NT Server with IIS later without having to change the way your site works at all. Those Microsoft guys — always thinkin'!

Even if your final platform is going to be a Windows 2000/Windows NT IIS server, it may be easier for you to set up an environment using Windows 95/98 and PWS just to figure things out. And even after you have ASP down pat, you can use this platform to develop and test new pages before you deploy them on the "real" server.

Whichever you use — IIS on Windows 2000/NT Server or PWS on Windows 2000 Professional, Windows NT Workstation or Windows 95/98 — you must have your operating system and web server software installed and working properly before you go any further.

Microsoft Personal Web Server 4.0 for Windows 95/98 and Microsoft Peer Web Services for Windows 2000 Professional/NT Workstation are both available for free download from the Microsoft Web site. Look for the NT Option Pack. Even if you don't run NT, installing the NT Option Pack will install PWS on your machine.

About Your Language, Young Man. . . .

Another topic that you have to think about before you begin on your ASP journey concerns language. Which scripting language do you want to use to create ASP pages?

The hosting option

If you don't want to go through the hassle of setting up your own web server (and believe me, it can be a hassle), you may want to think about finding a Web hosting site that supports ASP.

Hosting sites are companies that provide room on their server for you to place your Web site. You can even get a domain name that jumps right to your hosted site, so that no one ever knows it's not on its own machine.

But hosting sites aren't all created equal. So be sure to ask about all the things that are important to you:

✓ Do they host on a Windows 2000/NT machine?

✓ Do they support ASP development?

✓ Can they create DSNs mapped to your Access database files?

✓ Can they provide space on their SQL Server for your database?

Some of these features may require extra setup fees or extra monthly charges. But the good news is that there are a lot of hosting sites out there and you can always shop around.

You have several options. IIS and PWS come with the ability to use either VBScript or JScript (the Microsoft implementation of JavaScript).

But these aren't your only choices. Microsoft has built its scripting engine to be very flexible — so flexible that other companies can actually create new scripting languages and plug them right in. That means that if you are already familiar with Perl or REXX, you can find third parties that have created these scripting languages (and probably lots of others) that plug right into IIS or PWS and allow you to create ASP pages with them.

But suppose that you aren't a programming guru and you are just looking for an easy way to make your Web site really cool. In that case, I suggest you go with VBScript. It is based on Visual Basic, probably the most popular computer language ever created. VBScript is very English-like and straightforward. Not a lot of weird, incomprehensible symbols and strange three- or four-letter commands. After you get set up, you'll want to flip over to Chapters 3 and 4 to explore VBScript. And you can skip right over Chapter 5 because it's written for those who want to use JScript.

If, on the other hand, you like weird, incomprehensible symbols and strange three- or four- letter commands, then I'd be willing to bet you are already a C, C++, Java, or JavaScript programmer. If that's the case, then you'd probably feel more comfortable with JScript. Chapter 5 clues you in on the biggest differences between JScript and C, C++, Java, and JavaScript so that you can get started scripting right away. You can skip Chapters 3 and 4 unless you want to learn VBScript, too.

The examples I use throughout the rest of this book (after Chapters 3, 4, and 5) are usually in VBScript. I use VBScript because it's the most popular ASP scripting language and because I'm guessing that if you already know C, C++, Java, or JavaScript, you've probably got enough programming under your belt that you'll be able to translate the VBScript examples into JScript.

But no matter which language you pick, they all have roughly the same capabilities, so that you can do anything you want from any one of them.

Where's the Development Environment?

For most computer languages, you can buy complete development environments that put at your fingertips every tool you need to write, run, and test applications you create. ASP is a development technology that is still independent of any one development environment.

You have a number of development environments that allow you to create ASP pages or that generate ASP pages themselves based on what you tell them. Here are the three most commonly used development environments for ASP:

- ✔ Notepad
- ✔ Microsoft Visual InterDev
- ✔ Drumbeat

All right, maybe Notepad doesn't exactly qualify as a development environment. But I put it here to remind you that many, many developers use Notepad or some other simple text file editor to create ASP pages. You don't need a lot of complex tools and mystical icons to make ASP work. ASP is a simple language combined with standard HTML. What could be more elegant?

However, if you must be surrounded by lots of cool bells and whistles, then you have companies out there with products to accommodate you. The most obvious is Visual InterDev by Microsoft. Visual InterDev is a part of the Microsoft Visual Studio suite of development tools. Visual Studio also includes Visual C++, Visual Basic, and Visual J++.

If you are interested in Microsoft Visual InterDev, flip to Appendix A for more information and an example of using it to create an ASP application.

Drumbeat is an interesting product that goes beyond the typical development tool to provide you with a totally visual interface for creating Web applications that access a database. After you've designed what you want visually, Drumbeat generates the ASP pages to do it. Although this approach generally provides less hands-on control, it does simplify and speed development.

Creating and Testing Your ASP Pages

After you've tested HTML pages or pages that include client-side scripting, you may have gotten into the habit of just dragging and dropping the page onto the Internet Explorer browser. Or you may have used File⇨Open in the browser to open the page. You can't use either of these techniques if testing ASP pages. Both techniques open up the page directly without any web server involvement. Because ASP works on the server side, you have to let the server find the page, run the code, and then send the results to the browser.

One of the best ways I've found to do this is to set up a launch page with a list of links to all of your test pages. You can drag and drop this launch page onto the browser, because it contains only HTML. But then after you click a link, the server handles it by getting the associated ASP page.

Where to work

IIS creates a folder on your hard drive that is, by default, named Inetpub. If you are using PWS, the name may be Inetpub or WebShare. Under Inetpub or WebShare is another directory called wwwroot. The wwwroot directory is the root directory for your Web site.

If you place a new Web page in wwwroot or any subdirectory under wwwroot, your web server has access to the page and you can make links to it from other pages on your Web site.

For PWS users only

If you are using PWS on your local machine and creating a new site that is all your own, then you can use the Personal Web Manager's Web Site Wizard to create your link page for you automatically.

Just launch the Personal Web Manager by double-clicking on the Personal Web Server icon at the right of your Taskbar. (Or click the Personal Web Manager icon in the Start menu group for Microsoft Personal Web Server.)

Click on the Web Site icon and a wizard appears and walks you through creating your own home page. One of the options on this home page is a list of links you can add. Just start adding links to /test1.asp, /test2.asp, and so on.

Then simply create your ASP files in the www.root directory and you can link to them from your page.

We're clear for liftoff: Creating the launch page

If you are working on a corporate server where there are procedures in place about how new pages can be added, where you can and cannot put test pages, and so forth, you can follow these guidelines.

If you are the one in control of the Web site or you are creating your own site on your machine using PWS, then the process is much simpler. Create the page that will serve as your launch pad, linking to all the pages you create as you experiment with ASP.

If this isn't a server anyone else is using, you can make your launch page the `Default.asp` or `Default.htm` file in the `wwwroot`. If the site is being used for other things, you can make a new subfolder under `wwwroot` and then create a Default page for that folder.

After you've created your launch page with links, all you have to do is begin creating the pages to link to.

Always remember to save your files with the `.asp` extension. This is how the server software knows that it should interpret the code inside the page rather than just sending it on to the browser.

If you use Notepad as your editor to create ASP files, be aware that it virtually insists that you name your files with a `.txt` extension. In fact, if you try to create a new file and save it as `test.asp`, the file's name will end up `test.asp.txt`. Here's how you fix that problem: If you type in the filename, put it in quotes like this: `"test.asp"`. The file will be saved with exactly the filename you give it.

If you do accidentally save one with the wrong extension, just go out in Explorer and rename the file. Notepad only pulls this trick if you are creating new pages. After you edit an existing page, it always saves the page with the name it had originally.

Get Your ASP in Gear: Creating Your First ASP Page

Now that you have your environment set up to edit files on your Web site, and you know how to save them and test them through your launch page, you're ready to create your first ASP page.

1. **Verify that your server software is running. For PWS, an icon appears on the right side of your Task Bar. For IIS, you can go to** `Control Panel`, **double-click** `Services`, **and make sure** `World Wide Web Publishing Service` **appears and has a status of** `Started`.

2. **Create your launch page as described in the previous section.**

3. **Add a link from your launch page to a page named** `welcome.asp`. **Be sure it links to the page in the right directory.**

4. **Create a new page in the editor of your choice.**

   Most HTML editors work fine, as long as they let you work with the raw HTML tags and don't try to hide them from you. If you are using Microsoft Front Page, choose View⇨HTML from the menus to edit the raw HTML and add your scripts.

5. **Enter the following code.**

   Be sure to type it exactly as it is listed. Don't worry about whether something is entered in upper or lower case. It will work either way.

   By the way, even though I'm using VBScript for this example, the process for creating and testing a page is exactly the same if you were using JScript.

```
<html>
<head>
<title>Hello and Welcome</title>
</head>
<body>

<center>

<% Dim ftsize, ftcolor %>

<% For ftsize = 1 To 7 %>
<font size = <%=ftsize%>>
Hello and Welcome!<br>
<% Next %>

</center>

<h3>It is <% =WeekdayName(Weekday(Date)) %>, <% = Date %>.
The time is now <% = Time %>.<p>
</h3>
</body>
</html>
```

6. **Locate the directory where you have decided to place your test pages. This may be** `wwwroot` **or one of its subfolders. Save the page with the name** `welcome.asp`. **If you are using Notepad, remember to put quotes around the name so that it doesn't add the** `.txt` **extension.**

7. **Minimize your editor and open your browser. Now open the launch page.**

If you are working on the web server machine itself, you can do this in one of several ways:

- Drag and drop the launch page onto Internet Explorer.

- Use File⇨Open in Internet Explorer and then locate and load the page.

- Type `http://localhost` into the Address line at the top of the browser to see the Default page for your site, if that is your launch page.

- Type `http://localhost/yourfolder` into the Address line to see the Default page for `yourfolder` (replace `yourfolder` with the appropriate folder name).

If you are *not* working on the web server machine itself, then you should access your page by simply typing its complete URL, as in: `http://bigserver/myfolder/welcome.asp`.

8. **After you see your launch page, click on the link you created to take you to** `welcome.asp`.

9. **You should see the page you created in the browser. It looks a lot like Figure 2-1.**

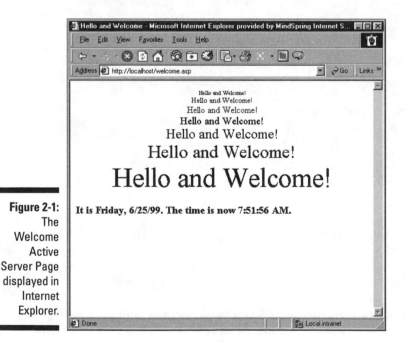

Figure 2-1:
The Welcome Active Server Page displayed in Internet Explorer.

If you don't see this, go back and check to make sure you entered the page exactly as it appears after Step 5.

It didn't WORK!

If this is the first time you've tried to set up your system to create and test ASP pages, you have a lot of things that could go wrong.

The most common problem is that the ASP page is not processed on the server as it's supposed to be, but is downloaded as-is to the client instead. This problem can manifest itself in a number of ways:

✔ Instead of displaying the results of the ASP as in Figure 2-1, you get a dialog box asking you if you want to download the .asp page.

✔ Either Front Page or Visual InterDev is launched editing the .asp page.

✔ The page appears in the browser but all the script is still in the page.

If one of these things (or something like it) is happening to you, then your server is not processing the page as an ASP. Several things can cause this to happen. Turn to Appendix D: "Troubleshooting Your ASP Projects." The reasons this can happen and information on how to fix them can be found there.

How Does It Work?

I've had you create this Web page so that you'll understand the process for creating and testing pages. Unless you already know VBScript or are a proficient programmer, you probably don't understand exactly how the page works just by looking at it. I explain exactly what it does here. For more information on any of the commands on this page or VBScript commands in general, see Chapters 3 and 4.

The first line of VBScript (beginning with `Dim`) creates a variable that will be used on this page: `ftsize`. The next line identifies the beginning of a `For` loop. This loop sets the value of the `ftsize` variable to one the first time through the loop. Everything inside the loop is executed until the `Next`. `Next` identifies the end of the loop. The second time through the loop, `ftsize` is set to two, the third time it is set to three and so on through seven, when the loop ends.

Inside the loop, the font size is set equal to `ftsize` and `Hello and Welcome!` is displayed on the page. Because `ftsize` gets bigger each time the loop executes, the same line is printed again and again in increasingly larger sizes. And that's exactly what you saw in Figure 2-1.

The next part of the page prints the day of the week, the date, and the time. The date and time are easy because VBScript has functions built in that return that information. The functions are called, oddly enough, `Date` and `Time`.

But before these are printed, the weekday is printed. VBScript requires you to call a couple of functions to make this happen. If you use the `Weekday` function, you send it a date by putting it in parentheses after the function name. In this case, I sent today's date by using the `Date` function.

The problem with `Weekday` is that it returns a number indicating which weekday the date falls on, not the name of the day. So I send the result returned from the `Weekday` function immediately to another function called `WeekdayName`. `WeekdayName` takes the weekday number and returns a string with the name of the day.

Don't feel like you need to completely understand this example before you go on. I cover all the intricacies of VBScript in Chapters 3 and 4. For now, make sure you understand the process used to create, test, change, and retest the page.

Modifying, Retesting, Creating New Pages, and Converting Old Pages

If you want to make modifications to `welcome.asp` and then test it again, follow these steps:

1. **If you've minimized your editor, restore it and make the changes.**
2. **Save the file. Save the file. Don't forget to save the file.**
3. **Minimize the editor again and find your browser window.**
4. **Click `Refresh` on the browser window.**

   The server gets the newly saved ASP page, re-executes it, and sends the results to the browser again.

Whenever you want to create a *new* ASP page:

1. **Create the page in your editor and save it with the `.asp` extension to the appropriate folder.**
2. **Add a link to the new page on your launch page.**
3. **Open the launch page in the browser and click on the link.**

Later, after you're ready to start working on your own Web site, you'll probably want to convert some of your existing HTML pages into ASP pages. That's easy, too.

1. **Rename the `.htm` or `.html` file. Remove the extension and replace it with `.asp`.**
2. **Edit the page in your editor and add any scripting code you like.**

Part II
Speaking Like a Native

The 5th Wave By Rich Tennant

ROOM 101

"I failed her in algebra but was impressed with the way she used Boolean variables with If.. Then conditions on her Active Server Pages."

In this part . . .

ASP is cool because it allows you to use a real scripting language right alongside your HTML — which provides a lot of power and capabilities you wouldn't have otherwise. But you can't begin until you know one of the scripting languages that ASP supports. The most popular scripting languages for ASP are VBScript and JScript.

Because you need to know only one or the other, you don't need to read all the chapters in this section. If you don't have a lot of programming experience or if you've programmed in Visual Basic before, the easiest language for you to pick up would be VBScript. In that case, read Chapters 3 and 4 and skip Chapter 5.

However, if you are already familiar with C, C++, Java, JavaScript, or Perl, you'll probably feel more at home with JScript. Skip Chapters 3 and 4 and go directly to Chapter 5. There you can discover how JScript is different from the language you are already familiar with — and how it's the same.

Chapter 3

Understanding VBScript Basics

● ●

In This Chapter

▶ Defining *programming language* and *scripting language*

▶ Using delimiters and comments

▶ Creating variables and constants

▶ Assigning and using variables

▶ Passing arguments to functions

▶ Receiving data back from a function

▶ Exploring common commands and functions

● ●

*T*his chapter and Chapter 4 explore the VBScript language and how to put it to use creating ASP pages. If you don't have much scripting or programming experience, you'll want to read these two chapters and skip over Chapter 5.

If you do have programming experience in C, C++, Java, or JavaScript, it will probably be easier for you to use JScript when you create your ASP pages. Feel free to skip this chapter and the next one and go straight to Chapter 5. There you discover all the differences between the language you are used to and Microsoft JScript, and how JScript works with ASP.

Getting Started with Programming and Scripting

The next few sections are for people who have very little or no computer programming experience. They define some terms and describe some basic concepts you need to know to get started. If you've done scripting or programming in the past, feel free to skip these sections.

What is a programming language?

A computer programming language is a lot like a human language. Like human languages, computer languages have a vocabulary of words. And both types of languages also have syntax rules for putting the words together into sentences.

The biggest difference between computer and human languages is that computer languages are very precise. Human languages may have five different words that mean the same thing, whereas a computer language only has one. And, in a human language, you can put together the same sentence in a number of different ways, reordering the words or even bending the rules of syntax now and then, and still be understood. Computers require you to follow their syntax to the letter. If you don't, an error occurs.

The other big difference between computer and human languages is that human language is designed for two-way communication. On the other hand, computer languages are designed so that you can tell the computer exactly what it is supposed to do and how it should respond to every situation. The only way the computer responds is by doing what you tell it to do. The computer can't argue with you — although when it throws error messages your way, you may *feel* like it's being argumentative! In this sense, the *programs* or *scripts* that you write are very much like a recipe or a to-do list. That's why the words in a computer language's vocabulary are often called *commands* or *statements*.

After a program is entered into the computer, the programmer will *run* or *execute* the program. For an ASP Web page, this happens when the *user* (the person sitting in front of his browser) requests an ASP page. The server finds the page and runs it. Then the resulting HTML page is returned to the user's browser so that he can see it.

What is a scripting language?

A scripting language is very similar to a programming language. Everything I said in the last section applies to scripting languages, too. The difference is that the scripting language has been scaled down and trimmed up so that it only has the bare essentials. Instead of having a vocabulary of hundreds of commands, a scripting language may have several dozen. But the ones that are left are the key commands that you use every day.

Microsoft Visual Basic is a computer programming language that has a vast array of commands and capabilities. Visual Basic is one of the most popular programming languages ever, primarily because it is so productive and so easy to use. VBScript is a scripting language that was created as a scaled-down version of Visual Basic.

You won't ever see the hottest new computer game or a company's account-ing system written in VBScript. Those kinds of large-scale applications require features that only a full-blown computer language can provide.

But for your Web applications, VBScript is perfect. It has all the essentials and none of the fat. And if you ever do need more powerful capabilities, you can always use server components written in a computer language like C or Visual Basic to give your ASP pages that extra boost. I tell you all about server components in Chapter 9.

What are all of those strange words?

Programmers are absolutely notorious for using lots of strange words that no one else can understand. It's like when you were a kid and you started a secret club with a secret handshake and a secret language.

I won't bore you with most of the terms that programmers use, but some of them are so common that you can't get by without knowing them. Here are a few of those:

- ✔ **code or source code:** A programmer may say, "That's a pretty hot piece of code you have there." Don't let the word throw you. It just means a computer program listing or part of a listing.

- ✔ **user:** No, it doesn't have anything to do with drugs. It's just the word programmers use to refer to the person who ultimately will be running and using the computer program. When you are referring to a Web site, the user is a person who is visiting the Web site.

- ✔ **active or activated:** You usually hear these words when referring to the Internet. Active distinguishes boring pages that just provide text and pictures from those that let you take part and play with them. Boring pages are out. Activated pages are way cool.

Power — In Time. . . .

Using ASP scripting on the server side provides many capabilities that would be difficult to implement any other way. But one odd thing about first discov-ering VBScript or JScript in the context of ASP is that you are somewhat limited in what you can do at first.

So, as you read this chapter, some of the examples may seem a little con-trived or less powerful than you were hoping for. Don't judge yet! These commands and their power will become a lot clearer as you discover more about ASP in later chapters. In Chapter 6 you find out about objects that are built into VBScript and JScript that extend the language's power. In Chapter 7

No MsgBox or InputBox

If you have used VBScript or Visual Basic before, you are probably familiar with the MsgBox and InputBox functions. These functions allow you to give information to the user and receive information back from the user using standard dialog boxes.

Because ASP pages are designed to run on the server before the page is sent to the user and displayed, these functions don't really make much sense and are therefore not available to you when you are creating ASP pages.

you discover all the server objects that give you information about the user, about the browser they're using, about fields submitted from forms, and about the server itself. And in Chapter 8 you can actually see real-world Web examples at work.

Delimiters — Keeping Your Tags and Your Code Apart

Because your VBScript code is a part of your HTML page and coexists right alongside the HTML tags, you need some way to separate the HTML from the VBScript code. That's what *delimiters* are for.

```
<html>
<head>
<title>Hello and Welcome</title>
</head>
<body>

<center>

<% Dim ftsize, ftcolor %>

<% For ftsize = 1 To 7 %>
<font size = <%=ftsize%>>
Hello and Welcome!<br>
<% Next %>
</center>

</body>
</html>
```

The tags appear and work in the document just as they would in a normal HTML page. The only difference is that interspersed throughout the page are lines of code that are surrounded by <% and %> signs. These are the delimiters. And the lines delimiters surround are lines of VBScript code.

But delimiters can contain more than one line. The first two lines of VBScript code could have been written like this instead:

```
...
<% Dim ftsize, ftcolor
For ftsize = 1 To 7 %>
...
```

Or like this:

```
...
<%
Dim ftsize, ftcolor
For ftsize = 1 To 7
%>
...
```

How you organize your delimiters and your code is up to you. The code will work as long as all VBScript code is inside the delimiters and all HTML tags are outside the delimiters.

Keep Your Comments to Yourself

Comments, also called _remarks_, are the way you include notes to yourself or others inside your page without changing the way the page works.

Delimiters inside an HTML tag

Look at the second line of code in this listing.

```
<% For ftsize = 1 To 7 %>
<font size = <%=ftsize%>>
Hello and Welcome!<br>
<% Next %>
```

It appears as though delimiters are inside of the font tag itself. And, in fact, they are. Why? I get into it in more detail later in this chapter when I discuss variables, but for now, I'll tell you this: You can insert the value of a VBScript variable inside an HTML tag by using this syntax. In this case, the value of the `ftsize` variable determines the font size each time `Hello and Welcome!` is printed.

In HTML, you use <!-- and --> to enclose comments that you want to include in the page, but don't want to display in the browser.

You can still use the HTML comment symbols in your pages. But if you want to comment VBScript code as you are creating it, you can also use the VBScript-style comment.

```
<%
' This code loops seven times
' and prints the same line on the page
' at seven different font sizes.
For ftsize = 1 To 7 %>
<font size = <%=ftsize%>>
Hello and Welcome!<br>
<% Next %>
```

Instead of enclosing the comment with two different symbols as HTML does, the VBScript comment always begins with an apostrophe and ends at the end of the line. So a new apostrophe is necessary at the beginning of each new line.

You can also put a comment on the same line as code. Again, the comment part starts with the apostrophe and ends at the end of the line.

```
<% For ftsize = 1 To 7 ' All 7 font sizes %>
<font size = <%=ftsize%>>
Hello and Welcome!<br>
<% Next %>
```

The VBScript comments, like all the rest of the ASP code, are removed before the page is sent. So, unlike the HTML comments, these comments cannot be seen when the person browsing your page chooses View⇨HTML from the Internet Explorer menus.

Up Your Case!

When you type in commands and variable names in VBScript, you can use uppercase and lowercase characters however you like. These three lines work exactly the same way in VBScript:

```
<% FOR FTSIZE = 1 TO 7 %>
<% for ftsize = 1 to 7 %>
<% FoR fTsIzE = 1 tO 7 %>
```

But the fact that case doesn't affect how the code works doesn't mean that you should be careless about which case you use. Throughout this book, I capitalize the first letter of all VBScript commands. The capitalization makes them stand out and keeps the code easy to read, and it's also similar to the way lots of other VBScript and Visual Basic developers write their code. It looks like this:

Deleting without really deleting

When you're testing a new page, you may want to delete some lines you've written, but still want to be able to easily get them back later if you need to. The best way to do that is to put an apostrophe in front of the line. The apostrophe turns the line into a comment. The line of code no longer affects the way the page works, but it's there if you want to bring it back. All you have to do is remove the apostrophe. Adding an apostrophe is called *commenting-out* a line of code. Removing the apostrophe is referred to as *un-commenting* the code.

```
<% For ftsize = 1 To 7 %>
```

I recommend doing it that way mostly because it is consistent with what other developers do.

As I Was Saying: Line Continuation

Sometimes a line of code gets really long and a little difficult to deal with. Fortunately, VBScript has a way of breaking your line in two without confusing VBScript into thinking it's supposed to be two separate lines.

```
<%
If Weekday(Date) > 3 And _
    Weekday(Date) < 6 Then
%>
```

The underscore character (_) is on your keyboard on the same key as the dash — just use Shift along with it. You can use this character anywhere you would normally put a space in your VBScript code.

If you use the underscore, it's a good idea to indent the second line three spaces or so to make it clear that the second line is a continuation of the previous line.

Creating and Using Variables

Think of variables as boxes that temporarily hold information for you to use later. Variables are very handy in all kinds of scripting situations.

Making your own variables with objects you can find around the house

In VBScript you create (or *declare*) a new variable by using the Dim statement. In the code below, three variables called Cost, Tax, and Total are created.

Go ahead and type this page in and give it a try. I label examples like this where I want you to actually try them out with the *Try This* icon. You can type the information into the page exactly as it appears below and then use the process I describe in Chapter 2 to test it.

Notice that I only use the HTML tag in the listing. You can go ahead and include HEAD, TITLE, and BODY tags that you commonly see in a page, but they aren't necessary. HTML is the only tag that is required.

```
<HTML>
<%
Dim Cost, Tax, Total
Cost = 40
Tax = 2
Total = Cost + Tax
%>
</HTML>
```

After they are created, Cost and Tax are immediately assigned a value. Cost is set equal to 40 and Tax to 2. Then the values held by Cost and Tax are added and the sum is placed in the variable Total. Simple enough.

You can do this kind of math with any combination of numbers and variables. You use the normal + and - for addition and subtraction. Multiplication uses the * symbol, and division uses the / symbol. Exponents are created using the ^ symbol.

So, what does this page do when you run it? The answer? This page does absolutely nothing. Or at least that's the way it seems. If you haven't already, try it out!

What DIMwit came up with that idea?

Dim? What the heck is Dim? Wouldn't something like Variable or Var be a better command for creating new variables? Yes, it would!

Dim stands for *DIMension*. Why? It's a long and boring story, but suffice it to say that it's a holdover from way back, when they were carving Basic programs on cave walls. And now we're stuck with it. Sorry.

Actually, the page did exactly what it was told to do. The page creates three variables, assigns values to two, and then adds them and puts the sum in the third variable. You never told the page to display any values, though. I show you how to do that later in this chapter in the section called "Displaying variable values."

Can you use a variable you didn't create?

Do you always have to create a variable using the Dim statement before you can use it in your script? Actually, no, you don't. If you just start using a variable name that's never been used before, VBScript will automatically create it for you. Is this a good idea? Absolutely not!

With these simple scripts, using a variable name that's never been used before is probably not a big deal. But when scripts start to get complicated, it can be a real pain to figure out what all the variables are and what they do. If you start using variables that you haven't even created, it gets even more complicated. As a general rule, always declare your variables with Dim before you use them.

Forcing the point

If you want to force yourself to always create your variables before you use them, VBScript has a command to do that. It's called Option Explicit. Just include this line as the very first line of your page, even before the <HTML> tag.

```
<% Option Explicit %>
```

From that point on, you actually get an error if you try to use a variable that wasn't created first. This can be really handy if you accidentally misspell a variable name. VBScript flags the misspelled variable as an error if you use

What! No variable types?

If you have programmed using other computer languages before, you may be startled to notice that VBScript doesn't seem to have any variable types! When you declare variables, you just declare their name, not what type of information they hold, like strings or whole numbers or fractional numbers.

This is one of the compromises that Microsoft made when scaling down Visual Basic into this much, much smaller package. Variable types and enforcement of variable types in the interpreter take a lot of code and make VBScript bigger than they wanted it to be.

This means, of course, that the programmer has to be more vigilant in making sure that variables don't end up being misused or confused.

`Option Explicit`. If you don't, VBScript just assumes you are creating a new variable, not misspelling an existing one.

It's a very good idea to always use `Option Explicit`.

Displaying variable values

In the section earlier in this chapter called "Making your own variables with objects you can find around the house," I showed you a page that did some math, but didn't display its result. Change the page (or create a new page) that looks like this:

```
<% Option Explicit %>
<HTML>
<%
Dim Cost, Tax, Total
Cost = 40
Tax = 2
Total = Cost + Tax
%>
<%=Total%>
</HTML>
```

What happens when you run it now? The number 42 appears in the upper left corner of an otherwise blank page.

But how did you do that? What kind of funky syntax is that in the second to last line? Basically, what you see is the normal delimiters <% and %> surrounding a variable name with an equal sign in front of it. This little VBScript shortcut allows you to replace that short section of code with the value in the variable. So if you do a View⇨Source in the browser, you see this:

```
<HTML>
42
</HTML>
```

Using this syntax is a very handy technique. Not only can you use it to print the value in a variable, but you can also use it within HTML tags themselves.

```
<% Option Explicit %>
<HTML>
<%
Dim ftsize
ftsize = 3
%>
<font size = <%=ftsize%>>
All creatures, big and small...<p>
</HTML>
```

When you try this page out, you see the phrase `All creatures, big and small. . .` printed on the page in the font size specified in the `ftsize` variable. Try changing the number, saving the page, and then refreshing the browser to see the result.

Using View⇨Source in your browser, you can see what happened.

```
<HTML>

<font size = 3>
All creatures, big and small...<p>
</HTML>
```

The `<%=ftsize%>` was replaced by the value of the `ftsize` variable — 3.

Don't string me along. . . .

In addition to holding numbers, variables can hold *strings*. A string is a bunch of letters put together to form words or sentences. Or maybe just nonsense.

```
<% Option Explicit %>
<HTML>
<%
Dim First, Last, Whole
First = "Bill"
Last = "Gates"
Whole = First & Last
%>
<% =Whole %>
</HTML>
```

Strings are always contained between quotes so that you know exactly where they begin and end, even though the quotes aren't actually a part of the string. The variable First is assigned the string Bill, and Last is assigned Gates. Whole is assigned to be equal to both First and Last. Notice the & separating the First and Last variables on the right side. In VBScript & is used to stick two strings together, or *concatenate* them.

What's wrong with this page (see Figure 3-1)?

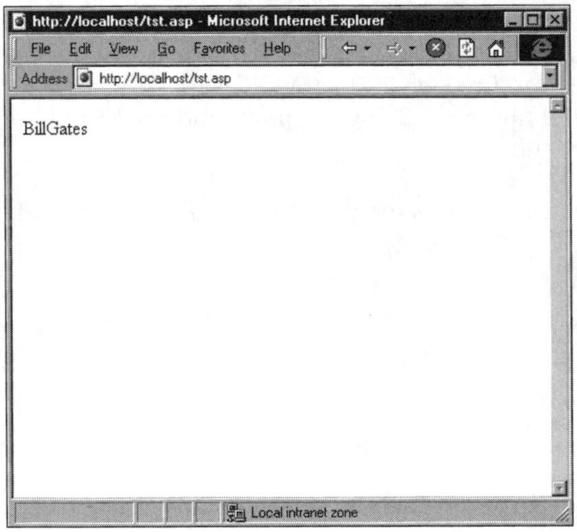

![Microsoft Internet Explorer window showing http://localhost/tst.asp with the text "BillGates" displayed]

Figure 3-1:
First and last names concatenated without a space.

No space exists between the first and last names. You have to add the space when you stick them together.

```
<% Option Explicit %>
<HTML>
<%
Dim First, Last, Whole
First = "Bill"
Last = "Gates"
Whole = First & " " & Last
%>
<% =Whole %>
</HTML>
```

In this listing, three strings are being concatenated — the one in `First`, a space, and then the one in `Last`. You can see the result in Figure 3-2.

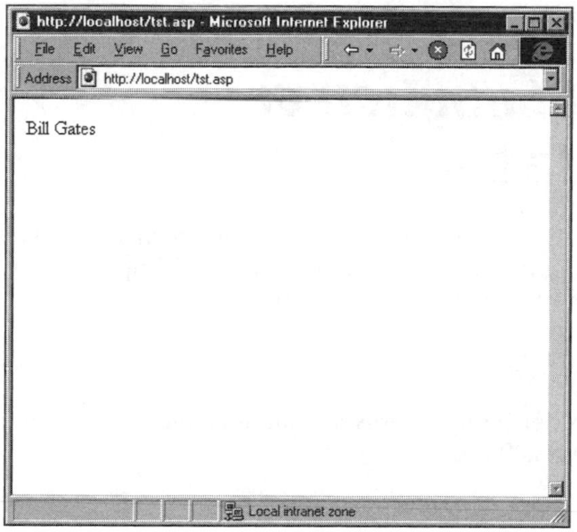

Figure 3-2:
First and
last names
separated
by a space.

Cantankerous Constants

A constant is like a variable except that you give it a value once, when you create it, and from then on, you're not allowed to change its value.

If you have a common number that you'll be using in several places throughout your page, you can assign that number to a constant at the top of your page and then use the constant name everywhere you'd normally use the number. This has two advantages.

  ✔ Because you're giving the number a name, the code is more understandable.

✔ If that number ever changes in the future, you won't have to hunt it down everywhere you use it on the page. You can simply change the constant declaration, and you're ready to go!

You declare a constant in much the same way you declare a variable, replacing `Dim` with `Const`.

```
Const Temperature = 98.6
Const CompanyName = "Colonial Computer Systems, Inc."
```

You may want to create a naming standard to differentiate between constants and variables so that you can keep them straight. One idea is to put constants in all upper case, while using mixed case for variables. Or you may want to put a prefix before all constants like `con`.

How Functions Function or How to Get a Date

Commands in VBScript come in two flavors — *statements* and *functions*. A statement is a command that stands on its own and simply does something. `Dim`, which declares variables, is a statement.

```
Dim Artist, CD
```

A function, on the other hand, *returns a value* for you to use in your code. An example of a function is `Date`.

What do you mean it "returns a value"?

If you haven't used a computer language with functions before, the concept of a function returning a value can be confusing. When I say a value is returned, what do I mean?

I mean that the built-in VBScript function `Date` is called when its name is used in the code. The function goes out to the system clock and finds out the current date. Then that current date is passed back to this script and the value is placed in the code right where the `Date` function appears. So the date returned by the function is assigned to the `CurrentDate` variable.

```
CurrentDate = Date
```

This line, then, does two things.

✔ It calls the `Date` function.

✔ It assigns the date returned from the `Date` function to the `CurrentDate` variable.

```
<% Option Explicit %>
<HTML>
<%
Dim CurrentDate
CurrentDate = Date
%>
The current date is <% =CurrentDate %>.<p>
</HTML>
```

In this code, the variable `CurrentDate` is created and then assigned the value which is *returned* from the `Date` function. Then the value of `CurrentDate` is used within a sentence to inform the user of the current date.

Let the Arguments Commence!

A function can also have *arguments* or *parameters*. An argument is a value that you can send *to* the function when you call it. This allows you to give the function information to work on. For instance, take a look at the `Weekday` function.

```
<% Option Explicit %>
<HTML>
<%
Dim ThisDay, ThisDate

ThisDate = Date
ThisDay = Weekday(ThisDate)
%>

It is day number <% =ThisDay %>.<p>

</HTML>
```

After `ThisDay` and `ThisDate` are declared, two VBScript lines are executed.

The first line calls the `Date` function. The `Date` function gets the system date and returns it. The value returned is assigned to `ThisDate`.

The second line calls the `Weekday` function and passes the value of `ThisDate` as an argument. `Weekday` uses this date to determine what weekday the date falls on. Notice that arguments are passed by placing them after the function name and putting them in parentheses. If this function had taken two arguments, they would both be inside parentheses and separated by a comma.

The value returned is a number from 1 to 7, indicating Sunday through Saturday.

If you want to make this code more concise, you could do it this way:

```
<% Option Explicit %>
<HTML>
<%
Dim ThisDay

ThisDay = Weekday(Date)
%>

It is day number <% =ThisDay %>.<p>

</HTML>
```

The `Date` function is called first, and then the value it returns is immediately sent to the `Weekday` function as an argument.

Rolling Dice and Cutting Cards — Using Functions in Formulas with Rnd and Int

One of the handiest things about functions and the way they return their values is that you can use them right in the middle of larger formulas. To illustrate how this works, I'm going to introduce you to two new functions: `Rnd` and `Int`.

```
<% Option Explicit %>
<HTML>
<%
Dim RandNum
Randomize
RandNum = Rnd
%>
<% =RandNum %>
</HTML>
```

Look at it in your browser. Now click Refresh. Click it again. If everything went well, you see a new number popping up in the upper-left corner of your page each time you refresh. The numbers look something like these (although not exactly):

```
0.1525385
0.9985163
8.871096E-02
0.4291651
```

The `Randomize` statement gets the process started. Any time you use `Rnd` on a page, you always put `Randomize` somewhere before the first `Rnd` is called.

Why Randomize?

Okay, here's the deal. You know about right-brained and left-brained people, right? Right-brained people are creative and usually become starving artists. Left-brained people are analytical and usually become accountants. Well, computers are left-brained, with a vengeance. The Rnd function is about as creative as computers can get. But even picking a number out of the air isn't easy for the computer.

The computer actually has a complex formula that it goes through to generate a "random" number. But to get the process started, the computer has to have a number to stick into the formula — what programmers call a seed value. If you don't use the Randomize statement, the computer always starts with the same seed. And, therefore, the computer ends up with the same series of "random" numbers every single time. Not very random, right?

So Randomize goes to the system clock and takes the numbers from there and uses them as the seed to stick into the complex formula. That way, the seed and the random numbers are different every time you run your page.

The Rnd function returns a fractional number between 0 and 1. The numbers that it gives you are completely different every time you run the program. Random numbers come in very handy when creating games and some types of cool graphics.

But these numbers aren't very useful, are they? If you wanted to create a program that simulates drawing cards or rolling dice, you want numbers between 1 and 13 or between 1 and 6. Numbers between 0 and 1 aren't useful very often.

Yeah, but what about 8.871096E-02?

Some of the random numbers generated have an E in them, such as 8.871096E-02. That isn't a number between 0 and 1, is it? Actually, it is. If you keep hitting refresh you're bound to see a number that looks like that every now and then. What you're seeing is a special mathematical notation that the computer likes to use on some numbers. The E-02 at the end is how you can tell it is using that notation (sometimes it's E-03 or E-04). To figure out what it means, move the decimal point two places to the left (or however many places to the left the number after E indicates). That makes it .08871096.

So why didn't it just say that to begin with? Who knows!

Unfortunately, no other function gives you random numbers in VBScript. So you have to use this one and tweak it a little. Take a look at this:

```
RandNum = (Rnd * 6) +1
```

The Rnd function is called and the value between 0 and 1 is returned. Then that value is multiplied by 6. After that, 1 is added to the number and then the final number is assigned to the RandNum variable.

The parentheses help VBScript decide which calculations it does *first*. In this case, it multiplies 6 times the number returned from Rnd first because that's in parentheses. (Actually, in this case, even if the parentheses weren't there, VBScript would always do the multiplication before the addition, but the parentheses make it clearer.)

Try plugging the preceding line of code into your page in place of the RandNum = Rnd line. Now you get numbers like this:

```
1.105081
5.167642
6.594674
```

Great! Now you're getting numbers between 1 and 6, just like you want. Except that annoying fractional part of the number is still hanging on. If there was some way we could just chop that off. . . .

And, of course, there is. It's called Int , which stands for *integer,* the word math teachers use when they mean a whole number. The Int function expects one argument: a number with a fractional part. Int returns the exact same number with the fractional part chopped off.

Notice I didn't say that Int rounded the number off because it doesn't. Int simply, unceremoniously chops off any fractional part and returns the whole number.

Replace the RandNum = (Rnd * 6) +1 line in your page with this new one:

```
RandNum = Int(Rnd * 6) + 1
```

Now you get numbers like this:

```
2
3
6
1
```

Perfect. Now you can create random numbers between 1 and any number you like. Want to simulate pulling cards off a deck? Use this line:

```
RandNum = Int(Rnd * 13) + 1
```

The 1 is an Ace, 11 through 13 are Jacks through Kings, and the rest are number cards. Easy enough.

All you have to do is replace the number after Rnd * with the highest number you want to generate.

Common Commands and Functions

In the sections throughout the rest of this chapter, I introduce you to some of the most commonly used functions in VBScript. Some of them have already been introduced earlier in this chapter, but many of them haven't.

You certainly don't have to memorize them all. You don't even have to read through them all. But if you at least skim over them, you get a good idea of all the things VBScript can help you do. And you know where to look when you want to read more detail.

Also, keep in mind that this isn't an exhaustive list of functions — not by a long shot. And I won't even tell you every detail about the functions I do list here.

Think of this as a quick jump-start to get you off and running with the most common commands and functions in VBScript.

And, if you need more, you can check out the VBScript documentation, which has a full rundown of every function and every option.

Downloading the VBScript documentation

The VBScript documentation is available from the Microsoft VBScript Web site for you to download for free. It's at www.microsoft.com/vbscript.

When you download it, it's a single file, but when you install it, it breaks itself into several *hundred* little Web pages that take a total of about 1.5MB of disk space.

This documentation includes a complete tutorial as well as an exhaustive reference for every command, function, and argument.

Doing Math

Computers are really good at doing math. So, of course, are VBScript and your ASP pages. And not all math is dull. In this section, I describe the more exciting math functions and leave the rest for your own research, if you are so inclined.

Rnd *and* Randomize

You can use Randomize and Rnd to add a creative or unexpected element to your Web pages. They are particularly useful when creating games or puzzles.

Randomize and Rnd are introduced earlier in this chapter, in a section called "Rolling Dice and Cutting Cards — Using Functions in Formulas with Rnd and Int". Look there for more details and examples.

Int *and* Round

Int and Round are the functions VBScript uses to convert numbers that include a fractional part (like 5.2 or 3.14159 or 7.632) to whole numbers. You can do that a couple of different ways, so that a couple of different functions exist (actually, there are a lot more than a couple, but these are the important ones).

I introduce Int earlier in this chapter, in a section called "Rolling Dice and Cutting Cards — Using Functions in Formulas with Rnd and Int." Look there for more details and examples.

Int

Int takes the most straightforward solution to this problem:

```
var = Int(expression)
```

The *expression* can be any formula that ends up producing a number with a fractional part.

Think of Int as the meat-cleaver approach to converting fractional numbers to whole numbers. Don't like the fractional part? Here, let me chop it off. Kachunk! There, no fractional part.

Int does no rounding or finessing of any kind. It simply removes the fractional part and returns the whole number part.

Round

The general form for Round looks like this:

```
var = Round(expression)
```

Again, the expression can be any formula that ends up producing a number with a fractional part.

Round is the kinder, gentler, more enlightened way of transforming fractional numbers into whole numbers. It rounds the fractional number just like you learned to do in sixth-grade math class. If the number is 6.7, it's rounded to 7. If it is 5.3, it's rounded to 5. If it is 2.5, the rule says that it goes to the higher number: 3.

Other math functions

All the standard math functions you may want are here, in all their gory detail. I didn't want to drone on about things only a math teacher could love, so I just list some of the other math functions you find in VBScript. You can look up the details in the VBScript documentation.

> **Trig Stuff:** Atn, Cos, Sin, Tan
>
> **Other Stuff:** Exp, Log, Sqr, Abs, Sgn, Mod, Hex, Oct

String Manipulation

Strings are letters, words, and numbers that can be stored in a variable. Information like names, addresses, and book titles are all stored in the computer as strings. Because strings are so important, many commands and functions exist to deal with them. Some of the most important ones follow.

FormatCurrency, FormatDateTime, FormatNumber, FormatPercent

You can look up all the different arguments that are available for each of these functions. Believe me, there are a lot of them.

The important thing for you to know is that you can format the look of a string holding currency values, dates and times, numbers, and percentage values in almost any way imaginable. These functions are very flexible. All four of them also give you the option of simply formatting the information based on the computer's regional settings.

InStr

InStr is a really handy one. It searches a long string to see if it can find a shorter string within it. If it finds the shorter string, it returns the position within the larger string where the shorter string can be found. The general form for InStr looks like this:

```
var = InStr(searchedstr, strtofind)
```

The var is a variable that holds the position where strtofind was found within searchedstr.

Here's an example:

```
<%
Dim BigString, FindString, Position
BigString = "I do not like green eggs and ham."
FindString = "eggs"
Position = InStr(BigString, FindString)
%>
<%=Position%>
```

Position would hold the value 21, because "eggs" appears 21 letters from the beginning of BigString.

Len

The general form for Len looks like this:

```
var = Len(stringvar)
```

You send a string to Len as an argument, and it returns a number indicating how long stringvar is.

```
<%
Dim MyString, MyLength
MyString = "Butter side down"
MyLength = Len(MyString)
%>
<% =MyLength%><p>
```

MyLength would hold 16, because that's how many letters are in the string.

LCase, UCase

The general forms for LCase and UCase look like this:

```
var = LCase(stringvar)
var = UCase(stringvar)
```

LCase and UCase both take one string argument. They both return that same string converted to lower case or upper case, respectively.

LCase("This Is A Scary Story") **returns** "this is a scary story".
UCase("This Is A Scary Story") **returns** "THIS IS A SCARY STORY".

LTrim, RTrim, Trim

The Trim functions — LTrim, RTrim, and Trim — each receive a string as an argument and return a string. The string returned is the same as the string sent except:

- ✔ LTrim chops off any spaces that appear on the left side of the string (at the beginning). These are often referred to as *leading* spaces.
- ✔ RTrim chops off any spaces that appear on the right side of the string (at the end). These are often referred to as *trailing* spaces.
- ✔ Trim chops off both leading and trailing spaces.

Space, String

The Space function provides an easy way for you to create a string with lots of spaces in it. Just send a number indicating the number of spaces you want and Space returns a string of that length, filled with spaces. For example, Space(15) **would return** "   " (15 spaces).

String is an enhanced and more generalized version of Space. It allows you to create a string of any length with any character. You simply send the number of characters you want and the character you want to use. String(3,"@") returns "@@@", while String(7,"!") returns "!!!!!!!".

Left, Mid, Right

Left, Mid, and Right are three of the most useful string functions in VBScript. They allow you to tear apart a string into smaller strings.

Left and Right have these general forms:

```
var = Left(stringvar, num)
var = Right(stringvar, num)
```

Left takes two arguments — a string and a number. It returns a string, which is comprised of the left-most characters of the string sent. For example, Left("Dog bones",3) returns "Dog". Left("Rubble",4) returns "Rubb".

Right works exactly the same way, but it takes the characters from the right side of the string.

Mid takes characters from anywhere within a string. It has this general form:

```
var = Mid(stringvar, start, num)
```

The second argument, start, determines where in stringvar to begin, and num determines how many characters to use. Mid returns the string that results. Mid("Quick brown fox",7, 5) returns "brown". It starts with the seventh character ("b") and takes five characters total (including the seventh).

Dates and Times

These VBScript functions provide key date and time access and manipulation functions.

Date, Time, Now

Date, Time, and Now are all functions, which take no arguments and return a single value, swiped from the system clock.

- ✔ Date returns today's date.
- ✔ Time returns the current time.
- ✔ Now returns the date and time together.

Weekday, WeekdayName

Weekday accepts a date as an argument. It returns a number between 1 and 7, indicating the number of the day that date falls on.

WeekdayName conveniently accepts a number argument between 1 and 7 and returns the name of the associated weekday.

```
<% =WeekdayName(Weekday(Date)) %>
```

This line would display the current day of the week in the browser.

Other Date/Time Functions

VBScript provides a broad variety of date and time commands and functions. Here are some of the rest of the date/time functions you may find interesting.

- ✔ DateDiff: Returns how many days, weeks, months, or years exist between two dates.
- ✔ DateAdd: Adds a certain number of days, weeks, months, or years to a date and returns the new date.
- ✔ Day, Month, Year: Each of these takes a date and returns a number, which indicates the part of the date associated with their name. That is, if MyDate holds 10/5/67, then Day(MyDate) returns 5, while Year(MyDate) returns 67.
- ✔ MonthName: Takes a month number (1 to 12) and returns the name of the month (January through December).

Whose time is it?

If you plan to put the date and time on your Web page, be aware that Date, Time, and Now in an ASP page return the date and time from the *server's* system clock, not the client machine where the browser is running. And because people from around the world will be accessing your site, you're probably giving them misleading information.

The better way to put the date and time on your page is to use functions like these in a client-side script using VBScript or JavaScript. That way, it pulls the information from the client machine and is a lot more likely to be the correct local time.

Chapter 4

Real VBScript Programming

● ●

In This Chapter

▶ Writing a simple If..Then condition

▶ Writing a compound If..Then condition

▶ Using ElseIf to ask several questions at once

▶ Cleaning it up with Select..Case

▶ Creating loops using For..Next

▶ Creating loops using Do..Loop

▶ Nesting loops inside other loops

▶ Declaring and using arrays

▶ Creating your own subroutines and functions

● ●

*I*n this chapter, you begin to see the real power that ASP scripting gives you. You discover the VBScript If..Then statement, in all its forms, and how you can use it to control which HTML is sent back to the browser and which isn't.

You also explore the various looping mechanisms offered by VBScript. You can use the For..Next loop for counting, or integrate If..Then-like decision-making with the Do..Loop.

Decisions, Decisions, Decisions: Using If..Then

Your Web pages can make decisions on their own based on information they gather. But first you have to tell your Web pages which decisions to make and how to make them. The statements you use to do that, naturally enough, are If and Then.

```
If condition Then statement
```

This If..Then structure is often called a *conditional*. A conditional has two parts:

- The *condition,* or the question part
- The *statement,* or the thing-to-do part

IF you want cool Web pages THEN use conditionals

This conditional stuff is all pretty simple, right? But how are you going to use conditionals in your Web pages? Good question.

```
<% Option Explicit %>
<HTML>
<%
Dim Temperature, Boiling
Temperature = 220
%>
The water is heated for 5 minutes.<p>
<%
If Temperature = 220 Then
  Boiling = True
%>
The water is boiling!<p>
<% End If %>
Then the stew is done.<p>
</HTML>
```

In the preceding lines, the condition part of the If..Then asks the question, "Does the Temperature variable hold a value that equals 220?" Everything between the Then and the End If is part of the *statement* portion, whether it is additional VBScript statements or HTML. If the condition is true, the statement portion is done. If the condition is not true, the statement portion is not done. So, in this case, if the Temperature variable equals 220, the Boiling variable is set to True, and then this HTML becomes part of the Web page that is sent back:

```
The water is boiling!<p>
```

When you create an ASP page, you are not creating the Web page itself. You are creating a set of instructions that tells the server *how to create* the Web page when it is requested. (For more information on this topic, see the section titled "ASP As Easy As 1, 2, 3" in Chapter 1.)

If the condition is true

If the page is executed as it is, the final Web page sent to the browser looks like this (which you can see by choosing View➪Source):

```
<HTML>
The water is heated for 5 minutes.<p>
The water is boiling!<p>
Then the stew is done.<p>
</HTML>
```

If the condition is false

Now change the Temperature = 220 line so that it now says Temperature = 190.

The page sent from the server looks like this:

```
<HTML>
The water is heated for 5 minutes.<p>
Then the stew is done.<p>
<HTML>
```

Using Boolean variables with conditions

Boolean variables hold only two possible values — True or False (for more information on Boolean variables, see Chapter 3). You can use these variables in an If..Then statement, too.

```
<% If AccountBalanced = True Then %>
```

In fact, when you are working with Boolean variables like this, you don't even need the = True part. Why does this work? Well, because the condition part of the If..Then is looking for a True or False anyway, you can just use the variable by itself.

```
<% If AccountBalanced Then %>
```

If **without the** End If

If you have a simple If..Then statement that has only one VBScript command as its statement, you can get by without using an End If, if you put the whole thing on one line.

```
If Length > 15 Then LongTail = True
```

Inequalities: A fact of life

If..Then statements use what math professors call *inequalities*. Inequalities are ways of comparing numbers to see if they are greater than or less than each other. And, to keep it simple, VBScript uses the same symbols as you did in your sixth-grade math class.

> Greater than

< Less than

Here's how it works in an If..Then:

```
<% If Grade > 90 Then %>
You get an A!<p>
<% End If %>
```

If the variable Grade is greater than 90, the You get an A! message appears. Otherwise, it doesn't. Suppose you don't get greater than 90, but you get 90 right on the nose. Shouldn't that be an A, too? How do we fix that? Well, one way would be to do this:

```
<% If Grade > 89 Then %>
You get an A!<p>
<% End If %>
```

But it makes more sense to stick with round numbers. A better way would be to use another symbol: >=, which you read *greater than or equal to*.

```
<% If Grade >= 90 Then %>
You get an A!<p>
<% End If %>
```

As you may expect, there is also a <= that stands for *less than or equal to*. These symbols are a little different from the ones you learned in sixth-grade math, but these are easier to remember anyway.

You can use one final symbol to compare variables: <>, which means *does not equal*.

```
<% If Grade <> 100 Then %>
You did not get a perfect score.<p>
<% End If %>
```

Table 4-1 summarizes the comparison symbols you use in If..Then statements.

Table 4-1	Conditional Operators for If..Then Statements
Symbol	*Description*
=	Equals
>	Greater than
<	Less than
>=	Greater than or equal to
<=	Less than or equal to
<>	Does not equal

Creating compound If..Then statements

You can also use what programmer-types like to call a *logical expression* in an If..Then statement. This simply means that you can put more than one question together inside the same condition by using an And or an Or. This creates a *compound* If..Then statement.

A compound If..Then statement works just like you may expect. If an And is between the two conditions, it succeeds only if *both* conditions are true. If either one or both is false, then the statement portion is ignored. If an Or is between the two conditions, it succeeds if *either* condition (or both) is true.

In VBScript, you can connect together as many conditions as you like as long as they are all separated with an And or an Or.

```
<% If Temperature <= 32 And Liquid = "Water" Then %>
Looks like ice...<p>
<% End If %>
```

Of course, too many conditions can make your statement very confusing. When you're writing scripts, one rule always applies: As much as possible, keep it simple.

Lies! All lies! Or . . . what to do if it isn't true

All the If..Then statements you've seen so far only tell the computer what to do if a condition is true. What if you want it to do something else when the condition is not true? That's where Else comes in.

```
<% If Grade >= 60 Then %>
You passed!<p>
<% Else %>
You failed...<p>
<% End If %>
```

Now you not only have the choice to include some HTML or not include it based on the condition, but you can also choose to include one set of HTML if it is true and a different set of HTML if it isn't.

Multiple conditions

You can ask one question, why not more? Well, of course you can always just write one If..Then statement after the other. For instance, if you want to translate a percentage grade to a letter grade, you write code that looks like this:

```
<% If Grade >= 90 Then %>
<%   LetterGrade = "A" %>
You got an A! Congratulations.<p>
<% End If %>
<% If Grade >= 80 And Grade < 90 Then %>
<%   LetterGrade = "B" %>
You got a B. Good job.<p>
<% End If %>
<% If Grade >= 70 And Grade < 80 Then %>
<%   LetterGrade = "C" %>
You got a C. Not bad.<p>
<% End If %>
<% If Grade >= 60 And Grade < 70 Then %>
<%   LetterGrade = "D" %>
You got a D. Try harder next time.<p>
<% Else %>
<%   LetterGrade = "F" %>
You Failed. I'm sorry.<p>
<% End If %>
```

The problem with the preceding code is that it's wordy and you end up repeating yourself a lot. To make the process easier, VBScript includes another statement to help you in situations like this: ElseIf. If you use ElseIf, your page begins to look simpler and is easier to understand.

```
<% If Grade >= 90 Then %>
<%   LetterGrade = "A" %>
You got an A! Congratulations.<p>
<% ElseIf Grade >= 80 Then %>
<%   LetterGrade = "B" %>
You got a B. Good job.<p>
<% ElseIf Grade >= 70 Then %>
```

```
<%  LetterGrade = "C" %>
You got a C. Not bad.<p>
<% ElseIf Grade >= 60 Then %>
<%  LetterGrade = "D" %>
You got a D. Try harder next time.<p>
<% Else %>
<%  LetterGrade = "F" %>
You Failed. I'm sorry.<p>
<% End If %>
```

Now the whole thing is part of one big long If..Then statement. You know that because there is only one End If — all the way at the end.

Here's the way the If..Then..ElseIf works:

1. If the Grade is greater than or equal to 90, the LetterGrade variable is set to A, the first HTML statement is displayed, and then the statement ends. The rest of the conditions are ignored after a condition is met.

2. If the first condition is false, the second condition is checked. Here you only have to check to see if the Grade is 80 or better. You don't have to specify that it is less than 90 because if it had been 90 or greater, you wouldn't be executing this condition. Right?

3. Likewise for the third and fourth conditions.

4. If you get through all the conditions and there still isn't a match, the Else catches everything else — which, in this case, is bad news.

Developing your nesting instincts

Another trick you can do is to put an If..Then statement inside of another If..Then statement. Programmers call this *nesting*.

```
<%
If CoffeeIsHot = True Then
  If CoffeeBlack = True Then
    AddCream
    AddSugar
    DispenseCoffee
  Else
    DispenseCoffee
  End If
Else
  HeatCoffee
End If
%>
```

The If CoffeeBlack = True Then statement is nested inside the Then portion of the If CoffeeIsHot = True Then statement. VBScript only checks to see if the coffee is black if it *first* determines that the coffee is hot. Otherwise, it doesn't bother.

An If..Then can also be nested inside the Else portion of an If..Then..Else statement.

```
<%
CheckPassword
If PasswordCorrect = True Then
 AllowAccess
Else
 CheckPassword
 If PasswordCorrect = True Then
  AllowAccess
 Else
  DenyAccess
 End If
End If
%>
```

The preceding code first calls the CheckPassword procedure. Then if PasswordCorrect = True, access is allowed. Otherwise, the user is given one more chance to enter a good password when the CheckPassword procedure is called again. If the user gets it right this time, he is allowed in. Otherwise, the DenyAccess procedure is called to inform the user that access is denied.

As you can expect, the second If..Then in the Else portion isn't executed unless the first If..Then condition is false.

I know someone out there will ask the question, so I'll answer it here: Yes, you can nest an If..Then statement inside an If..Then that is itself nested inside another If..Then. In fact you can nest as deeply as you like. But I warn you. Nesting gets *really* confusing after a while.

Get Off My Case!

As in the If..Then statement, the Select Case statement is used for decision-making. Select Case allows you to use one variable throughout the whole statement to do a variety of comparisons against it.

Indenting makes it clearer

Notice how the lines of code are indented when I use an If..Then statement in an example? All the lines in the Then and Else portions of the examples are indented about three spaces. Then, in the nested If..Then statements, the Then and Else portions are indented an additional three spaces. VBScript doesn't require you to indent at all, but doing so makes the code much easier to read. Indenting

also makes it clear which Else and End If go with which If.

One exception: If there are lines of HTML inside the Then or Else portions of your If..Then statement, you probably won't want to indent them, because in some cases, this may throw off your formatting. Just leave them as they are.

```
<% Select Case EmployeeStatus %>
<% Case "G" %>
Employee is employed in good standing.<p>
<% Case "L" %>
Employee is on leave.<p>
<% Case "F" %>
Employee no longer works here.<p>
<% End Select %>
```

Here's how VBScript interprets this code:

1. Always begin your Select Case statements with the words Select Case (easy enough?).

2. After that comes a variable name. Here, the variable is EmployeeStatus. This variable is used throughout the rest of the Select Case statement.

3. Next comes a series of lines that start with the word Case and then are followed by a number. Select Case automatically compares the first value ("G") to the variable at the top (EmployeeStatus) to see if they are equal.

4. If the first value is equal to the variable at the top, the lines after Case "G" and before Case "L" are executed. After those lines are finished, the statement is done and any other Case line is ignored. If anything is after the End Select, *that* is what happens next.

5. If the first value isn't equal to the variable at the top, the next Case statement is checked (Case "L") and that value is compared with the variable at the top (again, EmployeeStatus). If there is a match, the lines under Case "L" are executed. If not, it goes on.

It is possible that none of the `Case` statements may match. If that happens, none of the lines within the `Select Case` get executed, and you just go on after the `End Select`. This situation would happen in the preceding statement if the `EmployeeStatus` was something different than `"G"`, `"L"`, or `"F"`.

Notice that you don't need to repeat the variable name or even the equal sign again and again as you would in an `If..Then` statement. Both are automatically assumed. This strategy makes the `Select Case` much cleaner and easier to understand if you are continually comparing against one variable over and over again.

When Should You Use Select Case *Instead of* If..Then..ElseIf?

`Select Case` and `If..Then..ElseIf` do very similar things. How do you know which one to use? Here's an example that helps clear this dilemma up for you.

Suppose you want to create a Web page that rolls two dice and informs the user how they turned up. How would you create a little Craps ASP page?

Well, first off, you want to roll the dice. For this task, you probably want to use the `Rnd` function. (For more information on the `Rnd` and `Int` functions, see the section titled "Rolling Dice and Cutting Cards — Using Functions in Formulas with `Rnd` and `Int`" in Chapter 3.) The formula you use to get a random number between 1 and any number looks like this:

```
Num = Int(Rnd * HighNum) + 1
```

`Num` is the random number, and you replace `HighNum` with the highest number you want to generate. In this case, the highest number is 6.

```
<% Option Explicit %>
<HTML>
<%
Dim Dice1, Dice2, Total

Randomize
Dice1 = Int(Rnd * 6) + 1
Dice2 = Int(Rnd * 6) + 1

Total = Dice1 + Dice2
%>
<% If Dice1 = 1 And Dice2 = 1 Then %>
Snake Eyes<p>
<% ElseIf Dice1 = 6 And Dice2 = 6 Then %>
```

```
Box Cars<p>
<% ElseIf Total = 7 Then %>
You rolled 7! You're lucky!<p>
<% ElseIf Total = 11 Then %>
You rolled 11! You're lucky!<p>
<% Else %>
Dice 1: <% = Dice1 %><p>
Dice 2: <% = Dice2 %><p>
Total: <% = Total %><p>
<% End If %>
</HTML>
```

You roll two dice and store their values in Dice1 and Dice2. You also store the total for the two dice in Total. But having the information is no good unless you tell the user about it. How do you do that? With If..Then..ElseIf.

Now every time this page is loaded or refreshed, it rolls two dice and tells the user the results (see Figure 4-1).

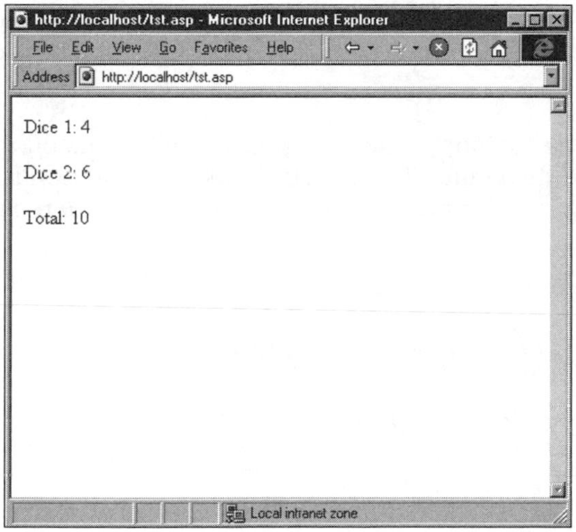

Figure 4-1:
Rolling two dice and telling the results.

So here's the big question: Why didn't I use a Select Case for the dice-rolling page instead of an If..Then..ElseIf? The biggest reason was because I was working with more than one variable. I was checking Dice1, Dice2, and Total in my If and ElseIf clauses. With a Select Case, you can only check for different values of *one* variable. In addition, if you need the flexibility to compare using the greater-than and less-than signs, you must use If..Then..ElseIf because Select Case doesn't support those kinds of comparisons. Those are the factors you need to use to decide whether to use Select Case or If..Then..ElseIf.

Speed champ: `Select Case` versus `If..Then..ElseIf`

In some computer languages the `Select Case` statement actually runs faster than an `If..Then..ElseIf`. If you have programmed in C or C++, you know that this is true for those languages — and because of that factor, you are encouraged to use `Select Case` whenever possible. With no significant difference in execution speed between the two statements in VBScript, you can use whichever makes your code easier to understand.

Loop the Loop

As in the `If..Then` and `Select Case` statements, loops change the order that lines are executed in your pages. `If..Then` and `Select Case` allow you to choose one of several different possible sections of code to execute based on a condition. Loops allow you to execute the same section of code again and again.

VBScript has two types of loops. The `For..Next` loop counts off a certain number of times and then quits. The `Do..Loop` uses a condition similar to an `If..Then` statement to determine whether it can continue looping each time or not.

Counting with `For..Next`

The `For..Next` loop makes it easy to execute a loop a set number of times while keeping track of which loop you are on.

```
<% Option Explicit %>
<HTML>
<%
Dim DiceNum, DiceValue
Randomize
For DiceNum = 1 To 5
DiceValue = Int(Rnd * 6) + 1
%>
Dice #<% =DiceNum %> rolled a <% = DiceValue %><p>
<%
Next
%>
</HTML>
```

This code rolls five dice and tells you the value of each one. When you run the code, your browser looks something like Figure 4-2.

Figure 4-2:
Rolling five
dice.

How does it work? The For line marks the beginning of the loop. For also identifies the *index variable* (DiceNum), the number of the first loop (1) and the number of the last loop (5). The Next line marks the end of the loop. Everything between the For line and the Next line is a part of the *body* of the loop (the stuff that gets executed again and again).

The first time through the loop, DiceNum is set to 1. The second time it is set to 2, and so on, up through 5.

An index variable can be any variable that you declare. The index variable is simply assigned the loop value each time the loop is executed. You can use the index variable and even display it as I've done in the example. Changing its value is never a good idea. The For loop really gets confused when you do that.

Most of the time your loops start with 1. But they don't have to. You can create a loop like this:

```
For Items = 10 To 100
```

This loop sets the variable Items to 10 the first time through, to 11 the second time through, and so on, up to 100. Here's another example:

```
For Counter = 0 To 5
```

Again, the first time through, `Counter` is set to 0, then to 1, and so on up to 5. This loop executes 6 times.

You can even do this:

```
For Coordinate = -5 To 5
```

The first time through, the loop is set to -5, then to -4, then on up through 0 and ending with 5. This loop executes 11 times (counting 0).

Watch where you Step

When you use the keyword `Step` with your `For..Next` loops, you can tell VBScript what number the `For` loop counts by.

```
For Num = 2 To 10 Step 2
```

In this loop, the first time through, `Num` is assigned 2, then 4, then 6, then 8, and finally 10.

```
For Weeks = 0 To 36 Step 7
```

`Weeks` is assigned 0 the first time, then 7, then 14, and so on up to 36.

Nesting loops

Just as you can nest an `If..Then` statement inside another `If..Then` statement, so that you can nest a loop inside another loop.

```
<% Option Explicit %>
<HTML>
<%
Dim OuterLoop, InnerLoop
For OuterLoop = 1 To 3
  For InnerLoop = 1 To 5
%>
OuterLoop = <% =OuterLoop %>, InnerLoop = <% =InnerLoop %>
<p>
<%
  Next
Next
%>
</HTML>
```

The result in your browser looks like Figure 4-3.

OuterLoop begins at 1 as does InnerLoop. The information is displayed, and then you run into Next. The first Next goes with the inner loop. That's why it is indented to line up with the inner loop's For line. The Next causes control to jump back up to the inner loop's For line and execute again. The inner loop executes all five times before the outer loop can continue. Then the outer loop is incremented and the inner loop executes five more times.

So when you have a loop within a loop, the innermost loop executes all its times and ends before the outer loop has a chance to loop a second time.

What do you think the HTML for this page looks like?

```
<HTML>
OuterLoop = 1, InnerLoop = 1
<p>
OuterLoop = 1, InnerLoop = 2
<p>
OuterLoop = 1, InnerLoop = 3
<p>
OuterLoop = 1, InnerLoop = 4
<p>
OuterLoop = 1, InnerLoop = 5
<p>
OuterLoop = 2, InnerLoop = 1
<p>
...
```

There is no indication of a loop at all in the HTML — that is all done on the server in VBScript. The only thing sent to the browser is the results.

*Doobee-Doobee-*Do..Loop

The VBScript Do..Loop is a very different kind of looping structure from the For..Next loop. Do..Loop allows you to loop *while* a condition is true or to loop *until* a condition becomes true. A Do..Loop looks like this:

```
<% Option Explicit %>
<HTML>
<%
Dim CoinToss, Heads, Tails, Tosses
Randomize
Heads = 0
Tails = 0
Tosses = 0
Do While Heads < 3
  Tosses = Tosses + 1
  CoinToss = Int(Rnd * 2) + 1
  If CoinToss = 1 Then
%>
Heads!<p>
<%
    Heads = Heads + 1
  Else
%>
Tails!<p>
<%
    Tails = Tails + 1
  End If
Loop
%>
It took <% =Tosses %> tosses to throw 3 heads.<p>
</HTML>
```

In this example, a random number between 1 and 2 is generated. If it is 1, it signifies that heads is thrown on a coin toss. And 2 indicates tails.

The Do..Loop causes a coin to be tossed again and again until a total of three heads are tossed. Then the total number of tosses to get three heads is revealed (see Figure 4-4).

The Do line indicates the beginning of the loop and the Loop line indicates the end. The condition follows the word While on the Do line. In this case, the loop continues as long as Heads has a value less than 3.

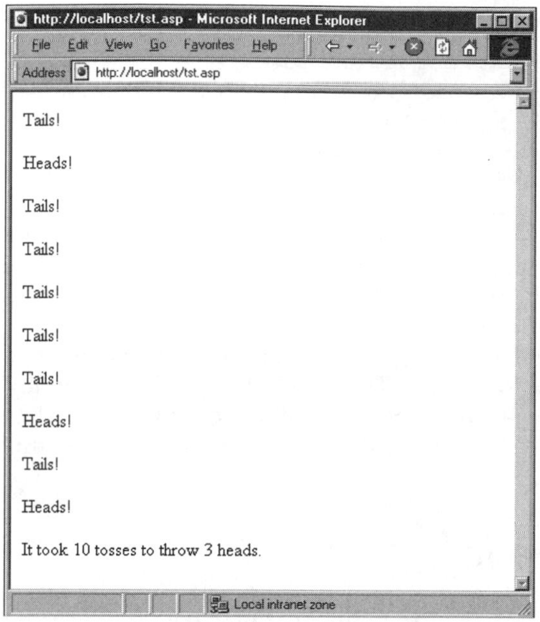

Figure 4-4:
How many
tosses does
it take to
get three
heads?

You can change the Do line to use Until, instead.

```
Do Until Heads = 3
```

If you use While, the loop continues as long as the condition is *true*. If the condition is false, the loop ends. Until is the logical opposite. The loop continues as long as the condition is *false*. As soon as the condition is true, the loop ends.

So to change this program to use Until, I have to change the condition so that the program still works the same way.

You need to know about one more wrinkle to the Do..Loop. The While or Until can appear at the bottom of the loop on the Loop line as well as at the top of the loop.

```
Do
  Tosses = Tosses + 1
  CoinToss = Int(Rnd * 2) + 1
  ...
Loop While Heads < 3
```

Or:

```
Do
  Tosses = Tosses + 1
  CoinToss = Int(Rnd * 2) + 1
  ...
Loop Until Heads = 3
```

What's the difference? Well, in the first examples, the condition is checked first, before the first loop even executes. In these examples, the condition isn't checked until everything in the loop has executed at least once.

Thus, in a top-tested loop, it is possible that the code inside the loop would never execute — not even once. That would happen if the condition failed the first time. In a bottom-tested loop, the stuff inside the loop is always executed once. Then if the first condition fails, it simply isn't executed again.

Exit, stage left

You may at times discover, right in the middle of a loop, that you want to get out of the loop entirely — no matter what else is going on. VBScript makes this action possible with the Exit command.

```
For Count = 1 To 100
  ...
  If Temp > Threshold Then Exit For
  ...
Next
```

Usually Exit For can be found within an If..Then statement that discovers some special case why the loop needs to end. Exit Do can be used in exactly the same way to exit a Do..Loop.

Arrays

An *array* is a way of declaring a whole group of variables at once. An array declaration looks like this:

```
Dim Names(20)
```

This single line creates 20 different variables. Each of these 20 variables has the same name — Names. You refer to the variables individually by using their number. You can assign a value to the fifth name by using this syntax:

```
Name(5) = "Brad Jones"
```

Why would you want to do this? Why not create 20 different variables the normal way?

```
Dim Names1, Names2, Names3, Names4, Names5
```

And so on. Well, being able to refer to variables by number has a couple of advantages. One advantage is that you have the ability to search through them one-by-one, using a loop.

```
<%
Dim CurName, Found
Found = False
For CurName = 1 To 20
  If Names(CurName) = "Mike Lafavers" Then
    Found = True
    Exit For
  End If
Next
If Found = True Then
%>
I found Mike Lafavers!<p>
<% Else %>
I didn't find Mike Lafavers.<p>
<% End If %>
```

Assume that this code is executed after all twenty names are filled in some-how. Now this code searches through the entire list to find one particular name. All you need is a For..Next loop. Just use the index of the loop for the array, and you check each variable in the array one at a time.

In fact, using a For..Next loop with an array is so common that VBScript has a special version of the For..Next loop designed for arrays — the For Each..Next loop.

Using For Each..Next *with arrays*

The For Each..Next statement works just like a For..Next loop, except for one thing. Instead of specifying the numbers, you simply specify the array's name, and it knows to go through all the elements — no matter how many there are.

The example in the preceding section can be re-coded with a For Each..Next loop by changing the loop to look like this:

```
For Each CurName In Names
 If CurName = "Mike Lafavers" Then
   Found = True
   Exit For
 End If
Next
```

Two things change.

- ✔ The For line changes to For Each. The array name comes last in the For Each. The variable after the Each is not, however, the index variable. It is a variable that is assigned the value of the *current element* in the Names array.

- ✔ The If on the second line doesn't index the Names array with CurName. If simply checks CurName itself because now CurName is used to hold the current element in the Names array.

For Each is handy to use and is safer than For..Next in the long run. If, in the future, the number of elements in Names changes, you won't have to change this loop. The For Each automatically goes through all of them no matter how many there are.

The Array *function shortcut*

The Array function provides a quick and easy way to assign values to a number of items in an array at the time it's created.

```
<%
Dim Names
Names = Array("Fred Smith", "Paul Keller", _
 "Mike Lafavers, "Steve Barron", "Melanie Moore", _
 "Patti Everhart")
%>
```

You create the array with as many elements as it needs to hold the values you enter.

Dynamic arrays

A *dynamic array* is an array that doesn't have a set number of elements defined when it's created. When you declare a dynamic array, it looks like this:

```
Dim Codes()
```

The empty parentheses after the variable indicate that it is a dynamic array. This option allows you to wait and determine later how many elements you need. After you know how many you need, you use ReDim.

```
ReDim Codes(15)
```

If you find out later that you actually need more elements than that, you can even ReDim again.

```
ReDim Preserve Codes(20)
```

The Preserve keyword asks VBScript to preserve any data that has been put into the array previously. If you don't use Preserve, all the data will be wiped out when you use ReDim.

UBound

When you are working with dynamic arrays, you don't always know what the highest array element is, especially if you keep ReDim-ing it. So VBScript offers a solution.

```
Dim Codes()
...
ReDim Codes(15)
...
HighElement = UBound(Codes)
```

After the ReDim, HighElement would hold 15.

Multidimensional arrays

Arrays are a list of variables that all use the same name. But arrays can be more than a list. They can be a *grid,* too.

```
Dim GameBoard(10,10)
```

This array has two *dimensions.* Instead of thinking of it as a list of values that each have a number, think of this as a grid of variables, each with its own two coordinates. GameBoard(5,5) is right in the middle of the grid while GameBoard(1,1) is in the upper left and GameBoard(10,10) would be in the lower right.

And, yes, you can have a three-dimensional array, too, if you want.

```
Dim Rubics(3,3,3)
```

Part II: Speaking Like a Native

A three-dimensional array is a little harder to picture. Think of a cube made of little boxes — three little boxes on a side. Each little box is a separate variable. How many little boxes are there total in a 3 x 3 x 3 cube? That's right, there are 27. Each one is referenced by 3 coordinates.

And, believe it or not, VBScript lets you create four- and five-dimensional arrays — and even more. Don't ask me to help you picture that because I'm all out of ideas!

But when you actually start using this stuff, you use one-dimensional arrays pretty often, two-dimensional arrays sometimes, and the rest almost never. Remember: Whenever possible, keep it simple.

Creating Your Own Subroutines and Functions

VBScript offers a wide array of commands and functions to meet all of your basic programming needs. But sometimes what VBScript offers isn't enough. That's when it's time to create your own subroutines and functions.

Creating subroutines

A subroutine is like a VBScript command — it does something for you, but it doesn't return a value. You create a subroutine using the Sub command.

```
Sub DisplayValues(FirstValue, SecondValue)
...
End Sub
```

The Sub line identifies the name of the subroutine, and the parentheses specify the arguments that the subroutine expects to have passed in. The End Sub line identifies where the subroutine ends. All the lines of code between Sub and End Sub are part of the subroutine.

Creating functions

A function, as you may expect, works like a VBScript function — it returns a value, and when a function is called it can be included as part of a formula.

```
Function CalculateCost(FoodCost, HotelCost, HourlyRate)
Dim TotalCost
...
CalculateCost = TotalCost
End Function
```

Just like a subroutine, the Function identifies the name of the function and the arguments. End Function comes at the end. You need to assign a value to the *name* of the function sometime before the End Function. This value assigned to the name of the function is the value that is *sent back* to the calling routine. In the preceding code, all the calculations use a variable, TotalCost, and then you assign the code to CalculateCost, the name of the function just before the function ends.

Note that the name of the function isn't declared as a variable anywhere. The name of the function is always automatically declared for you.

Keep in mind that the names you use inside the subroutine or function are the names you give them in the Sub or Function line. But that isn't necessarily the name the variables will have when they are sent. In fact, when you call a subroutine or function, you may not send variables at all, but supply actual values instead.

A better random number function

Now that you finally have a way of creating your own function, perhaps a good first project would be to create a function to replace the VBScript deficient random number function.

One way to do this is to create specifically what you need for a page. If you are creating a craps or Yahtzee page, you may be able to put this function to use.

```
<%
Function RollDie
RollDie = Int(Rnd * 2) + 1
End Function
%>
```

If you need to flip a coin, this function works well:

```
<%
Function CoinFlip
Dim Toss
Toss = Int(Rnd * 2) + 1
If Toss = 1 Then
 CoinFlip = "Heads"
Else
```

```
    CoinFlip = "Tails"
End If
End Function
%>
```

This function is convenient because you don't have to do any calculations, and it returns a string that says "Heads" or "Tails". Notice that `CoinFlip`, the name of the function, is assigned in a couple of different places. `CoinFlip` can even be assigned and then reassigned a different value in the course of the function. Whatever the value is when the function ends is what is sent back.

Or, if you are going to use random numbers in different ways throughout a page, you may want to create a more generic random number function.

```
<%
Function RandNum(LowNum, HighNum)
RandNum = (HighNum - LowNum + 1) * Rnd + LowNum
End Function
%>
```

Calling subroutines and functions

Calling subroutines and functions works in about the same way as calling built-in VBScript commands and functions.

```
Roll = RollDie
Flip = CoinFlip
AdultAge = RandNum(18, 75)
```

You need to know one tricky thing about subroutines. When you call a subroutine, you *don't* use parentheses even if the subroutine has arguments. If you have a subroutine named `DisplayValues` that takes two arguments, calling it looks something like this:

```
DisplayValues 100, FinalSum
```

You do, however, always use parentheses when calling a function that has arguments. Why? It's just one of those VBScript quirks!

Chapter 5

JScript for Geeks

*I*f you're the type of person who prefers the obscure and mysterious syntax of Java, C, or C++, then some people may call you a geek. Not me, of course. I would never say something bad about you. But some people might.

Either way, this chapter is definitely for you. It builds on what you already know about Java, C, or C++ and shows you how JScript is different. With your foundation and these guidelines, you'll be ASP scripting in no time.

Who Should Read This Chapter?

This chapter is for you if you have some programming experience in C, C++, Java, or JavaScript.

If this doesn't describe you, I think you'll find VBScript much easier to learn and use for creating ASP pages. You can find information on VBScript in Chapters 3 and 4. Feel free to skip this chapter if you're sticking with VBScript — you don't need the information here.

But if you do have experience in C, C++, Java, or JavaScript, you're in the right place. Building on the experience you already have, JScript is a snap.

If you have used JavaScript before, perhaps to do client-side scripting, you already know JScript. Congratulations! Your class is already over. JScript is identical to JavaScript, and you can probably safely skip most of this chapter. Be sure to read the section titled "JScript and ASP," though, because that has ASP-specific information in it. And you may want to skim over the rest of this chapter quickly to see if there's anything new you aren't aware of.

What Is JScript?

JScript is the Microsoft implementation of JavaScript. I use the word *implementation* instead of *version* because the JScript syntax and functionality is identical to the syntax of JavaScript. A program written in JavaScript will always run in JScript, and vice versa (at least that's the theory). But because the original JavaScript was created by Netscape, Microsoft had to write its own implementation of the JavaScript language so that you could use it in the Microsoft products. The result is JScript.

JScript and ASP

JScript and VBScript are the two languages that come with Internet Explorer and IIS that allow you to do client- and server-side scripting. You can get other languages that plug in to the Microsoft scripting engine, including Perl and REXX. But the popularity of JavaScript in the Internet arena makes it among the most popular choices.

In this section I discuss all the ASP-specific JScript information you need to know. Even if you already know JavaScript, you can find valuable information in this section.

Delimiters

You use the <% and %> delimiters to separate your code from your HTML tags. You use these same delimiters regardless of the scripting language you use.

Delimiters for multiple lines

You can use delimiters on each line individually, as I do in the examples in Chapters 1 and 2, or you can enclose several lines with one set of delimiters, like this:

```
<% var count
count = 15 %>
```

Often, when enclosing more than one line of code, you can make it look cleaner by putting the delimiters on a line by themselves:

```
<%
var count
count = 15
%>
```

Delimiters and curly braces

Your delimiters and your curly braces work independently. By that I mean that you can have HTML inside a block of code. For example:

```
<%
if (count > 15)
{
 Warning = True
%>
Count exceeded!<p>
<%
}
%>
```

In this example, a line of HTML is included in the body of the `if` statement. Notice how you use the delimiters to enclose the JScript code wherever needed. You may prefer a more compact method:

```
<% if (count > 15) {
 Warning = True %>
Count exceeded!<p> <% } %>
```

However you decide to organize your curly braces and your delimiters, just be consistent so that your code is more readable.

Delimiters for displaying variable values

A special syntax exists that allows you to replace a JScript variable with its value right in your HTML. The syntax looks like this:

```
The answer is <% =result %>.<p>
```

In the preceding line of HTML, the delimiters and the code inside are replaced by the `result` variable's value when the HTML is sent to the browser. You can display the value of any variable — numeric or string — using this notation. If the value of `result` is 5, the HTML sent back looks like this:

```
The answer is 5.<p>
```

You can even use this notation within an HTML tag:

```
<font size=<% =fontsize %>>
```

If the `fontsize` JScript variable has the value of 4 at this point in the script, the HTML sent back looks like this:

```
<font size=4>
```

Picking your parlance, locating your language, choosing your chatter

Although both VBScript and JScript come with your web server, only one of them can be the default, and that one is VBScript. You can change this default several ways.

Selecting JScript as your default language on IIS

If you are using Windows NT and IIS and you want to set JScript as the default language for all ASP pages on your entire site, follow these steps:

1. **Launch the** `Internet Service Manager` **(accessed through the Microsoft Management Console).**

2. **Open the** `Internet Information Server` **folder.**

3. **Find your** `Default Web Site` **and right-click. Choose** `Properties` **from the pop-up menu.**

4. **Click the** `Home Directory` **tab.**

5. **Click the** `Configuration...` **button. The** `Application Configuration` **dialog box is displayed.**

6. **Click the** `App Options` **tab (see Figure 5-1).**

7. **In the edit labeled** `Default ASP language`, **delete VBScript and type** `JScript`.

Selecting JScript as your default language on PWS

If you are using Windows 95/98 or Windows NT Workstation and PWS, I've got bad news for you: You can't change the default ASP language when you're using PWS. You have to use the technique described in the next section to identify each page individually as a JScript page.

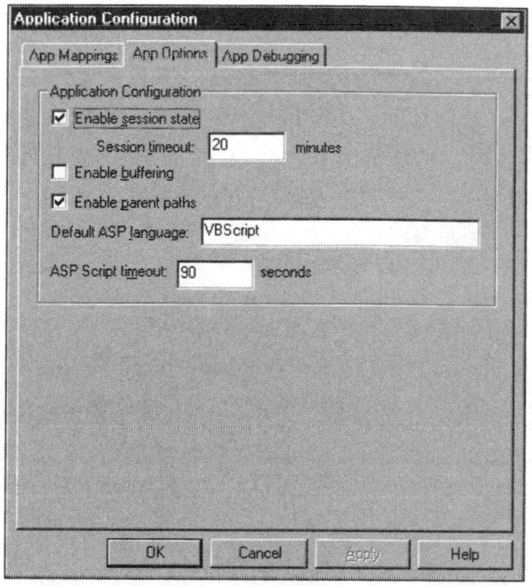

Figure 5-1:
The App
Options tab
of the
Application
Configuration
dialog box.

Selecting a different language for just this page

If you want to be able to choose your ASP language on a page-by-page basis, all you have to do is include this line at the top of your page:

```
<%@ LANGUAGE=JScript %>
```

Use the preceding line when VBScript is the default scripting language for your Web site, but you want to use JScript for this one page.

Alternately, if JScript is the default for your Web site, and you want to use VBScript for this page only, include this line at the top of your page:

```
<%@ LANGUAGE=VBScript %>
```

Here's What You Can't Do

I hate to start off on a downer, but when you're learning a language that is similar to something you know already, sometimes it's easier to describe what a language can't do before you learn what it can do. If you are a C or C++ programmer, you'll definitely find a few things that have been *left out* of JScript.

Is JavaScript like a Java Jr.?

So is it fair to say that JavaScript is a scaled-down version of Java in the same way that VBScript is a scaled-down version of Visual Basic? No, it isn't.

Java was created by Sun Microsystems. JavaScript was created by Netscape and was initially named LiveScript. Because of the cozy relationship of Netscape with Sun and because

of the popularity of Java, LiveScript became JavaScript at the last minute.

JavaScript shares the same syntax and basic commands as Java and, in turn, C and C++. This makes JavaScript easy to learn for all of those C and C++ developers out there. But the way JavaScript handles variable typing and objects is very different from Java, C, or C++.

Java, on which JScript is loosely based, attempts to simplify and fix some of the things that are overly complex, confusing, and potentially bug-causing in C and C++. The changes that the Java development team made are very controversial. And some people inevitably feel that they compromised too much away. But the overwhelming popularity of Java seems to confirm that the majority of developers feel they did the right thing.

JScript, in turn, is even slimmer than Java. JScript is an attempt to create a simple, small language that is, nonetheless, still very powerful.

No compiler

JScript is a completely interpreted language. It is not compiled in the traditional sense like C and C++. And JScript isn't compiled in the non-traditional sense (into byte-codes) like Java is.

JScript runs in the web browser when used in client-side scripts. And it runs on a web server when using ASP pages. The scripts are interpreted when they run.

The biggest downside to interpreted language is that they usually run more slowly than compiled languages. But you barely notice how slowly a small script runs after it took you several minutes just to download the page on your 56K modem!

No preprocessor

Both C and C++ have a preprocessor that goes through the source code before it is compiled and responds to compiler directives in the code like the #define and #include directives.

Java and JScript have no preprocessor. Some features in JScript help make up for some of the things you used to do with a preprocessor, though, so don't worry!

No pointers

C and C++ programmers often argue that pointers are powerful and necessary to do real programming. But even the most hard core C/C++ developers have to admit that pointers are often the source of some truly ugly bugs.

Because of the bugs that often result with pointers, Java and JScript have no pointers. There are, however, *references*. References are more carefully managed by the language than pointers are, and, because of this, it is not nearly as easy to get yourself into trouble with them.

No structures or unions

When you think about it, there's a lot of overlap, conceptually, among classes, structures, and unions. So why not collapse them together into one thing? That is what Java and JScript have done. In Java that *one thing* is a class. In JScript, it is an array (believe it or not). See Chapter 6 for more information on JScript objects and arrays.

No constants

In C, sometimes #define is used to give a name to a number that is used over and over again. That number can then be referenced throughout the program. In fact, this practice became so popular that the ANSI standard for C built this capability into the language with the const keyword. Java uses the keyword final to do the same thing.

Unfortunately, JScript does not yet support constants. I say *not yet* because const is a reserved keyword in JScript, even though it isn't implemented. So there's a chance you'll see it in the future.

No classes or inheritance

C is not an object-oriented language, so you pure C developers won't miss this, but C++ and Java developers will. JScript does not support classes or inheritance. But it does have objects. The way it handles objects, however, is quite — what word shall I use? — *unique*. For more information on how Java uses objects, see the section called "JScript Objects" in Chapter 6.

No operator overloading

Operator overloading is a feature that only C++ developers will have grown accustomed to. It is handy, but not essential. And not a part of JScript.

No variable number of arguments

In C and C++, you can create functions that can accept different numbers of arguments at different times, depending on how the calling routine wants to use the function. Both Java and JScript leave this functionality behind.

No goto statement

The goto statement has been the bane of structured programmers everywhere. At one time, when computer languages were much more primitive, you had no way around using goto statements for certain situations. But today's modern languages offer all the looping and branching structures you need to cover any situation. Therefore, in both Java and JScript, goto statements are history.

One Thing You Can (Finally!) Do: Strings

After all those *can'ts*, here's a really positive addition to both Java and JScript: full and complete support for strings! No longer do you have to deal with null-terminated arrays of characters (huh?). Strings are now a first-class citizen of data types!

But because of the very different ways data types in general are handled between Java and JScript, keep a sharp eye out in the coming sections for how strings are best put to use in JScript.

Common Comments

You'll be happy to know that comments are handled exactly the same in JScript as they are in modern C, C++, and Java.

//	Begins a line comment that ends at the end of the line.
/* and */	Begin and end multi-line comments.

These comments, like the rest of your JScript code, don't appear on the page when the user chooses View⇨Source in Internet Explorer. They are removed. If you want to add comments that can be seen on the page after it is sent, use the HTML comment tags `<!--` and `-->`.

Be Gentle. He's Case Sensitive.

JScript *is* case sensitive, just as C, C++, and Java are. That sensitivity means several things to you:

- ✔ Keywords, such as commands, must be entered exactly as they appear in the documentation — usually that means in all lower case.

- ✔ Object names must also be entered as they appear in their documentation. Usually, the first letter is capitalized and the rest are lowercase. However, property and method names can be in any case. See Chapter 6 for more information on JScript objects.

- ✔ Variables are named as you declare them. So create a standard and stick with it!

Be sure to keep the case-sensitivity of JScript in mind — especially when working with variables — because, unlike the other languages you're used to working with, you *don't* get an error if you accidentally change the case of a variable halfway through. JScript just assumes that you are creating a brand new variable and goes on. This assumption can cause bugs that are very, very tricky to find. For more information on JScript variables and their optional declaration, see the section called "Variable Vagrants and Smooth Operators" later in this chapter.

The Terminator (Of Lines)

In C, C++, and Java, you have to end each line with a semicolon. In JScript, it's still a good idea to do this, but it isn't required. If you don't end a line with a semicolon, the line is assumed to end when you hit return. For those of us who always seem to forget to put the semicolon on the end, this is good news!

Variable Vagrants and Smooth Operators

No matter what your language background, you may want to carefully read the following sections on variables. The way they work in JScript is unusual.

I declare! These variables have no type!

Unlike C++ and Java, variables in JScript are *not* strongly typed. In fact, they're not typed at all! You create variables by using the var keyword.

```
var wordcount, pagecount
```

No indication of the variables' type exists. In fact, you can't declare a permanent type for a variable either when you create it or anytime later. The variable takes on the type of the data that it holds, but it is perfectly acceptable to assign a variable a string value at one time and a numeric value at another. (Although, you could argue it isn't the best programming practice.)

As with other languages, you can initialize the variables with a value when you declare them.

```
var age = 23, gender = "male"
```

Types for the typeless

Although variables have no intrinsic type when they are created in JScript, they do take on the type of the data they are assigned. And the types of values that you can assign to variables in JScript are much like the types you find in any language.

- Either single or double quotes surround strings.

- Numbers come in either the floating point or integer variety. Integers can be represented in decimal, octal (by using a leading 0), or hexadecimal (by using a leading 0x). Number variables can also hold one of these values: NaN (stands for Not a Number), positive infinity, negative infinity, positive 0, and negative 0.

- Boolean values of true and false are special values, and they do *not* evaluate to 1 and 0. Although, if you use a numeric expression where a Boolean value is expected, zero is understood to be false and non-zero is interpreted as true.

Finally, a variable can hold two other values that don't really fall under any data type:

- A variable holds an *undefined value* after it's created and before it's assigned a value. If you try to use a variable with an undefined value, you get an error.

- A variable can hold a *null*. This is different from undefined and also different from 0. A null means that the variable holds no value at all.

Scoping it out

If you declare a variable using the `var` keyword on a page *outside* of any function, the variable is global to that page. If you declare a variable *inside* a function, it is local to that function.

If you assign a value to a variable that hasn't been declared using the `var` keyword, it is automatically created then. And regardless of whether the assignment is made inside a function or not, that variable is global. This is why it's extremely important to avoid accidentally misspelling or miscapitalizing a variable name.

If you try to use a variable that hasn't before been created — to compare it to something else or to display its value — you receive an error when the script is run.

Local variables always execute faster and more efficiently than global variables. Slowest of all are global variables that are not declared using `var` before they are assigned a value.

Casting out the demons of coercion

Casting, conversion, and *coercion:* All three of these words are used when talking about roughly the same idea — variable types changing when they are used with other variable types. Fortunately, most of the time, JScript handles this for you. You don't usually have to worry about it.

```
<%@ LANGUAGE=JScript %>
<HTML>
<%
var rate, hours, total,info
rate = 9.75
hours = 40
total = rate * hours
info = "Working " + hours + " hours at a rate of " + rate
info += " totals " + total + "."
%>
<%=info%><p>
</HTML>
```

When the floating point number is multiplied by the integer, JScript converts the variable types as it needs to. When the numbers are combined within a string, the numbers are converted to a string (see Figure 5-2).

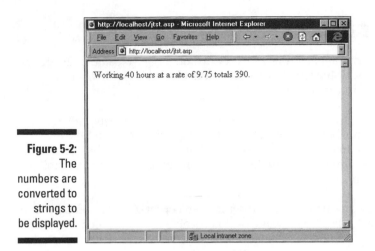

Figure 5-2:
The numbers are converted to strings to be displayed.

When you put numbers and strings together, as in the preceding code, JScript always assumes that you want to convert the numbers to strings — usually a good assumption. But for the times when it isn't the right assumption, JScript provides two functions to explicitly convert a string into either an integer or a floating point number: parseInt() and parseFloat().

```
<%@ LANGUAGE=JScript %>
<HTML>
<%
var length, feet
length = "20 yards"
feet = parseInt(length) * 3
%>
The length is <%=feet%> feet.<p>
</HTML>
```

Parse functions do another nice thing for you: They ignore any non-numeric stuff after the number (see Figure 5-3).

Operator? I'd like to make a call. . . .

The operators in JScript may look very familiar to you. The operators are all virtually identical to those in C. (See Table 5-1 for a list of the JScript operators.)

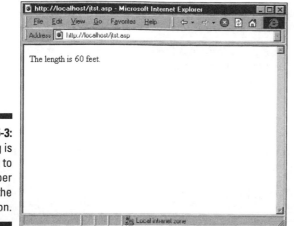

Figure 5-3:
The string is
converted to
a number
for the
calculation.

Table 5-1	JScript Operators
Operator	*Definition*
=	assignment
==	comparison
+, -	add, subtract
*, /	multiply, divide
%	modulus
++, —	increment, decrement
<, >	less-than, greater-than
<=, >=	less-than-or-equal, greater-than-or-equal
!=	not equal
&&, ||	logical and, logical or
!	logical not

All the bit-wise operators are the same, too.

Conditionals and Loops

The conditionals and loops in JScript all use the same keywords and work more or less the same way as those in C, C++, and Java.

if..else

The `if..else` statement is used to ask a question, and then branch based on the result.

```
if (cats >= 2 && husband == 0)
  oldmaid = true
else
  happily_ever_after = true
```

You can use the curly braces to create a block of multiple statements in either the `if` or `else` section.

switch..case

You use the `switch..case` statement to check one variable or expression against a number of possible values. It works just like the `switch..case` in C, C++, and Java, with the following exceptions:

- ✔ C and C++ don't allow you to switch based on a string variable. In JScript you can.
- ✔ The `switch` variable and the values it is compared to are required to be of the same type in C, C++, and Java. Because JScript is very loose with types, this restriction doesn't apply.
- ✔ C and C++ require the value in each `case` to be unique. JScript doesn't enforce this. It simply executes the first match it comes to.
- ✔ The `case` values you compare against must be literals in C, C++, and Java. In JScript you can use variables.

So, if you wanted to interpret a two-letter employee status code, you'd do something like this:

```
<%@ LANGUAGE=JScript %>
<HTML>
<%
var code, interpret
code = "XX"
switch (code)
{
case "OL":
 interpret = "On Leave"
 break
case "VA":
 interpret = "Vacation"
 break
case "GS":
 interpret = "Good Standing"
 break
default:
 interpret = "No longer employed here"
}
%>
<%=interpret%>
</HTML>
```

for..next, while, do..while

JScript supports all three looping statements supported by C++ and Java —
for..next, the top-tested while loop, and the bottom-tested do..while
loop. They work just as you expect them to.

```
<%@ LANGUAGE=JScript %>
<HTML>
<%
var squared
for (var x=1; x <= 10; x++)
{
 squared = x * x
%>
<%=x%> squared is <%=squared%><p>
<% } %>
</HTML>
```

All the numbers between 1 and 10 are displayed with their squares (see
Figure 5-4).

The while and do..while loops continue as long as a condition is true.

```
<%@ LANGUAGE=JScript %>
<HTML>
<%
var squared=0, x = 1
while (squared <= 100)
{
 x ++
 squared = x * x
<%=x%> squared is <%=squared%><p>
<% } %>
<%=x%> squared is greater than 100.<p>
</HTML>
```

Figure 5-4:
One through
ten and their
squares.

```
http://localhost/jtst.asp - Microsoft Internet Explorer
File   Edit   View   Go   Favorites   Help
Address  http://localhost/jtst.asp

1 squared is 1

2 squared is 4

3 squared is 9

4 squared is 16

5 squared is 25

6 squared is 36

7 squared is 49

8 squared is 64

9 squared is 81

10 squared is 100

                        Local intranet zone
```

The difference between the `while` and `do..while` loops is that the condition is checked *first thing* in the `while` loop. The condition isn't checked until the end of the loop in a `do..while` loop. This means that the stuff inside a `do..while` loop always executes at least once. The stuff inside a while loop will never execute if the condition fails the first time.

break, continue

The `break` and `continue` statements work identically to their counterparts in C++ and Java.

The break statement stops the execution of a loop or a switch..case and jumps out of it entirely, starting with the line immediately following the loop or switch..case.

The continue statement stops executing the body of a loop and begins the loop again from the top at the next iteration.

Arrays

Arrays in JScript are limited to one dimension.

But in many, many other ways arrays in JScript are very free from limitations. For example, because JScript doesn't support strict variable typing, it is perfectly legal to do something like this:

```
<%
player = new Array(4)
player[0] = "Fred Smith"
player[1] = 49
player[2] = "Jaguars"
player[3] = .225
%>
<%=player[0]%>
```

In other words, arrays aren't limited to holding only one variable type. A single array can hold many variable types in its different elements, much like a struct in C or C++.

Interesting, isn't it? But it's probably considered bad programming practice and one of those things you just shouldn't do. Don'tcha hate that?

Well, this time, the designers of JScript made it clear that they actually *do* intend for you to use this capability. In fact, they added other features to make it easier:

```
<%
player = new Array()
player["name"] = "Fred Smith"
player["number"] = 49
player["team"] = "Jaguars"
player["average"] = .225
%>
<%=player["name"]%>
```

Notice that this time I didn't give an array size. I didn't provide an array size because now I'm not even using numbers to reference the array elements. I'm using names, just like you do when you refer to the elements of a struct. In fact, the same syntax you use for a struct is valid here, too.

```
<%
player = new Array()
player.name = "Fred Smith"
player.number = 49
player.team = "Jaguars"
player.average = .225
%>
<%=player.name%>
```

Obviously, arrays in JScript are very flexible. In Chapter 6, I explore even more bizarre things you can do with them.

Creating Functions

In C and C++ you can create functions that are independent and can be called from anywhere in your application. Java, in an attempt to be more object-oriented, requires you to always create functions as part of objects. JScript works more like C and C++ in this respect. You can create normal, stand-alone functions that can be accessed from anywhere on a page.

You create a function by using the `function` keyword and specifying the name, arguments, and body of the function.

Array indexes don't have to come one after another!

Even when you do use numbers to index the elements of an array, you don't have to use *consecutive* numbers. For example:

```
<%
book = new Array()
book[52] = "Interesting quote"
book[103] = "Study for exam"
book[122] = "Very important"
%>
```

The array element numbers in the book array are used to indicate the page numbers in the book. You may think this would waste a lot of space by creating over a hundred elements, most of which aren't even used. But that turns out not to be true. JScript uses *sparse arrays,* which means that preceding code only creates three elements, even though the indexes aren't consecutive.

```
<%
function square_it(value_passed)
{
var squared_value
squared_value = value_passed * value_passed
return squared_value
}
%>
```

Variables declared within the function are local to the function. You use the `return` statement to identify the value that gets sent back as the result of the function.

To call this function, you simply mention its name, pass the right arguments, and be sure to receive the value returned, if you expect one.

```
<% sqr_val = square_it(15) %>
```

The `eval` *Function*

You need to know about one function in particular before you begin your JScript programming career — `eval`.

The `eval` function is a very interesting beast. `Eval` is the kind of function that you're most likely to find in an interpreted language, and it provides some benefits that are awfully hard to duplicate in a compiled language like C or C++.

What does it do? You can take a formula in the form of a string and evaluate it as though it were a line of code.

Passing by value or by reference

In C, C++, and Java, you usually explicitly identify how arguments are passed to a function — either by *value* or by *reference*. JScript makes some assumptions and always does it the same way.

Numbers and Booleans are always passed by value. Objects, arrays, and functions are always passed by reference.

These rules apply not only to arguments in a function but also to any time that one variable is assigned to another or compared.

Strings are a special case. They are copied and passed to functions by reference, but when they are compared, they are compared by value — just as you'd expect.

```
<%@ LANGUAGE=JScript %>
<HTML>
<%
var formula, result
formula = "15 * (300 / 7)"
result = eval(formula)
%>
<%=formula%> is equal to <%=result%>.<p>
</HTML>
```

The result is calculated as if it had appeared directly in the code (see Figure 5-5).

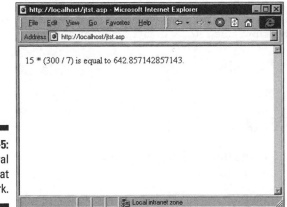

Figure 5-5:
The eval
function at
work.

Okay, that's interesting, but not earth shattering. Now look at this example:

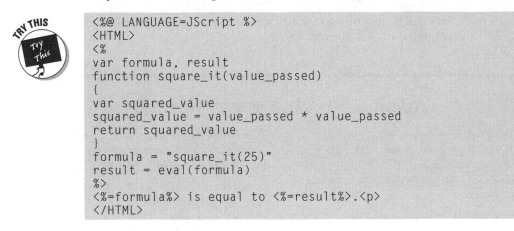

```
<%@ LANGUAGE=JScript %>
<HTML>
<%
var formula, result
function square_it(value_passed)
{
var squared_value
squared_value = value_passed * value_passed
return squared_value
}
formula = "square_it(25)"
result = eval(formula)
%>
<%=formula%> is equal to <%=result%>.<p>
</HTML>
```

The result looks like Figure 5-6. You can use JScript operators, you can use built-in JScript functions, and you can even use functions that *you* create. Calling `eval` is exactly like submitting the line of code contained within the string to the interpreter at that point in the script. Now your programs can begin to write themselves!

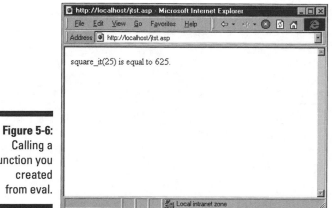

Figure 5-6:
Calling a
function you
created
from eval.

Part III
Getting to Know Your Objects

The 5th Wave   By Rich Tennant

"Hold on, that's not a problem with the ASP scripting, it's just a booger on the screen."

In this part . . .

*I*n this section, you learn about three different kinds of objects that you make use of in your ASP pages: scripting objects, server objects, and server components. These objects add a whole lot of exciting capabilities to your ASP scripts and make it possible to create very powerful Web applications.

In fact, to prove that you can start creating powerful Web applications, Chapter 8 begins doing it! There you can find five little applications that you can integrate and use to enhance your own Web site right away.

Chapter 6

Objects, Objects Everywhere!

. . . .

In This Chapter

▶ Dissecting an object

▶ Speaking the language

▶ Using objects, properties, and methods

▶ Working with scripting objects in VBScript and JavaScript

▶ Using scripting objects common to both VBScript and JavaScript

. . . .

*O*bjects are everywhere! Your car is an object, your computer is an object, even your mother-in-law is an object. An object is just a thing that you give a name. Most objects have attributes that describe the object, and most objects can do things and even interact with other objects. You deal with these kinds of objects every day. Using software objects to help describe the world that your script lives in helps make the software world easier to relate to.

I start off this chapter describing what a software object is and what it has inside it. Then I describe the objects that are built into the scripting language you've chosen for ASP development. Finally, I discuss the numerous scripting objects available to *both* VBScript and JScript and show you examples of putting them to work using both languages.

Okay, So What's an Object?

Computer programming-types love buzzwords. One of their favorites is *object-oriented programming*. What does it mean? Well, if you ask a programmer what it means, he usually starts waving his arms and throwing around even bigger buzzwords like *polymorphism* (say that three times fast!).

But the fact is, object-oriented programming is really a pretty simple idea. It takes all the functions that sort of go together and all the variables that those functions use and puts them together into one big pile.

For instance, if you have a payroll program, you may have several functions that go with an employee. Maybe you have a `PayEmployee` function, an `UpdateEmployeeInfo` function, and several others. You also have employee variables that those functions *use,* such as `EmployeeSalary`, `EmployeeName`, and `EmployeeAddress`. Why not put all of these functions and variables together into one big *thing*. You can call that thing an *object* — an *Employee* object.

Then you can start looking for other objects. Perhaps creating a `Check` object and an `ActivitySheet` object makes sense. These objects help bring organization to the hodgepodge of functions and variables in a big computer program.

So, what is an object? It's just a bunch of functions and variables that are brought together under one roof. Give the bunch a name, and you've got an object!

Getting the Patter Down

I hate to do this to you, but you absolutely have to know a few terms when you get into object-oriented programming. Don't worry. I won't give them all to you at once, and I won't give them to you at all if I think you can get by without them!

- ✔ **Object:** That's easy! It's just a pile of functions and variables to which you assign a name, right? Right!

- ✔ **Property (or Attribute):** No, I'm not trying to sneak two past you at once. Both of these terms mean the same thing. But you have to know them both because people use them both all the time. I told you that an object is made up of functions and variables, right? Well, a property or attribute is what you call one of those variables that is *inside an object*. That's it!

  You can think of the variables inside an object as properties or attributes that *describe* that object. Just like a flower has certain properties or attributes, such as a pretty color or a beautiful smell, your `Company` object has properties or attributes, such as `Name`, `Industry`, `Products`, and so forth that describe the company.

- ✔ **Method:** A method is simply a function that is *inside an object*. It is something the object can *do*, if you want it to. I know the name sounds very odd, but it is the name that all the programmer-types use, so I guess we're stuck with it.

Using Objects

Object-oriented programming has been around in universities for a long time, but just in the last few years it has taken hold in real-world computer programming. And it has *really* taken hold.

Your ASP pages use a lot of different kinds of objects:

- ✔ Objects that are built into the language and available only from the specific scripting language you are using.
- ✔ Objects that are designed to help with scripting but are available to be used from any scripting language.
- ✔ Objects that are a part of the web server.
- ✔ Objects that you create (in JavaScript).

But no matter what kind of object it is, you always work with it in the same way.

If you want to set the value of a property, you do it like this:

```
ObjName.PropName = Value
```

If you've used a `struct` in C or C++, this format should look very familiar. It's called *dot-notation* because you always refer to a property by first stating its object name, then a dot (period), and then the property name.

You can also use the property in a condition.

```
If ObjName.PropName > Value Then ...
```

If you want to call a *method* of an object, you do the same sort of thing.

```
ObjName.MethodName Arg1, Arg2
```

Call the function as you normally would, but be sure to use the object name and dot-notation. If the function returns a value, calling it looks like this:

```
Variable = ObjName.MethodName(Arg1, Arg2)
```

Using Scripting Objects

Both VBScript and JavaScript have objects that are built into the language, called *scripting objects*. These objects are designed to be language extensions that give you additional capabilities to write more powerful scripts. The trouble is, VBScript has some scripting objects that aren't available from JavaScript, and vice versa.

For example, a bunch of functions in VBScript work with dates (see Chapter 3). JavaScript doesn't have any date functions. Instead, it has a `Date` object that has all of these functions bundled together (see the section "Got a date? All the girls love a JavaScript geek. . . ." later in this chapter).

Because each language has its own set of language-specific objects and different ways of handling these objects, I discuss VBScript objects and JavaScript objects separately.

If you read Chapters 3 and 4 and are planning to use *VBScript* for your ASP pages, skip the section in this chapter called "JavaScript Objects." If you read Chapter 5 and are planning to use *JavaScript* for your ASP pages, skip the section in this chapter called "VBScript Objects." Got it?

But, regardless of which sections you read or skip, check out the last section titled "Scripting Objects Available to Both VBScript and JavaScript." There I show you how to access a set of common scripting objects from both languages.

VBScript Objects

In this section, I show you how to create your own simple objects in VBScript and then introduce you to one object which is specific to VBScript: the `Err` object. The `Err` object helps you with handling errors that happen when your script is running.

Creating and using VBScript objects

Objects are a great way to help you organize your subroutines, functions, and variables. So how do you create objects in VBScript? It turns out to be pretty easy.

```
<%
Class Employee
    Public FirstName, LastName

    Private Salary

    Function GetWholeName
        GetWholeName = FirstName & " " & LastName
    End Function
End Class
%>
```

The first thing you notice is that the whole affair is surrounded by Class and End Class. You probably expect something such as Object and End Object, but no such luck. A *class* in the object-oriented world refers to what an object is *before* it's an object. Until you actually make it and start using it, it's a class. As soon as you start using it, it is an object.

This class's name is Employee. It has three properties — FirstName, LastName, and Salary — and one method — GetWholeName.

In order to *use* this object, you first have to create it.

```
<%
Dim Emp1
Set Emp1 = New Employee

Emp1.FirstName = "Tom"
Emp1.LastName = "Wood"


Response.Write Emp1.GetWholeName
%>
```

You create the Emp1 variable to hold an Employee-type object. The Set line creates a New object of type Employee and then assigns Emp1 to represent that new object. From that point on, the new object can be referred to by the name Emp1.

Emp1 is just a variable, just like any other variable. If the variable is created on a page, it is local to that page and it can't be accessed on other pages.

To err is human. . . .

Normally, when your script is running on the server, if VBScript runs into an error, it simply gives up and sends the error message on the Web page to the browser, wherever the error occurred.

Obviously, this isn't the kind of thing you want happening on your Web page. So, you work hard to squash every bug you find before it has a chance to embarrass you. The problem is that there are some times when you can't anticipate an error. And no matter how much debugging you do, you can't prevent the possibility of an error (even if it is unlikely).

This kind of situation usually happens if you are depending on something outside of your program, such as the users putting a disk or CD-ROM in its drive. If they don't, an error is generated. Or perhaps you're using an object that someone else has created. Your code may work perfectly, but if their code causes an error, you need to try to handle the situation, if you can.

```
On Error Resume Next
```

If you can't stop errors from happening, the next best thing is to catch them and handle them when they do occur. Putting this line near the top of your page or at the top of your subroutine or function makes that possible.

```
<% On Error Resume Next %>
```

If VBScript runs into an error, this line tells VBScript, "Don't give up! Just keep on going to the next line."

The `Err` *object*

Of course if you tell VBScript to keep on going, then you'd better follow through and try to handle any errors that occur. This is where the `Err` object can help you. The `Err` object has several *properties:*

- `Number` **and** `Description`: Provide the error number and a textual, semi-English explanation of the error that occurred.

- `Source`: Identifies the place where the error occurred. If you are calling a method in another object when the error happens, often that object's name is placed in `Source`.

- `HelpFile` **and** `HelpContext`: Hold a help filename and an ID for a specific topic within the help file to display if the user clicks the Help button or presses F1 while looking at the error message dialog box.

The `Err` object also has two *methods:*

- `Clear`: Clears out all the properties in the `Err` object. You can do this after you've successfully handled the error in one way or another.

- `Raise`: Actually *generates* an error. You pass these arguments to the Raise method: `Number`, `Description`, `Source`, `HelpFile`, and `HelpContext`. You recognize this data — it's the properties of the `Err` object! All the arguments are optional except `Number`.

But if you call the `Raise` method and don't specify all the arguments, you should do a `Clear` first. Otherwise, you may end up with leftover values from a previous error!

Error trapping example

One short example shows you how to put VBScript error-checking to work. In the following code, the `AmountPerMonth` function calculates how much money you have to save per month to reach a goal to purchase an item. You pass the amount of the item and the number of months you're willing to wait, and it returns the amount per month you have to put back. It doesn't take into account any interest on your money, so the process is very simple.

```
<%
Dim Amt
Amt = AmountPerMonth(1000, 0)
%>
<%=Amt%>
<%
Function AmountPerMonth(Amount, Months)
On Error Resume Next
Dim MonthlyAmount
MonthlyAmount = Amount / Months
If Err.Number = 11 Then
   AmountPerMonth = -1
Else
   AmountPerMonth = MonthlyAmount
End If
Fnd Function
%>
```

Computers always croak if you try to divide by zero. It can't be done. But you don't want to show the user an ugly error message. `AmountPerMonth` uses the `On Error Resume Next` to stop VBScript from croaking and then immediately checks for the error after the calculation. A returned value of -1 indicates that an error occurred because of bad data sent to it.

Other VBScript-specific scripting objects

There is one more set of VBScript-specific scripting objects. They are the `RegExp`, `Matches` and `Match` objects. These allow you to quickly search a string with a very flexible set of wildcards to find exactly the pattern you are looking for. This search mechanism, called regular expressions, originally came from Unix and is a very popular way of doing complex searches. You can find more information on the regular expression objects in the VBScript documentation.

When to add `On Error Resume Next`

While you're developing your page, leave off the `On Error Resume Next` line until the end, or add it and immediately comment it out.

Why? Unless you are a much better developer than I am, you're going to get a lot of errors in the process of creating your page. You want to know about those errors right away. You don't want VBScript continuing on its merry way and not telling you about the errors it runs into.

Only after the rest of your page is totally debugged should you add the `On Error Resume Next` line and then test it.

Why aren't there more VBScript-specific objects? Well, it's not because Microsoft hasn't been hard at work creating a bunch of objects to make your scripting life easier — it has! It's just that instead of making those new objects specific to VBScript, Microsoft has generalized them so that they can be used from *any* scripting language.

Go ahead and skip to the section titled "Scripting Objects Available to Both VBScript and JScript" later in this chapter to discover more objects.

JavaScript Objects

VBScript was based on Visual Basic when it was created. Because JavaScript was created from scratch, the developers at Netscape could take the best from a number of different languages and even add their own creative touches to make JavaScript more object-oriented. Because of this, JavaScript is organized in a little more object-oriented manner than VBScript.

In the following sections I discuss:

- ✔ Creating and using your own objects in JavaScript
- ✔ Using the string object functions to manipulate strings like a master
- ✔ Calculating with the `Math` object
- ✔ Counting the days with the `Date` object

Arrays as objects as arrays as. . . .

JavaScript provides a rather unusual way for you to create your own objects. You do it with arrays!

Because the JavaScript variables don't have any type, you can use an array just like you would use a `struct` in C or C++ to store variables of different data types in different elements of the array. You can even refer to these elements the same way you do with structures. For more information on this topic, see the section cleverly titled "Arrays" in Chapter 5.

But you can go beyond that. You can create objects with arrays. Here's how you set it up.

First, create a function which will work as the *constructor* for the object. A constructor is a method that is called first when an object is created to set it up. It can look like this:

```
<%
function make_employee(first, last, addr, city, sal)
{
  this.first_name = first
  this.last_name = last
  this.address = addr
  this.city_state_zip = city
  this.salary = sal
}
%>
```

The this keyword is special. It refers to the current object — the one I'm working with right now. This function won't be called like normal functions. It's called in a special way, which creates a new object at the same time it is called. It is this newly created object that this refers to.

All you have to do to create properties for the object is assign them a value. The property values are all assigned from the arguments passed in.

Now, to create an employee object, all you have to do is use the new keyword along with the constructor function name to create an object and call the function. The property values you want are passed as arguments.

```
<%
var emp1, emp2;
emp1 = new make_employee("Buddy", "Tiger",
    "104 W. Main", "Boston, MA 33224", 30000)
emp2 = new make_employee("Coco", "Carmine",
    "5215 S. 5th", "Arlington, MA 66224", 50000)
%>
```

But, so far, this isn't any different from creating structures. An object is different because it has methods. How do you add methods to a JavaScript object? It's pretty easy.

First create a couple of methods:

```
<%
function format()
{
var layout
layout = this.first_name + " " + this.last_name + "<br>"
layout += this.address + "<br>"
layout += this.city_state_zip + "<br>"
layout += "Salary: " + this.salary + "<p>"
return layout
}
function raise(percent_amount)
{
this.salary = this.salary * (1 + percent_amount / 100)
}
%>
```

The first method, format, puts the information into a nice layout so that it can be easily printed on the Web page. The second method accepts a percentage amount and then raises the employee salary by that amount. For instance, if 15 were passed to the function, it would increase the salary by 15 percent.

I call these functions methods, but they aren't really methods yet. How do you build them into your object? Just modify your constructor method (make_employee) so that it looks like this:

```
<%
function make_employee(first, last, addr, city, sal)
{
   this.first_name = first
   this.last_name = last
   this.address = addr
   this.city_state_zip = city
   this.salary = sal
   this.format = format
   this.raise = raise
}
%>
```

New properties called format and raise are assigned to the names of the two functions we just created, also named format and raise. Now these functions are methods of this object and can be called using dot-notation.

Here I create some objects and put them to use.

```
<%
var emp1, emp2, emp1string, emp2string
emp1 = new make_employee("Buddy", "Tiger",
   "104 W. Main", "Boston, MA 33224", 30000)
emp2 = new make_employee("Coco", "Carmine",
   "5215 S. 5th", "Arlington, MA 66224", 50000)
emp1string = emp1.format()
emp2string = emp2.format()
%>
<%=emp1string%>
<%=emp2string%>
<%
emp1.raise(15)
emp2.raise(50)
emp1string = emp1.format()
emp2string = emp2.format()
%>
<%=emp1string%>
<%=emp2string%>
```

First off, I create two objects by using the new keyword while calling the constructor function make_employee. The new keyword creates the new object and the make_employee function creates the properties and assigns them their initial value.

Making quick functions

You can use a variation on the theme of using the new keyword with a function to create simple functions by using only a single line of code.

```
var CubeIt = new Function ("value_in",   "return value_in *
    value_in * value_in");
```

You can specify as many arguments as you like for the function, one after the other, separated by commas. The last argument is always considered the body of the function. Within the body, you can actually code more than one line by separating them with semicolons.

After the function is defined, you can use it just as you would any other function.

```
newval = CubeIt(weight) / num
```

This syntax is just a shortcut and is never required. You can always create the same functions using the normal function syntax.

Now I have two complete objects created and filled with data. Time to put them to work. The next two lines receive the nicely formatted string back from each object's format function. Then, of course, the strings are displayed.

To test the second method, I gave the first employee a 15 percent raise and the second one a 50 percent raise. Then I formatted and displayed them again. You can see the result in Figure 6-1.

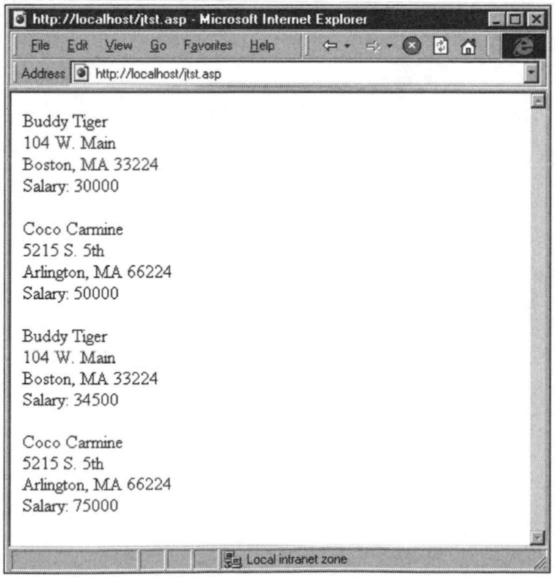

Figure 6-1:
The results
of the
employee
object
scripts.

Strings as objects

Every variable that holds a string in JavaScript is actually an object. And each of those objects has properties and methods that can be called to examine and manipulate the string in one way or another.

On the property front, only one is really important: `length`. It holds the current length of the string in characters.

Methods, on the other hand, are a different story. A lot of functions exist that do almost anything you'd want. I've divided them into two different categories: string manipulation, which allows you to examine and modify a string directly, and adding common HTML tags to a string automatically.

String manipulation

String manipulation methods allow you to directly examine and manipulate strings. Quite a few of these methods exist, so I only cover the most interesting ones here. You can look the others up if you need to in the JScript documentation. You can find complete JScript documentation in your web server's online help. You can also download a copy of the JScript documentation from the Microsoft JScript Web site at `msdn.microsoft.com/scripting/default.htm`.

Converting a string to upper or lower case

The `toLowerCase()` and `toUpperCase()` functions convert all the characters in the string to lower or upper case.

```
<% var banner = "Buy My Stuff!" %>
<%=banner%><p>
<%=banner.toLowerCase()%><p>
<%=banner%><p>
<%=banner.toUpperCase()%><p>
<%="Please Please Please!".toUpperCase()%><p>
```

After you execute this page, the browser shows this:

```
Buy My Stuff!

buy my stuff!

Buy My Stuff!

BUY MY STUFF!

PLEASE PLEASE PLEASE!
```

I've interspersed the normal banner string with the calls to the toUpperCase() and toLowerCase() functions to make a point. If you call a method on a string, the method returns the result of its manipulation. It does *not,* however, actually change the string.

Notice that I am displaying the result of the call to banner.toLowerCase(), and, as you'd expect, buy my stuff! is displayed. But then when I display banner again, it's normal. The actual string in the variable is not changed. This is the way all the string methods work.

If I wanted to write code that *would* change the original variable, I'd have to assign the value returned back to the variable, like this:

```
<% banner = banner.toLowerCase() %>
```

One more thing to note — that last line:

```
<%="Please Please Please!".toUpperCase()%><p>
```

What's happening here? Well, even string literals are objects. In other words, the string doesn't have to be in a variable before you call methods on it. In this case, it is just the literal text between quotes, then a period, and then the method name. You can call all the string methods from a string literal using this syntax.

Finding the index of a string within a string

The indexOf() and lastIndexOf() allow you to search through the string to find a substring that you pass in as an argument. You also pass the index where you want to begin searching. The function returns the index where it finds the first match. The only difference between the two functions is that indexOf() searches from left to right and lastIndexOf() searches from right to left.

```
<% var warning = "Death to all who enter here" %>
<%=warning.indexOf("enter",0)%>
```

This code begins searching for enter within the larger string, beginning at the first character (it always starts at 0). It displays the number 17, because that's the character where the word enter begins.

Dissecting strings

The substr() and substring() are two JavaScript functions that allow you to dissect strings. substr() accepts two arguments — an index to start and a length. The portion of the string specified is then returned:

```
<% var meet = "Meet the Flintstones" %>
<% =meet.substr(9,11)%>
```

This code displays in your browser:

```
Flintstones
```

The `substring()` function is similar, but you pass it a beginning and ending index and it returns the corresponding substring.

```
<% var meet = "Meet the Rubbles in person" %>
<% =meet.substring(9,15)%>
```

And you see this in your browser:

```
Rubble
```

Notice that the string begins at the first index and goes up to, but does not include, the character at the last index. That's why I get `Rubble` and not `Rubbles`.

Adding HTML tags

Many of the string methods are used to add HTML tags to the string. For example:

```
<%
var to_display
to_display = "Look At Me!"
to_display = to_display.big()
to_display = to_display.bold()
to_display = to_display.blink()
%>
<p>
<%=to_display%><p>
```

This shows a big, bold, blinking `Look At Me!` in your browser. (Actually, because Internet Explorer doesn't support the blink tag, it is only big and bold.) If you view the source, this is what you see:

```
<p>
<BLINK><B><BIG>Look At Me!</BIG></B></BLINK>
<p>
```

The only thing these functions do is take the string that was sent, add the appropriate tags, and return the result. Notice that the methods don't change the actual string you sent. They just add the tags to the result returned.

If you want to change the string you sent, you have to receive the value returned into the same variable, as I did in the preceding code.

A bunch of string methods add HTML tags like this. Table 6-1 has a list of the methods and the tags they add.

Table 6-1	String Methods and the Tags They Add
Method	*Tag Added*
anchor(name)	<a name=...>
link(url)	<a href=...>
big()	<big>
small()	<small>
blink()	<blink>
bold()	<b>
italics()	<i>
strike()	<strike>
fixed()	<tt>
sup()	<sup>
sub()	<sub>
fontcolor()	<font color=...>
fontsize()	<font size=...>

JavaScript does math

The math object contains a variety of properties and methods for doing all kinds of math calculations. I list the most common functions. If you're into math, you probably know what they do without me having to describe it. If you're not into math, you're probably skipping this section anyway.

Trig Methods: sin(), cos(), tan(), asin(), acos(), atan()

Other Methods: abs(), exp(), log(), min(), max(), pow(), round(), random()

And, so that you never have to remember pi to five digits again, the math object also provides these handy properties (see Table 6-2).

Table 6-2	The math **Object's Properties**
Property	*Value*
E	Euler's constant, approximately 2.718
LN2	Natural logarithm of 2, approximately 0.693
LN10	Natural logarithm of 10, approximately 2.302
LOG2E	Base 2 logarithm of e, approximately 1.442
LOG10E	Base 10 logarithm of e, approximately 0.434
PI	Ratio of circumference of a circle to its diameter, approximately 3.14159
SQRT1_2	1 divided by the square root of 2, approximately 0.707
SQRT2	Square root of 2, approximately 1.414

Got a date? All the girls love a JavaScript geek. . . .

Although *date* isn't a native data type in JavaScript, you can store dates and times by using the Date object.

```
<%
var rightnow, future
rightnow = new Date()
future = new Date(2000, 0,1)
%>
<%=rightnow%><p>
<%=future%>
```

This code displays your current date and the date of January 1, 2000:

```
Wed Oct 22 22:17:03 EST 1999
Sat Jan 1 00:00:00 EST 2000
```

After you create a new date object without passing any arguments, today's date and time are automatically filled in.

If you do want to pass in a value when you create it, you must enter the full four-digit year first, and then the month, and then the date.

Unfortunately, the months of the year are numbered from 0 to 11, not 1 to 12. Ugh! Like there isn't enough needless complexity in the world.

You can also enter the time by adding four more arguments: hours, minutes, seconds, and milliseconds. But if you don't want to be that precise, you can leave off whatever detail you like. You can specify just the hours, or just the hours and minutes, or whatever you want to specify.

Lots and lots of methods for the date object exist, but the vast majority of them are designed to let you get or set the different parts of the date object. Some of the methods are: `getDate()`, `getMonth()`, `getFullYear()`, `getHours()`, `getMinutes()`, `getSeconds()`, and `getMilliseconds()`. A corresponding set function exists for each of those `get` functions.

Finally, a handy `getDay()` method also exists that tells you what day of the week the date falls on — Sunday through Saturday. Of course, it returns 0 through 6 instead of 1 through 7.

Scripting Objects Available to Both VBScript and JScript

A number of scripting objects are available to any scripting engine you use. These objects include:

- `Dictionary` **object:** Provides another convenient way of storing and retrieving information.

- `FileSystemObject`, `Drive/Drives`, `Folder/Folders`, **and** `File/Files` **objects:** Make it easy to get information about and manipulate the drives, folders, and files on your server's hard drive.

- `TextStream` **objects:** Make it easy to create and read text files from the hard drive.

- `ScriptEngine`**:** Functions allow you to determine which scripting engine is being used and, more specifically, which build and version.

I discuss each of these topics in the following sections. And I show you examples in both VBScript and JavaScript, as appropriate. Again, feel free to skip right over those sections that don't apply to the language you're using.

What's a `Dictionary`? Look it up!

The `Dictionary` object provides a very handy way for managing lists. It's called a `Dictionary` because instead of organizing data by index numbers, as an array does, the `Dictionary` object organizes them by a word or phrase. So, for example, you can store state abbreviations like IN, OH, and CA with their associated state names, Indiana, Ohio, and California. Then whenever someone enters an abbreviation, you can look up the associated state name. The same can be done in a variety of other applications:

- ✔ Countries and their capitals
- ✔ HTML form controls and their values
- ✔ Article names and summaries
- ✔ Various preferences items (background image, text color, text size, and so on) and the user's choices for those items

Creating a `Dictionary`

You have to create the Dictionary before you can use it. I discuss how to do this in the following two sections. Read whichever is appropriate for your scripting language.

Creating a Dictionary in VBScript

The way the `Dictionary` object works is different from the way the `Err` object works. Only one `Err` object exists, and it is always available to you whenever you need to use it. But you may want to create several `Dictionary` objects on a page and none on another page. So you handle the creating of `Dictionary` objects whenever you like. You do this with the VBScript `CreateObject` function.

```
<%
Dim Capitals
Set Capitals = CreateObject("Scripting.Dictionary")
Capitals.Add "England", "London"
Capitals.Add "USA", "Washington"
Capitals.Add "France", "Paris"
Capitals.Add "Norway", "Oslo"
%>
```

Several new concepts are present in this example:

- ✔ The argument passed to `CreateObject` is "`Scripting.Dictionary`" because `Dictionary` is a scripting object.
- ✔ `Set` is used to assign the value returned from `CreateObject` to the variable `Capitals`. You don't normally use `Set` when you are assigning a value to a variable or receiving a value back from a function. The reason you use it here is because the thing returned isn't just a value, it is an object — a `Dictionary` object. Whenever you assign an object to a variable in VBScript, you have to use `Set`.
- ✔ After the new variable is set to the `Dictionary` object, you can use the variable to call methods of the object using the normal dot-notation. Here I call `Add` and pass a *key* (the first value) and an *item* (the second value). Every time I call `Add`, a new key/item pair is added to the `Dictionary`.

Creating a Dictionary in JScript

The Dictionary object doesn't provide as much to the JScript developer as it does to the VBScript developer. That's because the JScript array handling is so flexible that most of the things you'd use a Dictionary to do, you can do just as easily with an array.

However, some of the Server objects, which I discuss in Chapter 7, use a Dictionary to hold their information. So you want to have access to the Dictionary object and know how it works.

```
<%
var Capitals
Capitals = new ActiveXObject("Scripting.Dictionary")
Capitals.Add("England","London")
Capitals.Add("USA","Washington")
Capitals.Add("France","Paris")
Capitals.Add("Norway","Oslo")
%>
```

To create the Dictionary object, and other shared scripting objects, which you discover in later sections, you use new along with the ActiveXObject function. You pass to this function a string, which is identical to the string passed in VBScript to the CreateObject function. The string contains the type of the object, a period, and then the name of the specific object you want to create. The Dictionary object is a scripting object.

Looking up an entry

If Add makes Dictionary entries, how do you look something up? With the Item property, passing the key as an argument.

```
The capital city of France
is <%=Capitals.Item("France")%><p>
```

The Exists method returns true or false to let you know whether the key you pass exists or not.

```
<%
Dim Country
Country = "Iran"
If Capitals.Exists(Country) Then
%>
Yes, I know the capital of <%=Country%>.<p>
It is <%=Capitals.Item(Country)%>.<p>
<% Else %>
No, I don't know anything about <%=Country%>.<p>
<% End If %>
```

The JScript code for these examples are almost identical to the VBScript code.

Be careful with the Item property

The Item property is very powerful. You can use it to display the item associated with the key, but you can also use it to assign a new item to a key.

```
<% Capitals.Item("USA") = "New
   York" %>
```

And if you attempt to display or assign a value to a key that doesn't exist, VBScript goes ahead and creates a new entry for you with that key's name.

Walking through the entries one-by-one

Although Dictionary entries are made to be accessed by their keywords, there are times when you want to walk through all the entries one-by-one. Two methods and one property make looking through the entries one-by-one easy:

- Keys method: Returns an array holding all the keys in the Dictionary.
- Items method: Returns an array holding all the items in the Dictionary.
- Count property: Holds the number of entries in the Dictionary.

So, if you want to show a list of all the countries and their capitals, you do it like this:

```
<%
Dim CountryList, LastCountry, Num
CountryList = Capitals.Keys
LastCountry = Capitals.Count -1
For Num = 0 To LastCountry
%>
The capital of <%=CountryList(Num)%> is
<%=Capitals.Item(CountryList(Num))%>.<p>
<% Next %>
```

After putting the array returned from Capitals.Keys into CountryList, the last item in the array is calculated by subtracting 1 from the Count property. Notice that the array starts at 0, not at 1. So the For..Next loop then goes from 0 to Count - 1. Inside the loop, the country is displayed (the key) and, after that, the Item associated with the key. Again the JScript code is very similar.

Removing items from a Dictionary

To remove an item from the Dictionary, use the Remove method, passing the key.

```
Capitals.Remove("England")
```

To remove all the entries, use the RemoveAll method.

```
Capitals.RemoveAll
```

The FileSystemObject *and its* Drives, Folders, *and* Files

The FileSystemObject is the foundation of a whole bunch of other, smaller objects that enable you to look at and manipulate files on the server's hard drive. I won't bore you by detailing every property and method for all of these objects. If you need to, you can look up the details in your web server documentation. But I do want to show you the most important stuff, so that you know all the things you can do and where to look when you need more.

The FileSystemObject

The FileSystemObject gives you access to the drives, folders, and files on the web server. Like the Dictionary object, you have to create a FileSystemObject whenever you want to use it.

```
<%
Dim FileSystem
Set FileSystem = CreateObject("Scripting.FileSystemObject")
%>
```

Or, in JavaScript:

```
<%
var FileSystem
FileSystem = new
ActiveXObject("Scripting.FileSystemObject")
%>
```

The FileSystemObject itself has over twenty methods. Here are some of the most interesting of the group:

- CopyFile, MoveFile: Copy or move a file from one location to another. You can use wildcards to copy or move lots of files.
- CopyFolder, MoveFolder: Copy or move all folders and subfolders to a new location. You can use wildcards here, too.

- ✔ CreateFolder: Creates a new folder wherever you specify.

- ✔ DeleteFile, DeleteFolder: Delete the file or folder you specify. Again, you can use wildcards.

- ✔ DriveExists, FolderExists, FileExists: Allow you to check to see if a specified drive, folder, or file exists on the system.

- ✔ GetDrive, GetFolder, GetFile: Allow you to get Drive, Folder, and File objects that you specify.

So, for example, if you wanted to copy a file from one place to another, your script may look like this (the JavaScript is nearly identical):

```
<%
Dim FileSystem
Set FileSystem = CreateObject("Scripting.FileSystemObject")
FileSystem.CopyFile "c:\plans\*.*", "c:\backup\"
%>
```

All the files in the plans folder are copied to the backup folder. A third, optional argument to CopyFile exists. It is a true or false to indicate whether files with the same name in the destination folder should be overwritten. Because I didn't specify in the preceding code, I went with the default, which is true.

For a real-world example of using CopyFile, see the section titled "Creating a Radio: Music to Surf By" in Chapter 8. The user chooses his favorite style of music, and then background music in that style follows him to every page.

Drives and collections

The FileSystemObject has only one property — a *collection* called Drives.

What's a collection? A collection is a list, something like an array, that holds a bunch of objects of the same type.

The FileSystemObject's Drives property is a collection of individual Drive objects. Each Drive object in the collection represents a drive on the web server. It could be a hard drive, a floppy drive, a CD-ROM drive, or whatever.

Getting drive info with VBScript

You can use the For Each..Next loop in VBScript to go through each object in a collection one-by-one. (For more information on For Each..Next, see "Using For Each..Next with Arrays" in Chapter 4.)

```
<%
Dim FileSystem, Drv, Drvs
Set FileSystem = CreateObject("Scripting.FileSystemObject")
Set Drvs = FileSystem.Drives
For Each Drv In Drvs
%>
Drive: <%=Drv.DriveLetter%><p>
```

```
<%  If Drv.IsReady = True Then %>
Volume: <%=Drv.VolumeName%><p>
Space Free: <%=Drv.FreeSpace%> bytes<p>
<%  Else %>
Drive Isn't ready.<p>
<%  End IF
Next
%>
```

For Each..Next is handy if working with collections because it doesn't require you to figure out how many objects are in the collection before you start. It simply goes through each one of them.

In the preceding code, after the FileSystemObject is created, the Drvs variable is assigned the collection of drives in the FileSystemObject. The For Each..Next loop walks through the drives one-by-one. The drive letter for each is displayed. If the drive is ready, the volume name and amount of space free are also displayed. The IsReady returns false if the drive is removable (like a floppy or CD-ROM drive) and there is no disk in it.

Getting drive info with JavaScript

You can use the Enumerator object in JavaScript to go through each object in a collection one-by-one.

```
<%
var FileSystem, Drv, Drvs, EnumDrvs
FileSystem = new ActiveXObject("Scripting.FileSystemObject")
Drvs = FileSystem.Drives
EnumDrvs = new Enumerator(Drvs)
EnumDrvs.moveFirst()
while (! EnumDrvs.atEnd() ) { %>
Drive: <%=EnumDrvs.item().DriveLetter%><p>
<% if (EnumDrvs.item().IsReady == true) { %>
Volume: <%=EnumDrvs.item().VolumeName%><p>
Space Free: <%=EnumDrvs.item().FreeSpace%> bytes<p>
<% } else { %>
Drive Isn't ready.<p>
<% }
  EnumDrvs.moveNext()
}
%>
```

The Enumerator is an object that makes it easy to deal with collections. After you create an Enumerator, you send a collection to it. It then provides you with methods to navigate through the collection:

- moveFirst(): Moves to the first object in the collection.

- moveNext(): Moves to the next object in the collection.

- atEnd(): Returns true or false indicating whether you are at the end of the collection.

✔ `item()`: Returns the current object in the collection. (This is a method, not a property, so be sure to remember to always use the empty parentheses afterward.)

The `Enumerator` has no properties.

In the preceding code, after the `FileSystemObject` is created, the `Drvs` variable is assigned the collection of drives and enumerated in the variable `EnumDrvs`. The `while` loop, along with the `moveFirst()` and `moveNext()` `Enumerator` methods, walks through the drives one-by-one. The drive letter for each is displayed. If the drive is ready, the volume name and amount of space free are also displayed. The `IsReady` returns false if the drive is removable (such as a floppy or CD-ROM drive) and there is no disk in it.

The `Drive` *object's properties*

The `Drive` object has no methods, but quite a lot of properties. Here are a few of the most important properties, including the four that were used in the preceding code:

✔ `DriveLetter`: Used to access the drive on the system.

✔ `IsReady`: Returns true or false indicating whether the drive is ready to be accessed or not.

✔ `FreeSpace`: Gives the number of bytes free on the drive.

✔ `TotalSize`: Gives the total number of bytes on a drive.

✔ `VolumeName`: Provides the name the volume was given when it was created.

✔ `DriveType`: Returns a number indicating what type of drive it is. Possible return values are 0, Unknown; 1, Removable (such as a floppy or Zip drive); 2, Fixed (such as a hard drive); 3, Network drive; 4, CD-ROM drive; 5, RAM drive.

✔ `FileSystem`: Returns the type of file system used on the drive. Possible return values: "FAT", "NTFS", "CDFS".

✔ `RootFolder`: Returns the folder of the root directory for the drive. This is the property that allows you to get to all the other folders and files on that drive.

How drives and folders work together

Just as a `Drives` collection exists, which contains `Drive` objects for all the drives on the web server, so `Folders` and `Files` collections exist that contain the content on the drives. But, unlike the `Drives` collection, more than one `Folders` and `Files` collection exists for the entire system. For example, each `Folder` object has its own `Files` collection that represents the files that are in that folder.

All of these drives, files, folders, collections, and objects can get very confusing. So let me go through it step by step. Take a look at Figure 6-2 as you are reading this. It can help you follow along.

To get the root folder for a drive, you use the `Drive` object's property `RootFolder`. This gives you a `Folder` object that represents the root folder for the drive.

The `Folder` object has a `SubFolders` property that returns a `Folders` collection containing, oddly enough, all its subfolders.

In that `Folders` collection, each individual `Folder` object also has its *own* `SubFolders` property with a `Folders` collection. And each `Folder` there has a `SubFolders` property. This arrangement allows you to go to as many levels of folders and subfolders as you like.

I show you how to get to the *files* that are in each folder in the next section.

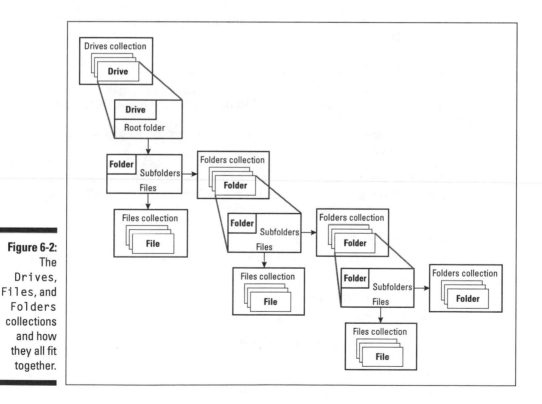

Figure 6-2:
The
`Drives`,
`Files`, and
`Folders`
collections
and how
they all fit
together.

The `Folder` object's methods and properties

The `Folder` object has `Copy`, `Delete`, and `Move` methods. These methods can be used to copy, delete, or move this folder.

The `Folder` object, like the `Drive` object, has a lot of properties to allow access to information about the folder.

- ✔ `Name`: The name of the folder.
- ✔ `DateCreated`, `DateLastAccessed`, `DateLastModified`: The dates the folder was created, last accessed, and last changed.
- ✔ `Size`: The size of the files in this folder and all the subfolders under it.
- ✔ `Drive`: The drive on which this folder sits.
- ✔ `ParentFolder`: The folder that contains this one.
- ✔ `SubFolders`: A `Folders` collection holding all the folders under this one.
- ✔ `IsRoot`: A true or false value indicating whether or not this is the root folder for this drive.

Getting the files in a folder

Each `Folder object` has a `Files property`. This property returns a collection of `File` objects that represent all the files in that folder (refer to Figure 6-2).

The `File` object has `Copy`, `Delete`, and `Move` methods, just as the `Folder` object does.

And, just like the `Folder` object, the `File` object has lots of properties to tell you everything you want to know about a file. In fact, most of the properties have counterparts in the `Folder` object.

- ✔ `Name`: The name of the file.
- ✔ `DateCreated`, `DateLastAccessed`, `DateLastModified`: The dates the file was created, last accessed, and last changed.
- ✔ `Size`: The size of this file.
- ✔ `Drive`: The drive on which this file sits.
- ✔ `ParentFolder`: The folder that contains this file.

A folders and files example

To pull all of these objects, properties, and methods together in your head, I've created an example. A drive letter is chosen and a list of all the files that are in the root of that drive is displayed in the browser.

Show files in root in VBScript

Here's what the code looks like:

```
<%
Dim fileSys, drv, f1, s, rootdir, rootfiles, fileobj
Dim drivelet
drivelet = "c:"
Set filesys = CreateObject("Scripting.FileSystemObject")
' Get the Drive object based on the drive letter
Set drv = filesys.GetDrive(drivelet)
' Get the Drive's root folder
Set rootdir = drv.RootFolder
' Get the files in the root folder
Set rootfiles = rootdir.Files
' Loop through all the files and display them
For Each fileobj in rootfiles
%>
<%=fileobj.Name%><p>
<%
Next
%>
```

After I declare some variables, the `drivelet` variable is set to "c:" and I create a `FileSystemObject`. Then I call the `GetDrive` method to get a drive object based on the value in the `drivelet` string. The `drv` variable ends up holding a `Drive` object for the c: drive.

I assign to the `rootdir` variable the `Folder` object returned from the `RootFolder` property of `drv`.

Then the `Files` collection returned from the `rootdir` object's `Files` property is assigned to `rootfiles`. The `For Each..Next` loops through this collection of files, each time assigning the current file object to `fileobj`. Inside the loop, the `fileobj`'s `Name` property is displayed.

Show files in root in JavaScript

Here's what the code looks like:

```
<%
var drivelet, fileSys, drv
var rootdir, rootfiles, enumfiles
drivelet = "c:"
filesys = new ActiveXObject("Scripting.FileSystemObject")
// Get the Drive object based on the drive letter
drv = filesys.GetDrive(drivelet)
// Get the Drive's root folder
rootdir = drv.RootFolder
// Get the files in the root folder
rootfiles = rootdir.Files
// Enumerate the root files collection
```

```
enumfiles = new Enumerator(rootfiles)
// Loop through all the files and display them
enumfiles.moveFirst()
while (! enumfiles.atEnd())
{
%>
<%=enumfiles.item().Name%><p>
<%
  enumfiles.moveNext()
} %>
```

After I declare some variables, the `drivelet` variable is set to "c:" and I create a `FileSystemObject`. Then I call the `GetDrive()` method to get a `drive` object based on the value in the `drivelet` string. The `drv` variable ends up holding a `Drive` object for the c: drive.

I assign to the `rootdir` variable the `Folder` object returned from the `RootFolder` property of `drv`.

Then the `Files` collection returned from the `rootdir` object's `Files` property is assigned to `rootfiles`. That collection is enumerated and stored in `enumfiles`.

The `while` loop loops through this collection of files. Inside the loop, `enumfiles.item()` gets the current `File` object, and its `Name` property is displayed.

Islands in the TextStream

All the `FileSystemObject` properties, methods, and objects I describe above allow you to navigate, view, and manipulate files and folders on your web server's drives.

`TextStream` objects allow you to actually create files from scratch or to append information to existing files. This is a very handy, easy way to store quick and dirty information you may need to access later.

For a real-world example of using the `FileSystemObject` and the `TextStream`, see the section titled "A Guest Book: Creating and Responding to Forms" in Chapter 8. I create an application there that accepts Guest Book information from a form and stores it in a text file. Another page retrieves and lists all the people who've signed the Guest Book.

Creating a new file

You get a TextStream object by calling the CreateTextFile method of either the FileSystemObject or the Folder object. This method actually creates a new file. Then a TextStream object is returned from the function, which serves as your reference to that file.

As soon as you have a TextStream object, you can write to the file. Here's an example (the JavaScript code is very similar):

```
<%
Dim filesys, txtfile
Set filesys = CreateObject("Scripting.FileSystemObject")
Set txtfile = _
   filesys.CreateTextFile("c:\temp\tempfile.txt")
txtfile.WriteLine("This is the first line of my new file!")
txtfile.Close
%>
```

After the FileSystemObject is created, CreateTextFile is called, passing as an argument a string that includes the path and name of a new text file to be created. After it is created, txtfile is assigned the TextStream object returned from CreateObject. Then, using TextStream methods, a line of text is written to the file, and then the file is closed.

The TextStream has four methods that are helpful when creating a file:

- ✔ Write: Writes a string to the file.

- ✔ WriteLine: Writes a string to the file and follows it with a new line character.

- ✔ WriteBlankLines: Accepts a number as an argument and then sends that number of new line characters to the file.

- ✔ Close: Closes the file.

Opening an existing file to append information

The FileSystemObject has another method called OpenTextFile. You pass as an argument the path and name of the file you want to open. (The JavaScript code for this example is very similar to this.)

```
<%
Dim filesys, txtfile
Set filesys = _
   CreateObject("Scripting.FileSystemObject")
Set txtfile = _
   filesys.OpenTextFile("c:\temp\tempfile.txt",8,0)
txtfile.WriteLine "P.S. You're the best!"
txtfile.Close
%>
```

The first argument is the path and filename. The second and third arguments are I/O Mode and Format.

The second, I/O Mode, has two possible values:

1 — Open for reading.

8 — Open for appending.

The third, Format, has three possible values:

0 — Open it as an ASCII file.

-1 — Open it as a Unicode file.

-2 — Open it using the system default.

ASCII is the normal way of saving text files and is the most widely used. Unicode is a relatively new way of saving text files, and it provides a lot more characters for use with other languages.

If you already have the File object for the file you want to open and append to, you can use the File object's OpenAsTextStream. Because OpenAsTextStream works on the file associated with the File object, you don't have to pass a filename or path. All you have to pass is the I/O Mode (1 for reading, 2 for writing, or 8 for appending) and the Format (with exactly the same options as OpenTextFile).

Opening an existing file to read

If you want to read information from a file, you use the same functions you do to open a file to append information: the FileSystemObject's OpenTextFile or the File object's OpenAsTextStream. (For more information on these functions, see the previous section.) Only instead of using I/O Mode 8 to append, you use I/O Mode 1 to read. (JavaScript folks: you can translate this one, too.)

```
<%
Dim filesys, txtfile, line
Set filesys = CreateObject("Scripting.FileSystemObject")
Set txtfile = _
   filesys.OpenTextFile("c:\temp\tempfile.txt",1, 0)
Do
   line = txtfile.ReadLine
%>
<%=line%>
<%
Loop Until txtfile.AtEndOfStream
txtfile.Close
%>
```

After creating the `FileSystemObject` and opening the text file to read, a `Do..Loop Until` loop begins. This loop continues until the `TextStream` property `AtEndOfStream` is true. Within the loop, `ReadLine` reads an entire line of text at a time and places it into the line variable which is then displayed in the browser.

The `TextStream` object has several methods you'll be interested in if you are trying to read information from a text file:

✔ `Read`: You pass a number to `Read` and it returns that many characters read from a file.

✔ `ReadLine`: Reads the next line in the file and returns it as a string.

✔ `ReadAll`: Reads the entire file and returns it as a string variable. This is really handy and can make quick work of your file reading. But if you are working with really large files, it is usually more efficient to read line-by-line.

✔ `Skip`: If you pass it a number, it skips over that many characters in the text file.

✔ `SkipLine`: Skips the next line in the text file.

✔ `Close`: Closes the file.

Several properties can also help as you're reading information from a file:

✔ `AtEndOfStream`: Contains true if you are at the end of the file.

✔ `AtEndOfLine`: Contains true if you are at the end of a line in the file.

✔ `Column`: Contains the number of the column you're on in the file.

✔ `Line`: Contains a number indicating the line you're on in the file.

Start up the `ScriptEngine` ... we're goin' to town!

Although the `ScriptEngine` functions aren't a part of an object, I do want to mention them here because they are shared between VBScript and JavaScript, and you should know a little bit about them.

Actually, they're very simple. They provide a way for you to figure out what scripting engine is running right now and what version of it is being used.

Knowing the scripting engine and version can be handy if you are writing scripts that may potentially run on several different web servers. By checking the current version of the scripting language, you can write scripts that can adapt themselves to whatever capabilities this version of the scripting language supports.

Here are the `ScriptEngine` functions:

- ✔ `ScriptEngine`: Returns a string to indicate which scripting language is in use. Potential values: "VBScript" or "JScript". If you are writing a script that could potentially run in an environment where Visual Basic for Applications is used (Microsoft Word or Microsoft Excel, for example), then this function may also return "VBA".

- ✔ `ScriptEngineBuildVersion`: Returns the build version number of the scripting engine.

- ✔ `ScriptingEngineMajorVersion`, `ScriptingEngineMinorVersion`: Returns the major and minor version numbers of the scripting engine.

Chapter 7

Using Server Objects

● ●

● ●

*M*ore objects? Yes, indeed! And these objects are going to help you begin to see the real power rumbling under the hood of ASP. Server objects are not a part of the scripting environment such as the scripting objects I cover in Chapter 6. Server objects are, instead, a part of the web server itself. They represent your entire server environment and they give you information that allows you to create some very interesting applications. In fact, in the next chapter, Chapter 8, that's exactly what I do! I take these objects and show you all the cool stuff you can do with them. Feel free to jump ahead to Chapter 8 and look at how these objects are used there as you discover more about them. I let you know at various points throughout this chapter where to go in the next chapter to find specific examples of the concepts demonstrated here.

I begin by describing the very important concept of the Web application and how it applies to your ASP pages. Then I give you an overview of each of the server objects and what their commonly used properties and methods are.

An Application, or Just a Bunch of Pages?

In the past, you probably thought of ASP as a simple way to enhance your Web pages by adding code. Although that definition is true, it's not the whole truth. You can use ASP to create more than just individual pages that are linked together in some way. With ASP, you can actually begin to create real *Web applications*.

What is a Web application? Well, at its most basic level, a Web application is a bunch of pages linked together in some way. But Web applications go further. The pages interact with each other and with the user. They can customize and adapt themselves based on this interaction so that they act more like a cohesive stand-alone computer program than a bunch of relatively unrelated pages.

In this chapter, I introduce you to several new concepts that help you tie your pages together in new ways. Many of the server objects play a role in tying your pages together because the same objects are shared among all the pages. But when it comes to sharing information, these four features probably have the biggest impact:

- ✔ The `Application` object
- ✔ The `Session` object
- ✔ The `Global.asa` file
- ✔ Server-Side Includes

These features allow you to share data and code among all the pages in your Web application so they can work together as a unit, rather than as separate entities.

I discuss all the server objects as well as `Global.asa` and Server-Side Includes in this chapter. In Chapter 8, I show you how to begin harmonizing these capabilities to compose your application symphony. How's that for a metaphor?

Using ASP Server Objects

In Chapter 6, I explore scripting objects which act as extensions to your scripting language. In this chapter, I introduce the *ASP server objects*. Scripting objects and server objects differ in several ways:

- ✔ The server objects are exactly the same no matter which scripting language you use.
- ✔ Server objects are not a part of your scripting language. They are built into the web server software you are using — either IIS or PWS.
- ✔ You do not need to create the server objects using `CreateObject` in VBScript or `new` in JavaScript. The server objects are always there for you, and you only ever need one of each.

But server objects are still objects, and, despite their differences, you still work with them by accessing their properties and calling their methods.

In the next few sections, I highlight each object, showing you its general purpose in life, and then pointing out some of the most interesting properties and methods of that object.

The Server *object*

The Server object represents the web server itself. It has just a few properties and methods.

Time's up: The ScriptTimeout *property*

Actually, to be precise, the Server object has only one property: ScriptTimeout. When an ASP script runs on the server, it can sometimes get fouled up and either get stuck or get caught in an infinite loop. If these things happen, you don't want your web server to simply freeze up, waiting for the script to finish. ScriptTimeout specifies the number of seconds the server should wait before giving up on a script.

The default value for ScriptTimeout is 90 seconds. IIS and PWS store this setting internally. Although you can change this setting with the server software to anything you want, you can only use the Server.ScriptTimeout property to *extend* the time a script has to execute. If it is set internally to 90, setting ScriptTimeout to 110 causes it to wait the extra 20 seconds. But setting it to 60 has no effect — it still waits 90 seconds.

And on the eighth day, He did CreateObject

The CreateObject method is used to create an instance of an ActiveX server component. It is similar to the VBScript CreateObject function and to the JavaScript ActiveXObject() function. But this server method should always be used when working with server components. See Chapter 9 for detailed information on server components and examples of CreateObject.

Finding your way with MapPath

The MapPath method receives a virtual or relative path and maps it to the actual, physical folder on the hard drive.

For example, imagine your Web site is at c:\inetpub\wwwroot\ and you call this function:

```
location = Server.MapPath("/letters")
```

After this line executes, location holds this:

```
"c:\inetpub\wwwroot\letters\"
```

HTMLEncode — *the Web master*

Usually, when you are writing HTML, you write things that look like this:

```
Groceries:<p>
Bread<br>
Vegetables<br>
```

But suppose you actually wanted the less-than and greater-than signs to appear on your page. How do you do it? You may already be familiar with the codes that enable you to do this: &lt for less-than and &gt for greater-than. A whole slew of other codes exist.

If you only need to use the special codes every now and then, it's no problem. But if you need to use the special codes a lot, you can use the HTMLEncode method.

```
Server.HTMLEncode("0 < x < 1")
```

produces this string:

```
0 &lt; x &lt; 1
```

If you put that in a Web page, it displays in a browser like this:

```
0 < x < 1
```

So, HTMLEncode is an easy way to display text exactly as you want it on the Web page without having to remember a bunch of silly codes.

Breaking the URLEncode

If you use a search engine to look for stuff on the Web, you may type something like this:

```
cow tipping recreational activity
```

You'd like to find a page that uses all of these words. After you click search, the URL is likely to look something like this:

```
http://find.com/search?p=cow+tipping+recreational+activity
```

Notice how the words are all stuck together on one line separated by plus signs? This is a standard way to pass information from one page to another through the URL itself.

The URLEncode method does this encoding for you, if you ever need to.

```
result = _
  Server.URLEncode("cow tipping recreational activity")
```

After this line is executed, `result` holds a value like this:

```
cow+tipping+recreational+activity
```

Big deal! `URLEncode` puts plus signs in place of strings. It actually does a lot
more than that. It converts symbols like : and > to %3A and %3E to make sure
everything on the URL line is a legal URL character.

The input object: Request

Because your scripts are executing on the web server, you can think of the
`Request` object as the *input* object. This object holds information that was
sent from the browser to the web server.

The `Request` object has only one regular property and one method. It has a
lot of collections, though. These collections hold objects that represent information sent to the web server from the browser — things like client
certificates, cookies, information from submitted forms, information from
queries sent via the URL, and finally, general information about the server
and the current session. The next several sections summarize these collections along with the single property and method. The most important
collections are the `Cookies` and the `Form` collections.

For more information on collections, see Chapter 6.

Can I have a byte of your Cookie?

Computer programmers may be geeks, but they have a way of coming up
with some pretty cute buzzwords. And they don't come any cuter than the
cookie.

A cookie is nothing more than a small text file that you can create and store
on the *client's* machine, where the browser is running. This text file is identified with your Web site and can hold any information you like.

Using cookies

One thing that cookies can do is identify someone and let you know that he
has been to your site before. Although cookies don't include any of the security measures that are built into certificates (see "I'll have to see your
`ClientCertificate`" later in this chapter), cookies are much more common
and easier to work with.

After you gather information such as a person's name, e-mail address, and possibly any preferences she has set about the kind of information she wants to
see or how she wants it presented when she is at your Web site, you can store
that information in a cookie for future reference. Then every time she comes to
your site, you can retrieve this information and adjust things to suit her.

Accessing cookie values

The `Cookie` collection in the `Request` object is used to look at the value in the cookie passed to the server from the browser.

Because a cookie is nothing more than a text file, you can display its entire contents as a string.

```
<%=Request.Cookie("Preferences")%>
```

But most of the time, the information stored in a cookie is stored like the information in a `Dictionary` object (for more information on the `Dictionary` object, see "What's a `Dictionary`? Look It Up!" in Chapter 6). In other words, a keyword provides access to an item, which holds a value. You can have as many key/item pairs in the cookie as you like. To get the value of a specific key, do this:

```
<%=Request.Cookie("Preferences")("BackgroundColor")%>
```

This code displays the item associated with the `BackgroundColor` key. You may also have `TextColor`, `Font`, `Size`, and other keys.

Why do they call it a cookie? No one knows.

For information on how to set the value of cookies, see the section titled "Tossing your cookies" later in this chapter.

For a real-world example of using cookies in your Web applications, see the section titled "A Personalized Welcome Page with Cookies" in Chapter 8.

The cookieless

It is a sad fact that not everyone has cookies. Some older browsers out there simply don't support cookies. And some people have newer browsers, but turn off the ability to do cookies (usually because they are concerned about security).

If the user's browser doesn't support cookies, then this collection of cookies and the one in the `Response` object won't do you much good.

I'll have to see your `ClientCertificate`

Certificates are another way that you can verify that a person is who he says he is. An authorized company issues a certificate, along with a serial number, to an individual. This identification information is unique and includes security measures to make it difficult to forge or copy someone else's certificate.

If your server is set up to request certificates from your users, you can use the `ClientCertificate` collection to verify that the user has a certificate and to look at the certificate information that was sent.

Form and function

HTML forms allow the user to enter data into controls on a Web page that work like edits, radio buttons, and check boxes. Then they can send the information to the web server by clicking a Submit button. On the server, you can use an ASP page along with the Form collection to handle the information sent.

When you create a form in HTML, you have to give it a method describing how the form is to be processed. The two options are GET and POST — POST being the most common. If the form's method is POST, the information entered in the form is accessed through this Form collection. (If the method is GET, the information can be found in the QueryString collection. See the next section for information on QueryString.)

If you create a form in HTML, you can also specify an action. If you intend to handle the form using an ASP page, put the page's name that will handle the form in the action attribute. The form tag may end up looking like this:

```
<form method="POST" name="GuestBook" action="gbproc.asp">
```

If you create the controls using the input tag, be sure to specify a name property for each of them.

```
First Name:<input type="text" size="20"
  name="FirstName"><p>
```

Then, in the page that is handling the form, you may want to display the values received from the form to verify that the information is correct.

```
<%=Request.Form("FirstName")%>
```

Or you can use the shortcut:

```
<%=Request("FirstName")%>
```

You don't actually have to specify the Form collection. When you use this syntax, the Request object looks in the Form collection for the name you send it.

You can use this same shortened syntax to access QueryString collection elements as well (see the next section for information on QueryString). So be careful using this shortened syntax when you are using both the Form and the QueryString collections at the same time. If you have elements with the same name in both, you have to actually specify the collection name to access those elements.

For a real-world example of using the Form collection, see the section titled "A Guest Book: Creating and Responding to Forms" in Chapter 8.

Using one page to both present the form and respond to it

The page you specify in the action attribute of the form tag is the one that gets called to respond to the form when the user clicks the Submit button. That can be another ASP page or it can be the *same* ASP page that presented the form in the first place. Here's an example. Suppose this page is named `newinfo.asp`:

```
<HTML>
<% If Request("Name")="" And Request("Address")="" And ... Then %>
<h1>Please Enter This Information:</h1>
<form action="tst.asp" method=POST>
Name: <input name=Name type=edit><p>
Address: <input name=Address type=edit><p>
...
<input type=submit value="Submit">
</form>
<% Else %>
<h1>Here's The Information You Entered:</h1>
<%=Request("Name")%><p>
<%=Request("Address")%><p>
...
<% End If %>
<HTML>
```

This page is divided into two parts using an `If..Then..Else` statement — the form and the form handler. The `If` statement checks each form element to see if it has been filled in. The first time the page is loaded, of course, none of the form elements will have any information in them. That causes the first part of the page to execute, and the form is displayed. Then when the user fills out the form and clicks the Submit button, this form loads another copy of itself on the server to handle the form. Only this time, there is information in the form elements, so that the second part of the page is executed — and this is where the form is handled. The only thing the handler does in the page above is simply display back to the user whatever he entered. But it can do anything you want — like store the information in a text file or database.

Of course, you don't have to do it this way. You can always use one page for the form and one for the form handler. But by combining them into one, you reduce the number of pages in your application and you make it easier to extend and update both the form and the handler in one place. For a real-world example of combining the form and form handler in one page, see Chapter 13. Several of the forms in this application are combined with their form handlers, including `PlaceAd`, `EditAd`, and `DelAd`.

Querying with QueryString

One way that a page can send information to the server or to another page is by putting the information right into the URL of the page being requested. That page can then be constructed or changed based on the information passed to the server. This technique is most often seen when you are using a Web search engine to look for stuff on the Web.

Imagine you go to Yahoo!, AltaVista, Excite, or one of the other search engines and type in something like this:

```
history soap
```

After you click the Search button, the page that is requested in the Address line at the top of your browser looks something like this:

```
http://find.com/search?Criteria=history+soap
```

Rather than simply requesting a page to be displayed, this URL is passing the information after the question mark to the server.

This information can then be accessed from your ASP pages using the QueryString collection. It works exactly like the Form collection.

```
<% SearchCriteria = Request.QueryString("Criteria") %>
```

For a real-world example of sending information from one page to another using QueryString, see Chapter 13. Several pages in that application pass information to other pages using QueryString.

- ✔ Content_Length: The length, in bytes, of the information sent back from a form. Can be used to check to see if any form information has been sent to this page. This is especially useful when you create a single page that serves as both the form and the response to the form. I describe how to do this in a sidebar called "Using one page to both present the form and respond to it" earlier in this chapter. Instead of checking each form element individually to see if it is empty, you can check the Content_Length like this: If Request.ServerVariables ("Content_Length") > 0 Then...

- ✔ Remote_Host: The client's IP address. Often this uniquely identifies a computer, but it isn't reliable. When people use a dial-up connection to the Internet, they are assigned an IP address from a pool of addresses used by that provider. So a computer using a dial-up provider probably has a different IP address each time the user logs in.

- ✔ Request_Method: If the client is submitting a form, this variable holds the value GET or POST to let you know the method used to submit the form.

- ✔ Script_Name: The name of the ASP page being executed.

If you know that the client's browser is Internet Explorer, version 3.0 or higher, you can also get some very specific information about the client's computer. Unfortunately, these variables aren't available if the client is using the Netscape browser.

 ✔ HTTP_UA_CPU: The type of CPU on the client's computer.

 ✔ HTTP_UA_OS: The operating system the client's computer is using.

 ✔ HTTP_UA_Pixels: The screen resolution of the client's computer.

 ✔ HTTP_UA_Color: The color depth of the client's computer. In other words, this indicates the number of colors the user's screen is capable of displaying.

Cut it out! I'm trying to BinaryRead

The TotalBytes property holds the number of bytes that the browser sent to the web server in the body of the request.

The TotalBytes property is most often used with the BinaryRead method. BinaryRead is an alternative way of getting information that was sent to the server through a POST. If the browser has not posted values entered on a form, but rather some other type of data, BinaryRead is a generic way of getting the data and depositing it in an array.

Unless you have a very specific reason to use BinaryRead, most of your interaction with the browser is probably done through the Form collection. If you do use BinaryRead, you cannot later access the Form collection. Likewise, if you access the Form collection, you cannot later do a BinaryRead — both give you an error.

The output object: Response

If the Request object is the *input* object (because it receives information from the browser that is sent to the server), then the Response object is just the opposite — the *output* object. The Response object allows you to send information from the web server back to the browser.

Unlike the Request object, the Response object has a lot of properties and methods, but only one collection. In the next several sections, I give you a quick overview of the most important aspects of the Response object.

Probably the most important parts are the Cookies collection, the Redirect method, and the Write method.

Tossing your cookies

Now wait a minute! The `Cookies` collection is in the `Request` object. What's it doing here in the `Response` object? Well, it turns out that there are two `Cookies` collections. You use the one in the `Request` object to *get* cookie information from the browser. You use the one here in the `Response` object to *create* new cookies and *change* information in the cookies you've already made.

So, how do you create cookie entries and change the data in existing cookies? Easy.

```
<% Response.Cookie("Preferences")("BackgroundColor")=_
   "Black" %>
```

`Preferences` is the name of your cookie. The `BackgroundColor` is a key in the cookie and `Black` is the value that is assigned to the `BackgroundColor` key. If the key already exists, it is assigned the new value. If it doesn't exist, the new key is created and assigned the value. If a cookie by that name (`Preferences`, in this case) doesn't exist, it is also created.

The `Response` object's `Cookies` collection itself also has a couple of properties you need to know about:

- ✔ `Expires`: A date that indicates when the cookie expires. By default the cookie expires when the Session ends, so if you really want to be able to access the information you are storing later when the user returns to your site, you need to set `CookieExpires` to a date in the future. It looks like this:

  ```
  <% Response.Cookie("Preferences").CookieExpires = _
     "January 1, 2000" %>
  ```

- ✔ `HasKeys`: Indicates whether the cookie is just a string (false) or is set up as a `Dictionary` with keys and items (true).

For a real-world example of using cookies in your Web applications, see the section titled "A Personalized Welcome Page with Cookies" in Chapter 8.

Let me `Redirect` *your attention*

The `Redirect` method is simple to use and very handy. It tells the browser where to go (so to speak). You call `Redirect` and send a URL as a string argument and the browser goes to the URL you send.

If you have ever gone to a page that has been moved to a different server, you've more than likely seen a page informing you of the move and then immediately been taken to the new page without clicking on anything. You're seeing `Redirect` (or its equivalent) in action.

```
Response.Redirect("http://rightpage.htm")
```

For an amusing application that makes use of Redirect, see the section titled "Web Site Roulette with Redirect" in Chapter 8.

You never call, you never Write

The Write method accepts a string as an argument and, in turn, writes that string to the Web page. This is especially handy in functions or subroutines that you create to add elements to your Web page.

```
Sub ShowHeader
Response.Write("<center><h1>The Weather Page</h1><center>")
End Sub
```

Your Web page is Expired . . . and it smells bad, too

Usually, when the browser goes to a page, it downloads the page and displays it. It also usually saves that page in a folder on the hard drive. The browser does this so that later, if you decide you want to go to that page again, it can just pull the page off the hard drive instead of downloading it again. This makes accessing pages you just recently visited much faster.

The problem with this scheme, of course, is that the page may have changed since the last time you downloaded it. If you just pull a copy off the hard drive, you won't see the changes. The Expires and ExpiresAbsolute properties offer ways for you to set an expiration date for your page so that the browser knows when it should start checking back again to see if you've actually changed the page.

Expires allows you to pass a number of minutes before the page expires. If you set this property to 1440, the page expires in one day (60 minutes times 24 hours). If the users come back to this page in a few hours, the page will be pulled off the hard drive. If they check back tomorrow, it'll be downloaded from the Web site again.

ExpiresAbsolute accepts an actual date and time, rather than a number. Before that date and time, the browser pulls the page from the hard drive, and after that, downloads from the Web site.

Chop log, AppendToLog

IIS keeps a log of all requests and pages sent out. If you want to write your own special information to that entry for this request, you can do it by calling the AppendToLog method. Just send the string you want to add as an argument.

Remember two important things when calling AppendToLog:

🖙 The string must be less than 80 characters long.

🖙 Don't use a comma anywhere in the string. The log separates entries with the comma, and if you put one in your log entry, you confuse it.

Buffer, Flush, Clear, End — *dodge, perry, spin!*

Normally, when a page is processed by the web server, it is sent out *as it is processed*. That means that the first part of the page may already be sent out while scripts near the end are still running.

You can change this default behavior by setting the Buffer property to true. When you do, the page is not sent until it is completely processed and all scripts have finished executing.

Because setting the value of Buffer affects how the rest of the page is processed, be sure to do it at the very top of the page.

It is often necessary to set Buffer to true when you manipulate information that is stored in the HTTP headers. For example, if you manipulate cookie information or call the Response.Redirect method later in your script, you almost always have to set Buffer to true at the top of your script because both of these manipulate the HTTP headers behind the scenes. If you don't set Buffer to true you get an error that looks like this: "The HTTP headers are already written to the client browser. Any HTTP header modifications must be made before writing page content." Any time you get this error, you can set Buffer to true at the top of the page to get rid of it.

Setting Buffer to true also makes it possible to use these three Response object methods: Flush, Clear, and End.

Flush sends whichever part of the page has been processed already. By using Flush, you control when the various parts of the page are sent.

Clear, on the other hand, completely clears the buffer of everything that it was getting ready to send. This is often useful if you are halfway through a page and realize that there is an error and you don't want to send the page after all. You can send an error message instead.

End actually stops all processing and stops all scripts from running. The current contents of the buffer are sent and the page is complete. If you don't want to send anything at all, you can call Clear before calling End.

BinaryWriter*'s block*

The BinaryWrite method sends a block of binary information using the HTTP protocol, but without any character conversion as you do for a Web page. This method can be used to pass information to a custom program other than the browser running on the client side which receives HTTP data.

BinaryWrite is not one you're likely to use in your everyday ASP development.

The Application *and* Session *objects*

The Application and Session objects work similarly and are used for similar tasks. The Application object is used to hold information about the ASP application. The Session object keeps track of each person who accesses the application, individually.

The application vs. the session

To help you see the difference, let me give you an example. You have a really cool real estate ASP application on your web server that allows users to look at a variety of homes and then pick one to calculate what their mortgage payment would be if they bought it. Only one copy of this application exists on the web server. The application starts up the first time someone accesses a page for that application. It doesn't end until the last person has left the Web application. That is the Application object's domain — the entire application for its entire life.

The session is much different. Suppose Sparky logs in to your real estate application and begins looking through the homes. Soon after, Judd pulls up a page and begins looking at houses, too. Now, two different people are running the same application. Two different applications do not exist. But there *are* two different sessions. Every time a new person accesses your ASP application, a new session is created. Even if Sparky gives up for the night and comes back tomorrow, he will be in a different session tomorrow than he was in tonight.

Application *and* Session *variables*

Variables in an ASP page have two levels of scope — local and global. Local variables are created in a function and can only be accessed in that function. They begin life when the function begins, and they die when the function ends. Global variables are declared outside any function and can be accessed from anywhere on the page.

If you've done much playing around with ASP, it won't be long before you find yourself wishing there were a *super-global* variable — a variable that kept its value from one *page* to the next. What you really want is a Session variable.

```
Session("HouseCost") = 175000
```

This code creates a new variable called HouseCost, if it didn't already exist before, and assigns it the value 175000. (If the variable already existed before, then this code just changed its value.) This variable is a session-level variable that can be accessed from any page as long as this person is using this application.

For a real-world example of using Session variables, see the section titled "Creating a Radio: Music to Surf By" in Chapter 8. There I create an application that allows the users to choose which style of music they like best and

TECHNICAL STUFF

How does the web server know what a session is?

The World Wide Web uses HTTP as its protocol language for communication. The trouble is HTTP is what techie-types call a *stateless protocol,* which means that, unlike other networks, you don't log on and log off of machines in order to use them. When you ask for a page, that is an independent request. The server sends you the page and then forgets about you. If you click on a link to go to another page on that server, the request is sent and the server sends that page to you — without any realization at all that you are the same person who asked for a page a minute ago.

So, if this is true, how can you talk about a session? Well, IIS uses cookies to keep track of sessions by uniquely identifying each person when he first makes a request. Then, after he makes another request in the near future, the server recognizes him and accepts this new request as part of the same session. After a request, the server waits up to 20 minutes for a new request. If a new request doesn't happen in that time, the server assumes that the user has gone to some other site or gotten off the Internet entirely, and it considers the session ended. If you want the server to wait a shorter or longer period of time, you can set the Session object's Timeout property to whatever you like.

You can also end a session yourself by using the Session object's Abandon method. It ends the session when the current script finishes executing.

Unfortunately, because the web server uses cookies to track sessions, if the user's browser doesn't support cookies, or cookie support is turned off, you won't be able to use the Session object.

Fortunately, most browsers used today do support cookies.

then plays it for them on each page. In the section titled "The Tuning Page: Plan A," I use a Session variable to store the user's choice and play the appropriate music.

As you may expect, application-level variables also exist. You create them and assign values to them just as you do with session variables.

```
Application("NumberOfHits") = 0
```

But don't forget that an application is universal. Only one application exists, no matter how many people use it. So, whenever you access an application variable you have to be careful that you are the only one accessing it at that time. The way you do that is by using the Application object's Lock and Unlock methods. Instead of just setting a value, as I did in the preceding code, I should have done this:

```
Application.Lock
Application("NumberOfHits") = 0
Application.Unlock
```

Now no other session is messing with the `Application` object for the millisecond or two that I need to change it.

The big difference between session-level variables and application-level variables is this: If five people are using your real estate Web application at the same time, five copies of the `HouseCost` session-level variable are present — one for each session. Only one copy of the `NumberOfHits` variable exists. This means that if you truly want to create a super-global variable to share information from one page to another, you definitely want to use the session-level variables.

Application-level variables tend to be used much less frequently. But they are great for keeping track of the number of hits a page has taken or other application-level statistics. They can also be used to share information among several sessions.

For a real-world example of using an Application-level variable, see Chapter 12. The key to sharing the same conversation among many different participants is an application-level variable that is displayed, and redisplayed as it is updated, in the browsers of all participants.

The `Global.asa` *File*

As you begin to create ASP pages and they become more sophisticated, what you end up creating is less like a hodgepodge of pages that are linked together and more like one cohesive application. That Web application does many of the same kinds of things that your normal applications like Word and Excel do, and some things those applications *can't*.

But when you are working with a bunch of separate files, how do you define which pages are a part of which applications? Microsoft defines an ASP application as any virtual folder on your Web site along with its subfolders. But that doesn't help very much. How do you tell where one application ends and another one begins?

One way of making the distinction between applications clear is the `Global.asa` file. For each Web application you have, you can have only one `Global.asa`. And it's always in the same place — in the root directory for that application. And while you can create ASP pages without using a `Global.asa` file, I recommend using one for each application just so that you can keep them straight.

What is the `Global.asa` file? Well, instead of the `.asp` extension (standing for *Active Server Page*) that all of your pages have, the Global file has an `.asa` extension that stands for *Active Server Application*. The Global file holds application-level and session-level variables and objects.

The application and session events

You may be surprised to find out that you can write ASP scripts in the Global.asa file. When do these scripts execute? Users never pull up the Global.asa file directly, do they?

No, they don't. You can create four subroutines (or functions in JavaScript) in the Global.asa file. Here's a list describing what they are and when they run:

- ✔ Application_OnStart: This routine is executed when the Web application itself first begins, which happens the first time someone requests a page from that application.

- ✔ Application_OnEnd: This happens when the application is finished executing. Practically, this will only get executed when the server is taken down.

- ✔ Session_OnStart: This one is executed each time a new person first requests a page from this application.

- ✔ Session_OnEnd: When the session for a particular person times out or is abandoned, this code runs.

Here's what a typical Global.asa file may look like:

```
<script language=VBScript runat=Server>
Sub Application_OnStart
Application("NumUsers") = 0
End Sub
Sub Application_OnEnd
End Sub
Sub Session_OnStart
Application("NumUsers") = Application("NumUsers") + 1
End Sub
Sub Session_OnEnd
Application("NumUsers) = Application("NumUsers") - 1
End Sub
</script>
```

This file has no ASP delimiters. Instead, I've used the <script> tag. If you've done client-side scripting, this tag will be very familiar to you. If not, it's simple enough. The begin and end <script> tags surround any ASP code. In the attributes for the tag, you can specify which language to use and that it should be run at the server.

It will always look similar to the preceding code, unless you are using JavaScript. If you're using JavaScript, you change the script tag's language attribute to JavaScript and use functions for each routine. Otherwise, the code works in exactly the same way.

I didn't write code for each subroutine, but I include the declarations for them all. Including the declarations is not required, but it's a good idea.

The code above keeps track of the number of users currently on the system. The `NumUsers` application-level variable is created when the application starts. It is increased by one every time a new session starts and decreased by one every time a session ends.

You may expect that you can write your own subroutines or functions in the `Global.asa` file and then call them from any of the pages in your application. That'd be nice. But it doesn't work. Subroutines and functions created in the `Global.asa` file are only accessible from within the `Global.asa` file.

Creating objects in `Global.asa`

The other thing you're likely to do in the `Global.asa` file, in addition to writing scripts, is creating objects.

ASP offers you the ability to create server components that can help you create your pages or add interesting features to them. Server components are the subject of Chapter 9.

For more information on creating objects in `Global.asa`, see Chapter 9.

Server-Side Includes

Suppose you create a common function that's really handy and you want to use it in a number of different pages. What's the best way to do that?

Well, one obvious way is to simply copy the function out of the page where you created it and paste it into every page where you want to use it. The problem with that approach is when you go to make changes to that function, you have to make those changes in a bunch of different places. And if you miss one, your application will begin acting inconsistently. That's bad.

How about this: You create a file that holds the function and then you *include* that file into all the pages where you want to use it. This will work. But, it will also take a bit more explaining.

How to do it

IIS and PWS have the ability to process Server-Side Includes (SSI), which means that you can include a line like this at the top of your ASP page:

```
<!--#include file="header.inc" >
```

Now, when this line is processed by the server, it loads the entire contents of the `header.inc` file into memory and replaces the previous line of code with those contents.

What does `header.inc` have in it? Anything you want! It may have an HTML table that you use to set up a common header for every page on your site. It may have ASP code in VBScript or JavaScript. Anything that you can put into your page at that point can be included into the page using the `#include` directive.

The preceding line includes a file that is in the same folder as the page including it. But often it is convenient to put common include files in a folder of their own.

```
<!--#include virtual="common/header.inc"-->
```

This line retrieves `header.inc` from a virtual folder on the web server called common. Notice that I use the virtual keyword in the above line and not the `file` keyword as I do in the previous example. If you use `file`, it assumes that you are starting from your current folder. If you use `virtual`, it assumes you are starting from the root of the Web site.

For a real-world example of using the `#include` directive, see Chapter 13. There I create an include file which contains a subroutine to print a header for each page in the application and one to format the output of a classified ad.

What it's good for

SSI is a very simple concept. So, what good is it? Actually, it's surprisingly useful. Here are some ideas:

- ✔ Any piece of HTML that you find yourself using more than a couple of times in different pages is a good candidate for SSI. Headers, footers, frames, tables — nearly anything.

- ✔ Common ASP subroutines or functions that you want to use in more than one page.

- ✔ A common set of constants that you want to use throughout the application to simplify the code or make it more readable.

Chapter 8

Creating ASP Applications

• •

In This Chapter

▶ Creating new Web applications

▶ Developing a Guest Book

▶ Providing a Radio for personalized music while you surf

▶ Personalizing a Web site and storing user preferences

▶ Using the system date to keep content current

▶ Spinning a Web Roulette page

• •

*I*n this chapter, you create real ASP applications. Now, working with ASP starts to get really fun. I won't show you too many new tricks in this chapter. Instead, I show you how to use what you already know to begin creating real, useful applications.

I begin by providing a step-by-step procedure to go through when you want to create a new application. After that, you're off!

The first application is a simple guest book. You see guest books on sites all the time. They allow those who visit your site to tell you a little about themselves, and they allow you to keep a list of the type of people who like to visit your site. I use forms, the `Response` object, the `FileSystemObject`, and `TextStream` objects to create the Guest Book.

The second application also uses a form and collects input. But this time, the input is just a set of radio buttons that allows a user to choose what type of music he likes best. The "Radio" then plays music for him for the rest of his visit.

Next, you take the Guest Book and extend it to use the information gathered to create a personalized Welcome page. The user chooses a background color, a text color, and so on. Then the Welcome page calls her by name and uses her preferences.

Gee, I could do better than that!

As you look at the applications I show you how to create in this chapter, you may find yourself thinking you could have made a page look nicer or more organized. Great! That's exactly what I want you to do. Go ahead and actually make the page better. After it's perfect, use it in your own Web site.

I intentionally keep these examples simple. I don't do a lot of fancy formatting with tables or frames to make the page look nice because I want you to focus on the techniques without being distracted by a lot of glitz. After you've got the technique down, you can go nuts with the glitz.

Keeping your content up-to-date all the time is tough. So why not get ASP to help you out? That's the idea behind the fourth application in this chapter, which is really just a Welcome page that presents a couple of useful techniques.

Finally, the last application is mostly just for fun. It is a Web Roulette page that allows the user to click on a link that takes them to a different, randomly selected site each time.

Creating a Home For New Web Applications

Creating a place for your new Web application to live is pretty easy. The procedures for the different web servers are a bit different, though, so just read the section that applies to the web server you're using.

Creating new Web applications with Personal Web Server

Use these steps if your web server is Personal Web Server running on Windows 95/98.

1. **Create a new folder under your current Web site's root folder.**

   By default, the Web site's root folder is `c:\webshare\wwwroot` or `c:\inetpub\wwwroot`. Name this folder something appropriate to your application.

2. **Open the Personal Web Manager and click the Advanced icon.**

3. **Click** `<Home>` **at the top of the Virtual Directories list.**

4. **Click the Add button.**

   The Add Directory dialog box appears.

5. **Click Browse and find the directory you created in Step 1. Then click OK.**

6. **Type the name of the folder you created in Step 1 into the Alias edit.**

   You can name the virtual folder something different from the actual folder it is associated with, but naming it the same helps keep you from getting confused.

7. **Be sure the Read and Script check boxes are checked and the Execute check box is not checked.**

   You want to be able to read HTML files and execute scripts, but not execute actual applications like .exe and .dll files from this folder.

8. **Click OK.**

   Your new folder should appear somewhere under <Home>.

9. **Copy a** Global.asa **file into your new folder.**

10. **Create a** Default.htm **or** Default.asp **to act as your opening page for the application.**

Creating new Web applications with Internet Information Server

Use these steps if you are running Internet Information Server or Personal Web Server running on any version of Windows NT or Windows 2000.

1. **Create a new folder under your current Web site's root folder.**

   By default the Web site's root folder is c:\inetpub\wwwroot. Name this folder something appropriate to your application.

2. **Open the Internet Service Manager.**

3. **In the panel on the left, open the Internet Information Server folder.**

4. **Under the Internet Information Server folder, open your server.**

5. **Under the server, open the Default Web Site.**

   All the virtual folders for the Web site are displayed.

6. **Right-click on the Default Web Site. Choose New⇨Virtual Directory from the pop-up menu.**

7. **Type the name of the folder you created in Step 1 into the Alias edit.**

You can name the virtual folder something different from the actual folder it is associated with, but naming it the same helps keep you from getting confused.

8. **Click the Next button. Click Browse and find the directory you created in Step 1. Click the Next button.**

9. **Put a check mark in all the check boxes except Allow Execute Access (includes Script Access).**

   If you know what you plan to do with this application, you may want to leave some of the other check boxes unchecked, too. But you must always check Allow Read Access and Allow Script Access if you want to use HTML and ASP pages.

10. **Click Finish.**

   Your new folder appears somewhere under Default Web Site.

11. **Copy a** `Global.asa` **file into your new folder.**

12. **Create a** `Default.htm` **or** `Default.asp` **to act as your opening page for the application.**

Your Web application's Default page

If you create a Web application that integrates with the rest of your site, the Default page in your Web application presents whatever capabilities your Web application offers. For instance, if it is a Guest Book, the default page presents the Guest Book form.

In the examples in this chapter, however, I don't integrate these Web applications into an existing Web site. So, the Default page I create for these applications represents a normal page on your Web site that isn't necessarily a part of this Web application, but provides a link to it. In this way, I show you how the application *can* be integrated into your site. I am also able to demonstrate any changes you may need to make to the pages on your Web site that are necessary to make the Web application work.

A Guest Book: Creating and Responding to Forms

The Response object's Form collection makes it easy to use your ASP pages to respond to and save form information. I introduced the Form collection in a section titled "Form and function" in Chapter 7. In this section I create a simple guest book application that allows the user to enter his name, age, e-mail address, and so forth. Then the application appends the new entry to a file that holds information on all the visitors.

The Default page

In the first step, you create a home for this new application. Follow the steps in "Creating New Web Applications," earlier in this chapter. Put the application in a folder named gb.

Here's a simple default page that provides a link to the guest book:

```
<HTML>
<HEAD>
<TITLE>Home Page</TITLE>
</HEAD>
<BODY>
<h1>Home Page</h1>
Welcome to my home page. I'm glad you decided
to stop by. Please take a couple of seconds to
sign my guest book. Thanks!
<p>
<a href=gb.htm>Sign My Guest Book</a>
</BODY>
</HTML>
```

Save it as Default.htm. In the browser, this page looks like Figure 8-1.

Figure 8-1:
The Default page with a link to the Guest Book.

The Guest Book form

Now create the page that provides a form for the user to enter her information. Notice that no ASP code is in it, so save this page with an .htm extension. I call it gb.htm.

```html
<HTML>
<head>
<title>Guest Book</title>
</head>
<body bgcolor="#FFFFFF">
<h1>Guest Book</h1>
Welcome to my guest book! Thank you for visiting
my site and thank you for taking the time to give me
just a little bit of information about yourself.<p>
<form method="POST" action="gbproc.asp">
First Name:<input type="text" size="20"
  name="FirstName"><p>
Last Name:<input type="text" size="20"
  name="LastName"><p>
Gender:
<input type="radio" checked name="Gender" value="Male">
Male
<input type="radio" name="Gender" value="Female">
Female<p>
Age:<input type="text" size="10" name="Age"><p>
<p>Email Address: <input type="text" size="30"
name="Email"><p>
<input type="submit" name="Submit" value="Thank You!"><p>
</form>
</body>
</HTML>
```

This is a fairly simple form. The form tag's method is "POST" and the action is "gbproc.asp". Also, notice that I give each control a name that makes sense.

The Guest Book form looks like Figure 8-2.

Responding to the form

Here's what the ASP page that processes the form looks like:

```asp
<% Option Explicit %>
<HTML>
<head>
<title>Guest Book Response</title>
</head>
```

```
<body>
<%=Request.Form("FirstName")%><br>
<%=Request.Form("LastName")%><br>
Gender: <%=Request.Form("Gender")%><br>
Age: <%=Request.Form("Age")%><br>
Email: <%=Request.Form("Email")%><p>
<p>
<%
Dim filesys, peoplefile
Set filesys = CreateObject("Scripting.FileSystemObject")
Set peoplefile = _
 filesys.OpenTextFile(_
 "c:\inetpub\wwwroot\gb\gbpeople.txt",_
 8, true)
peoplefile.WriteLine Request.Form("FirstName")
peoplefile.WriteLine Request.Form("LastName")
peoplefile.WriteLine Request.Form("Gender")
peoplefile.WriteLine Request.Form("Age")
peoplefile.WriteLine Request.Form("Email")
peoplefile.Close
%>
<h3>This information has been saved.</h3>
<a href="gblist.asp">See others who signed in.</a>
</body>
</HTML>
```

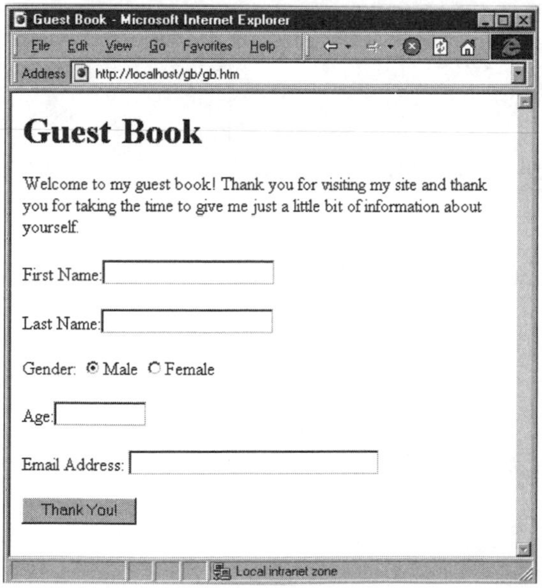

Figure 8-2:
The Guest
Book form.

Save this one as `gbproc.asp`.

The information entered in the form is displayed. Then I create a `FileSystemObject` and use that to open the text file named `gbpeople.txt`. Be sure to change the path to `gbpeople.txt` so that it matches the folder organization on your server. The second argument, `8`, tells the `OpenTextFile` function that I want to open the file and append new information to the end. The third argument, `true`, indicates that if the file doesn't exist, it should be created.

Then the `WriteLine` method writes each piece of information separately to its own line in the file. This makes it easy to read later.

The Guest Book processing page looks like Figure 8-3.

Figure 8-3:
The Guest
Book
processing
page.

That's all there is to it! You end up with a `gbpeople.txt` file that looks something like this:

```
Melanie
Hatfield
Female
29
melanie24@aol.com
Bill
Hatfield
Male
30
billhatfield@worldnet.att.net
Frisk
```

```
Fletcher
Female
35
friskem@worldnet.att.net
```

Listing the visitors

But to make it easier to read, you can create a Web page to read it for you. You probably noticed in the last listing that I included a link to such a page, named gblist.asp. Here's what that page may look like:

```
<% Option Explicit %>
<HTML>
<head>
<title>Guest Book List</title>
</head>
<body>
<h1>Guest Book List</h1>
Here's a list of all those who've been kind enough to
sign the Guest Book.<p>
<%
Dim filesys, peoplefile, fname, lname, gender, age, email
Set filesys = CreateObject("Scripting.FileSystemObject")
Set peoplefile = _
 filesys.OpenTextFile( _
 "c:\inetpub\wwwroot\gb\gbpeople.txt",1)
Do While Not peoplefile.AtEndOfStream
fname = peoplefile.ReadLine
lname = peoplefile.ReadLine
gender = peoplefile.ReadLine
age = peoplefile.ReadLine
email = peoplefile.ReadLine
Response.Write fname & "<br>"
Response.Write lname & "<br>"
Response.Write gender & "<br>"
Response.Write age & "<br>"
Response.Write email & "<p>"
Loop
peoplefile.Close
%>
</body>
</HTML>
```

This time I open the same file (again change the path to suit your server), but the second argument is 1 — open for reading. Then I begin a Do While loop that goes until it hits the end of the file. Within the loop, I use ReadLine to read the information for one person at a time into local variables, and then I display the local variables.

The Guest Book list page looks like Figure 8-4.

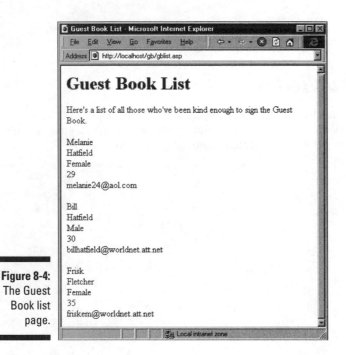

Guest Book List - Microsoft Internet Explorer

File   Edit   View   Go   Favorites   Help

Address | http://localhost/gb/gblist.asp

Guest Book List

Here's a list of all those who've been kind enough to sign the Guest Book.

Melanie
Hatfield
Female
29
melanie24@aol.com

Bill
Hatfield
Male
30
billhatfield@worldnet.att.net

Frisk
Fletcher
Female
35
friskem@worldnet.att.net

Local intranet zone

Figure 8-4:
The Guest
Book list
page.

Nothing to it!

Creating a Radio: Music to Surf By

Some sites offer music for you to listen to while you surf through the pages on the site. Music is a nice feature, unless you don't happen to have the same taste in music as the person who created the site. Then it's more annoying than a neon-colored background image.

I decided to create a way for the users who visit my site to select their own favorite style of music to listen to.

Many different technology options are available for providing music on your Web site, but just to keep it simple, I decided to use ASP and the `bgsound` tag with small MIDI files that download quickly.

First, you create a new home for this application. Follow the steps in the section titled "Creating a Home For New Web Applications," earlier in this chapter. Put this new application in a folder named `Radio`.

To make this idea a reality, you need four things:

- ✔ MIDI music files with several different styles of music.
- ✔ A Default page that kicks off the application with a link to the Radio page.
- ✔ A Radio page that provides a form with a list of radio buttons so that the user can choose a style of music and click Submit.
- ✔ A Tuning page that actually does the work of changing the music to what the user wants to hear. It also informs the users that it was successful and plays the music they selected. This page has a link back to the Default page, which continues to play the music.

Creating the MIDI music

I created the MIDI music files for you. You have many MIDI creation utilities available from commercial, shareware, and freeware channels. For this application, just steal the ones I include on the CD with this book.

The Default page

Next, I need a Default page to kick off this Web application. Here it is:

```
<HTML>
<HEAD>
<TITLE>Normal Page</TITLE>
</HEAD>
<BODY>
<h1>Welcome To A Normal Page On Your Web Site</h1>
This page represents any normal page on your site
where you want to support music from the radio.
<p>
<a href=radio.htm>Change Radio Station</a>
</BODY>
</HTML>
```

Name this file Default.htm and save it. The page ends up looking like Figure 8-5.

The Radio page

The form in which users can select from a variety of options and then click a button to indicate the one that they want comes next. I created a page that looks like this:

```
<HTML>
<head>
<title>Radio Tuner</title>
</head>
<body bgcolor="#FFFFFF">
<h1>Radio Tuner</h1>
Please tune to the radio station that plays
the music you like best.<p>
<form method="POST" action="/radio/radiotun.asp">
<input type="radio" checked name="Station"
value="Classical">
WCLAS - - Classical Music<br>
<input type="radio" name="Station" value="Rock">
WROCK - - Rock Music<br>
<input type="radio" name="Station" value="Country">
WCTRY - - Country Music<p>
<input type="submit" name="Submit" value="Tune It In!">
</form>
</body>
</HTML>
```

Figure 8-5:
The Default
page with a
link to the
Radio.

Save this one as `radio.htm`. No big surprises here. Three radio buttons and a Submit button.

The page looks like Figure 8-6.

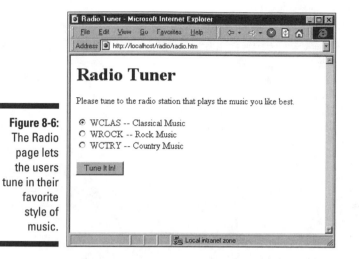

Figure 8-6:
The Radio
page lets
the users
tune in their
favorite
style of
music.

The Tuning page

The Tuning page is really the tough part. How am I going to make the music play on every page? The HTML tag I want to use looks like this:

```
<bgsound src=\radio\rock.mid loop=-1>
```

`src` identifies where the MIDI file can be found and a `loop` value of `-1` means that the music should be played over and over again forever.

I want the `bgsound` tag to appear in each Web page, but I want it to have a different MIDI file identified in `src`, depending on which option the user chooses in the Radio page.

So, why not just put the entire line in a session-level variable named `music`, and then display the value of `music` at the top of each page? Create this page and save it as `radiotun.asp`:

```
<HTML>
<head>
<title>Radio Tuning</title>
</head>
<body>
<h1>Radio Tuning</h1>
<%
If Request.Form("Station") = "Classical" Then
```

```
%>
You requested Classical Music. One moment while I
tune in WCLAS. <p>
<%
 Session("radio") = _
 "<bgsound src=\radio\class.mid loop=-1>"
ElseIf Request.Form("Station") = "Rock" Then %>
You requested Rock Music. One moment while I
tune in WROCK. <p>
<%
 Session("radio") = _
 "<bgsound src=\radio\rock.mid loop=-1>"
ElseIf Request.Form("Station") = "Country" Then %>
You requested Country Music. One moment while I
tune in WCTRY. <p>
<%
 Session("radio") = _
 "<bgsound src=\radio\country.mid loop=-1>"
End If
%>
<%=Session("radio")%>
When you hear your favorite music, feel free
to go to <a href="/radio/default.htm">another
page</a>.<p>
</body>
</HTML>
```

One of the last things I do is display the value of the session variable `radio`. This variable is replaced in the final page by the actual value of `radio` which should be the `bgsound` tag with `src` pointing to the right MIDI file. This tag makes the music begin playing on this page. (See Figure 8-7.)

But, in order to make this work, I have to go back and change `Default.htm` to `Default.asp` and add this line near the top of the body:

```
<%=Session("radio")%>
```

In fact, I have to go back and change every HTML page on my site to an ASP page and add the line. If I don't, the page doesn't play the music. Also, when you make those page name changes, don't forget to change all the links that refer to those pages, like the one in `radiotun.asp`.

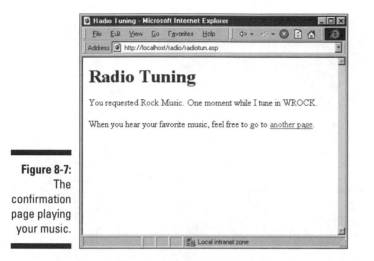

A Personalized Welcome Page with Cookies

After people sign your Guest Book, why not reward them with a little personal attention? In this application, I build on the Guest Book application you created earlier in this chapter. If you didn't build the Guest Book application, just steal the one that came on the CD in the back of this book and start with that.

Changing the Guest Book form

If you want to save the Guest Book as it is now, you may want to make a copy of the Guest Book application, put it in a new folder, and then work from the copy to create this application. To do that, follow these steps:

1. **Create a new folder. Name it** Personal.

2. **Copy the files from the GB folder into the Personal folder. Delete the gbpeople.txt file in the new folder.**

3. **Create a virtual folder on your Web site for the Personal folder as I describe in the section titled "Creating New Web Applications," earlier in this chapter. Name the virtual folder** Personal**, too.**

Open the `gb.htm` page. Change it to look like this:

```html
<HTML>
<head>
<title>Guest Book</title>
</head>
<body bgcolor="#FFFFFF">
<h1>Guest Book</h1>
<p>Welcome to my guest book! Thank you for visiting
my site and thank you for taking the time to give
me just a little bit of information about yourself.</p>
<form action="gbproc.asp" method="POST">
First Name:<input type="text" size="20"
 name="FirstName"><p>
Last Name:<input type="text" size="20" name="LastName"><p>
Email: <input type="text" size="30" name="Email"><p>
Web Page Preferences:<p>
Background Color:<select name="BackgroundColor" size="1">
 <option selected>White</option>
 <option>Yellow</option>
 <option>Silver</option>
 <option>Olive</option>
 <option>Teal</option>
 <option>Lime</option>
 <option>Aqua</option>
</select><p>
Text Color:<select name="TextColor" size="1">
 <option selected>Black</option>
 <option>Green</option>
 <option>Blue</option>
 <option>Maroon</option>
 <option>Red</option>
 <option>Purple</option>
</select><p>
Text Size:<select name="TextSize" size="1">
 <option value="1">Very Small</option>
 <option value="2">Small</option>
 <option selected value="3">Medium</option>
 <option value="4">Large</option>
 <option value="6">Very Large</option>
</select><p>
<input type="submit" name="Submit" value="Thank You!"><p>
</form>
</body>
</HTML>
```

I took out the age and gender questions and added questions under the heading `Web Page Preferences`. The new questions ask for the user's favorite background color, text color, and text size. I could have included a whole lot of other things, too, but I decided to do just enough here to give you an idea of the possibilities. I leave the rest to you.

The new Guest Book form looks like Figure 8-8.

Changing the Guest Book processing page

If you change the form, you always have to change the page that processes the form. The new gbproc.asp looks like this:

```
<% Option Explicit %>
<% Response.Buffer = true %>
<HTML>
<head>
<title>Guest Book Response</title>
</head>
<body>
<%=Request.Form("FirstName")%><br>
<%=Request.Form("LastName")%><br>
Email: <%=Request.Form("Email")%><br>
Background Color: <%=Request.Form("BackgroundColor")%><br>
Text Color: <%=Request.Form("TextColor")%><br>
Text Size: <%=Request.Form("TextSize")%><p>
<p>
<%
Dim filesys, peoplefile
```

```
Set filesys = CreateObject("Scripting.FileSystemObject")
Set peoplefile = _
 filesys.OpenTextFile( _
 "c:\inetpub\wwwroot\Personal\gbpeople.txt", 8, true)
peoplefile.WriteLine Request.Form("FirstName")
peoplefile.WriteLine Request.Form("LastName")
peoplefile.WriteLine Request.Form("Email")
peoplefile.Close
Response.Cookies("Personal")("FirstName") = _
 Request.Form("FirstName")
Response.Cookies("Personal")("LastName") = _
 Request.Form("LastName")
Response.Cookies("Personal")("Email") = _
 Request.Form("Email")
Response.Cookies("Personal")("BackgroundColor") = _
 Request.Form("BackgroundColor")
Response.Cookies("Personal")("TextColor") = _
 Request.Form("TextColor")
Response.Cookies("Personal")("TextSize") = _
 Request.Form("TextSize")
Response.Cookies("Personal").Expires = "January 1, 1999"
%>
<h3>This information has been saved.</h3>
<a href="gblist.asp">See others who signed in.</a>
</body>
</HTML>
```

One of the first things I did on the page is set the Response object's Buffer property to true. Usually the server sends out one portion of a page while it is still working on another portion. Setting Buffer to true causes the server to wait until the entire page is completely processed before it sends it out.

Why did I need to set the Buffer property for this page? When you change Cookie values, the information is sent back in a portion of the HTML page that you never see, called the *header*. If you don't turn buffering on, the header is already sent out by the time it gets to the bottom of the page, where I change the Cookie values. This causes an error. Setting Buffer to true makes the server wait to send out the header and gives me time to change.

As before, I display the information the user entered. This time I only write part of it — the name and e-mail address — to a file. I store all the information in a Cookie named Personal, though. I give the information the same name in the Cookie that it had in the form. Finally, I set the Cookie expiration date so that the Cookie remains on the client's machine when the session is over.

Figure 8-9 shows what the new form processing page looks like.

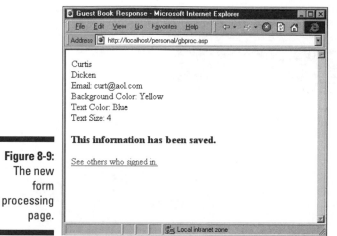

Figure 8-9:
The new
form
processing
page.

Changing the Listing page

The Listing page has to change because it has fewer items. Here's what the
new gblist.asp looks like:

```
<% Option Explicit %>
<HTML>
<head>
<title>Guest Book List</title>
</head>
<body>
<%
Dim filesys, peoplefile, fname, lname, email
Set filesys = CreateObject("Scripting.FileSystemObject")
Set peoplefile = _
 filesys.OpenTextFile( _
 "c:\inetpub\wwwroot\Personal\gbpeople.txt", 1)
do while not peoplefile.AtEndOfStream
fname = peoplefile.ReadLine
lname = peoplefile.ReadLine
email = peoplefile.ReadLine
Response.Write fname & "<br>"
Response.Write lname & "<br>"
Response.Write email & "<p>"
loop
peoplefile.Close
%>
<a href=default.asp>Home</a>
</body>
</HTML>
```

Also, notice that I change the link at the bottom to reference default.asp,
instead of default.htm. You work on that in the next section.

No other important differences here. Figure 8-10 shows the new list.

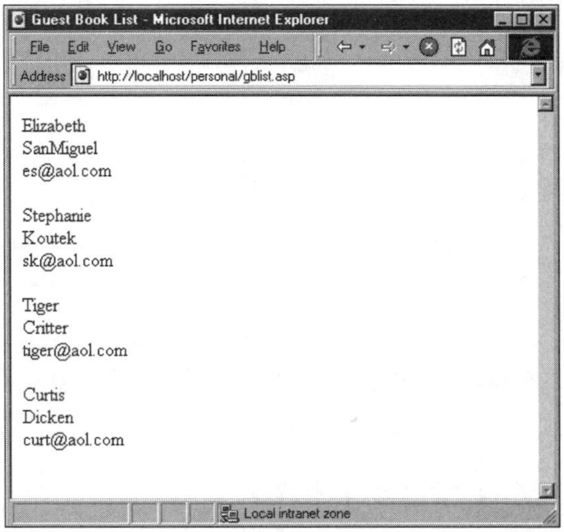

Figure 8-10:
The new list.

The new Default page

The real difference in this application, aside from the form, is the Default page. This is the page that is customized for the user. First, because it is now using ASP code, you have to rename it to `Default.asp`. After that, make changes so that it looks like this:

```
<HTML>
<head>
<title>Home Page</title>
</head>
<% If Request.Cookies("Personal")("BackgroundColor") = _
  "" Then %>
<body>
<font>
<% else %>
<body bgcolor=
  <%=Request.Cookies("Personal")("BackgroundColor")%>
  text=<%=Request.Cookies("Personal")("TextColor")%>>
<font size=<%=Request.Cookies("Personal")("TextSize")%>>
<% end if %>
<h1>Home Page</h1>
<% If Request.Cookies("Personal")("FirstName") = "" Then %>
```

```
<h2>Hello There! </h2>
<% else %>
<h2>Hello
<%=Request.Cookies("Personal")("FirstName")%>!</h2>
How is the <%=Request.Cookies("Personal")("LastName")%>
family doing?<p>
<% end if %>
Welcome to my home page. I'm glad you decided
to stop by. Please take your time. Look around
and enjoy. Thanks!
<p>
<% If Request.Cookies("Personal")("FirstName") = "" Then %>
<a href=gb.htm>Please Sign My Guest Book</a>
<% Else %>
<a href=gb.htm>Click Here To Change Your Guest Book
Information</a>
<% End If %>
</font>
</body>
</HTML>
```

Three If..Then statements are used to check to see if Cookie keys have values. If no values are in the Cookie keys, you end up with a very generic opening page that looks something like Figure 8-11.

Figure 8-11:
The generic
opening
page
displayed if
you don't
have any
cookies.

If you have signed the guest book and filled in all the information, however, the opening page looks very different. See Figure 8-12 for one example.

Serious personalization

This simple example was created to show you how Cookies work and present one of the ways they can be used.

If you are trying to create a site that takes user personalization and customization seriously, you probably want to check out the Microsoft Site Server package. Site Server is a supplement to

Internet Information Server and provides a variety of tools that make your Web site development, management, and maintenance much easier. One of those tools is a server component that is designed to make easy the getting, storing, and using of user personalization information.

This information is remembered from one session to the next. This feature is very powerful and could be used to customize the entire site to look just the way the user prefers — changing fonts, background graphics, and the way menus are presented.

But in order to use the information in that way on every page, you have to turn every page into an ASP page. No way around it exists in this application. If you want to make use of Cookies, you have to be able to access the values. And you can only do that from your ASP scripting language.

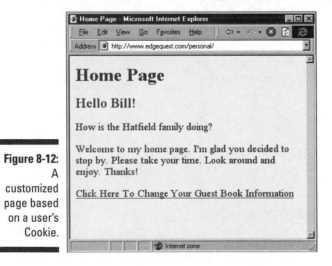

Figure 8-12: A customized page based on a user's Cookie.

Customizing a Page Based on the Date

If you want to attract new people to your Web site and keep them coming back often, you absolutely must keep your site updated on a regular basis.

Have you ever gone to a site that had text like this:

Don't forget about our contest — sign in with our Guest Book by December 1st and get a chance to win $100 cash in our Guest Book drawing!

Great idea. Except that it's December 15th, and they obviously haven't bothered to update their site in several weeks. Why should you waste your time here if they don't even keep it up-to-date?

On the other hand, if you're the person who has to keep a site constantly updated, it can be quite a task, especially with a big site. Why not use ASP to help?

Take a look at this welcome page:

```
<% Option Explicit %>
<% Response.Buffer = true %>
<HTML>
<head><title>Welcome</title></head>
<body>
<h1>Hello and Welcome to My Site</h1>
<% If Request.Cookies("Visit")("Last") = "" Then %>
We're happy you came to visit us.<p>
<% else %>
Thanks for coming back. Your last visit
was on <%=Request.Cookies("Visit")("Last")%>.<p>
<% End If %>
<% Response.Cookies("Visit")("Last") = Date %>
<h3>Important Information:</h3>
<% If Date < #12/1/1999# Then %>
Don't forget about our contest - - sign in with our
Guest Book by December 1st and get a chance to win
$100 cash in our Guest Book drawing!<p>
<% ElseIf Date = #12/1/1999# Then %>
Today's the last day you can sign in with our
Guest Book for a chance to win $100 cash. Don't
put it off a moment longer!<p>
<% Else %>
Our drawing to win $100 cash by signing in with
our Guest Book is officially over. Keep watching!
We'll be announcing the winner soon...<p>
<% End If %>
</body>
</HTML>
```

This page uses dates in two different ways. First, it uses a Cookie to keep track of the date of the user's last visit. Just telling a user when he last visited is somewhat interesting, but you can use this technique for more useful purposes. You could

- ✔ Give special instructions or information to people the first time they visit your site.

- ✔ Write the information out to the database or a text file so that you can keep track of not only how many people hit your site, but also how often a given person is likely to come back.

The second technique demonstrated in this page is even more useful. In fact, you should think about using this technique anywhere on your Web site where time-sensitive information is present.

Instead of just entering the message and then expecting that I'll have time to come back and update it in the future (yeah, right!), I put an `If..ElseIf` statement around three different messages — one for before the drawing, one for the exact day of the drawing, and one for after the drawing. That way, the site updates itself and the content always looks current — even if I forget to do the actual drawing on December 1st!

Figure 8-13 shows the page before the drawing, and Figure 8-14 shows it on the day of the drawing.

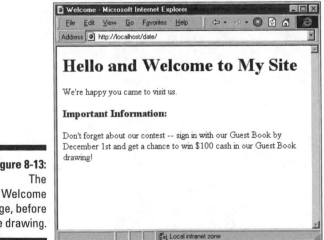

Figure 8-13:
The
Welcome
page, before
the drawing.

Figure 8-14:
The
Welcome
page, the
day of the
drawing.

Web Site Roulette with Redirect

I leave you with one final, entertaining application. You may have seen Web site roulette pages before. They allow you to "spin the wheel" and end up at a random Web site. Often the sites you end up at are silly, but sometimes this is a good way to begin browsing and finding sites on topics you never thought to search for.

To make it more interesting to the people who visit your site, you can create a *topical* Web Roulette by sending them to sites along a particular theme. If you have a gardening site, your Roulette could send them to other sites that would be interesting to gardeners.

Using ASP pages, a Web Roulette page is easy. First, you need a page to present to the user. If you have a good graphic of a roulette wheel, use it. Or perhaps a graphic of an old-fashioned revolver for a game of Russian Roulette. In this page, I just use some text as the link.

```
<HTML>
<head><title>Web Site Roulette</title></head>
<body>
<h1>Welcome to Web Site Roulette</h1>
Care to take a spin on the wheel? It's always a
gamble...<p>
When you're ready, just click...<p>
<p>
<a href=wheel.asp>Round and round she goes. Where
she stops, nobody knows.</a><p>
</body>
</HTML>
```

The real work is done in `wheel.asp`.

```
<%
Response.Buffer = true
dim sites(20), num
Randomize
sites(1) = "http://www.microsoft.com"
sites(2) = "http://www.borland.com"
sites(3) = "http://www.netscape.com"
sites(4) = "http://www.sun.com"
sites(5) = "http://www.ibm.com"
sites(6) = "http://www.lotus.com"
sites(7) = "http://www.discovery.com"
sites(8) = "http://www.comedy.com"
sites(9) = "http://www.futility.com"
sites(10) = "http://www.hbo.com"
sites(11) = "http://www.cnet.com"
sites(12) = "http://www.comedycentral.com"
sites(13) = "http://www.time.com"
sites(14) = "http://www.wired.com"
sites(15) = "http://www.gamesdomain.com"
sites(16) = "http://www.monopoly.com"
sites(17) = "http://www.moviecritic.com"
sites(18) = "http://www.cdnow.com"
sites(19) = "http://www.circlecity.com"
sites(20) = "http://www.ebay.com"
num = int(rnd * 20) + 1
Response.Redirect sites(num)
%>
```

An array of 20 strings is filled with the addresses for 20 different Web sites. (I'm sure you're able to come up with more imaginative ones than I have here.) Then a random number between 1 and 20 is chosen, and the `Redirect` is called, passing the randomly chosen string. You want to use at least 20 Web sites to keep it from getting dull. And the more the better.

The Power of ASP

The applications in this chapter begin to give you an idea of how easy it is to use ASP to empower your Web sites with more flexibility and more interactivity. For more examples of using ASP to create real web server applications, check out Chapters 12 and 13. In each chapter, I present one of the complete full-blown applications that I've included on the CD-ROM in the back of the book. The first is a real-time chat room that allows your guests to visit with each other and share ideas together. The second is a classified ads application.

Chapter 9

Using the Included Server Components

*T*he ancient writer Heraclitus said, "Nothing endures but change." Those words are nowhere more true than in the world of the Internet. But if change is a constant, then it makes the words of A. N. Whitehead all the more imperative: "The art of progress is to preserve order amid change." Of course, that's easier said than done.

One of the key ways software developers have tried to harness the change and preserve order through it is with objects. I discuss scripting objects, such as the `Dictionary`, `FileSystemObject`, and `TextStream`, in Chapter 6. Scripting objects extend the ASP script language and provide new capabilities. Server objects, which I discuss in Chapter 7, add additional capabilities by giving you access to the server itself and to the page being created through the `Server`, `Request`, and `Response` objects.

However, only a few scripting and server objects are available, and, if you need new capabilities, you can't add more objects. But there is a type of object that you *can* add: *server components*.

Server components work a lot like scripting objects. IIS and PWS offer a number of server components to get you started. But if you need some additional capabilities that you can't get from the scripting objects or the included server components, you can download *new* server components.

Many commercial, shareware, and freeware server components are available for you to install and use from ASP just as easily as you use the `Dictionary` object.

In this chapter, I introduce you to the concept of server components. You discover what they do and how to include them in your Web pages. You also find out how to integrate them with your page and with other server components to create even more powerful Web applications.

Finally, you explore several of the important server components that come with your server software. IIS and PWS include the same powerful server components, and this chapter helps you integrate these components into your own Web site.

A Rose by Any Other Name . . . Is Confusing!

For some reason, people seem unable to agree on a name for server components. Everyone calls them something different. You may hear people call server components by any of these names:

- ActiveX server components
- Active Server components
- Server-side ActiveX controls
- Design-time components

But don't be confused. All of these terms refer to *exactly* the same thing. And I call that thing a *server component.*

Also, don't confuse server *components* with server *objects*. Server objects, such as the `Request` and `Response` objects, are built into your web server itself. I discuss server objects in Chapter 7.

So What Is a Server Component?

A *server component* is a small program, written in C++, Visual Basic, or some other language, that uses ASP scripting to do some task that you either can't do or don't want to do. A server component is specifically designed so that it fits easily into the ASP scripting environment. You only have to create an instance of the object and use it — then everything it can do, you can do.

You can think of server components as the bricks you use to create your Web application and your script as the mortar that holds the bricks (server components) where they belong. With the right components and some cleverly written scripts, you can put together surprisingly powerful Web applications in no time!

You may be familiar with the Microsoft COM technology. COM is the umbrella under which you find the Microsoft OLE and ActiveX technologies. COM and subsequently OLE and ActiveX are standards that have been developed to provide a common way to create components as well as a standard way for applications to communicate with each other.

Server components are built on ActiveX technology. So server components are basically the same as an ActiveX control that is downloaded and used on a Web page (a *client-side* ActiveX control). But a couple of important differences between server components and client-side ActiveX controls do exist:

 ✔ Server components are specifically designed to help you create pages and scripts on the *server,* whereas client-side ActiveX controls are downloaded as part of a Web page, appear in the browser, and run on the client.

 ✔ Server components don't have any user interface. You use server components on the server, so that they don't need to present themselves to the user. Server components are simply engines that perform a task for your script.

If all of this is still a little fuzzy for you, hang in there. This concept makes a lot more sense after you see some examples of real server components in action. I describe the server components that come with IIS and PWS in the next section.

The Components Included with Your Server

Internet Information Server (IIS) and Personal Web Server (PWS) come bundled with a number of very handy server components that you can use right away. I list them here with a short description of each. In the remainder of this chapter, I describe some of them in more detail and show you how to use them in your ASP pages.

 ✔ **Browser Capabilities Component:** Determines the capabilities, type, and version of the user's browser. You can use this information to send different HTML tags to individual users based on the capabilities of each user's browser.

- ✔ **Advertisement Rotator Component:** Automatically rotates banner advertisements on a schedule you specify.

- ✔ **Content Rotator Component:** Automatically rotates HTML content strings on a Web page.

- ✔ **Content Linking Component:** Provides an easy way to tie pages together so that they can be viewed sequentially, like a book. It automatically generates appropriate links and a table of contents for newsletters and other publications.

- ✔ **Tools Component:** Provides a few handy utility functions that do things such as checking to see if a file exists or helping in handling submitted form information.

- ✔ **Page Counter Component:** Automatically increments and persistently maintains and displays the number of times a Web page has been opened.

- ✔ **Counters Component:** Allows you to create, store, increment, and retrieve any number of individual counters that are automatically and persistently maintained in a text file.

- ✔ **MyInfo Component:** Tracks information about the site, such as the site owner's name and address, and the company that owns the server.

- ✔ **File Access Component:** Provides access to file manipulation commands and the ability to create, read, and write text files. This component provides functionality identical to the `FileSystemObject` and `TextStream` scripting objects. Using the scripting objects is usually easier and preferable to using the server component. (See Chapter 6 for more information on using these scripting objects.)

- ✔ **Database Access Components or Active Data Objects (ADO):** Can be used to quickly and easily access your database. You can use it to retrieve and update data. (See Chapters 10 and 11 for detailed coverage of the ADO.)

Browser Performance Anxiety

Web developers always want to use the latest and greatest HTML tags and browser capabilities so that their Web sites are cutting edge. However, lots of people use older browsers that don't support all those fancy features, which becomes a real problem. You can't just leave those people out in the cold, can you?

One solution is to create two versions of your site: one that uses only basic HTML and another that uses all the latest tags. Then the users can choose on the opening page which version they prefer. Using two versions is a very common solution that is implemented on many different sites.

The Browser Capabilities Component makes it possible to offer a better solution than creating two separate versions. With it, you can use your VBScript or JScript code to find out which features are supported and which are not and then send the HTML that will work best in their browser. And you can do it all on a single page.

But before you can use *any* server component, you first have to create it.

Creating a new server component object

Here's the code you use to create a Browser Capabilities Component object:

```
Set browser = Server.CreateObject("MSWC.BrowserType")
```

A new sever component object is created using the Server's `CreateObject` method. `MSWC.BrowserType` is the name you pass to `Server.CreateObject` to create the Browser Capabilities Component. The component is placed in the `browser` variable. From this point forward, you access the component using the `browser` variable.

All server components work this way: You must first create an object by using the `Server.CreateObject` method and then receive that object as it is passed back into a variable using `Set`. Then you use the variable to refer to the component.

This should sound familiar to you because you do something very similar to this when you work with *scripting* objects like the `Dictionary`, `FileSystemObject`, and `TextStream`. However, when you work with scripting objects, you use the VBScript built-in function called `CreateObject`.

```
Set filesys = CreateObject("Scripting.FileSystemObject")
```

The big difference between scripting objects and server components is that you should *always* use the `Server.CreateObject` method instead of the VBScript `CreateObject` function when you are creating *server component* objects.

```
Set browser = Server.CreateObject("MSWC.BrowserType")
```

If you create scripting objects, you only use them within your script to enhance the language's capabilities. But if you use server components, they often need to interact with the web server itself. If you use the `Server.CreateObject` method, it informs the web server about the object and makes that interaction possible.

You can also create objects that can be accessed from other pages by storing them in application- or session-level variables.

```
Set Session("browser") = _
  Server.CreateObject("MSWC.BrowserType")
```

The other way to create a new server component object

In the preceding section, I describe one way to create a new server object. That method is best used when you want to create an object to be used on a single page.

But if you want to create objects for use throughout a session or across an application, a better way to do it is with the Global.asa file and the object tag.

```
<object runat=Server scope=Session id=BrowserCap
progid="MSWC.BrowserType">
</object>
```

This tag is included anywhere in the Global.asa file *outside* the script tag. It indicates that you want to create an object that runs on the server at the session level. The id indicates the name you'll use to refer to the object in your scripts. The progid indicates which object should be created. After this object tag is in Global.asa, a new Browser Capabilities Component is created every time a new session begins.

The scope can also be set to Application to create a single component for all sessions. Although setting scope to Application doesn't make any sense for the Browser Capabilities Component (because each session has a different browser), it does for other components, like the Page Counter Component, which stores application-level information (for more information on the Page Counter Component, see "Counting Page Hits" later in this chapter).

The object **tag versus the** Server.CreateObject **method**

Use the object tag in the Global.asa file whenever you want to create an object that is used throughout a session or an application. The object tag is the most efficient because it doesn't actually create the object until a Web page uses it. If you use Server.CreateObject and assign the object to a session or application variable (as described in the previous section) the object is created whether it ends up being used or not.

However, if you're creating an object to be used on one page only, Server.CreateObject is the better way to go.

Putting the Browser Capabilities Component to work

The Browser Capabilities Component has properties that allow you to find out what the user's browser can do. Here's an example of the component at work:

```
<HTML>
<head>
<title>Runs Per Inning</title>
</head>
<body>
<% Set browser = Server.CreateObject("MSWC.BrowserType") %>
<% If browser.Tables = True Then %>
<table border>
<caption>Number of Runs for the First Three
Innings:</caption>
<th>First<th>Second<th>Third<tr>
<td>1<td>3<td>2<tr>
<td>3<td>1<td>1<tr>
</table>
<% Else %>
Number of Runs for the <br>
First Three Innings:<p>
<pre>
First Second Third
1  3  2
3  1  1
</pre>
<% End If %>
<% If browser.BackgroundSounds = True Then %>
 <BGSound SRC=\radio\qwake.mid LOOP=-1>
<% End If %>
</body>
</HTML>
```

After the component object is created, the page checks to see if the browser supports tables. If it does, it creates a table. If the user's browser doesn't support tables, it uses the next best thing — the preformatted text tag.

The preceding listing also checks to see if background sounds are supported. If they are supported, the bgsound tag is used to play MIDI music. If the browser doesn't support the tag, it simply does nothing.

So now you no longer have to create and maintain two different pages — generic HTML and multimedia. You only need one. And the users don't have to choose which type of page they want to see. You already have all the information you need, using the Browser Capabilities Component to make all the decisions for them. Using the Browser Capabilities Component, you can provide all of your users with the highest fidelity experience their browsers will allow.

In the preceding listing, notice that you can check to see if the browser supports tables and background sounds. What other properties are available from the Browser Capabilities Component? Here's a list of the common ones:

- ✔ `Browser`: What is the browser's name?

- ✔ `Version`: What version of the browser is being used?

- ✔ `Frames`: Does it support frames?

- ✔ `Tables`: Does it support tables?

- ✔ `BackgroundSounds`: Does it support the `<bgsound>` tag?

- ✔ `ActiveXControls`: Does it support client-side ActiveX controls?

- ✔ `JavaApplets`: Does it support Java applets?

- ✔ `VBScript`: Does it support client-side scripting with VBScript?

- ✔ `JavaScript`: Does it support client-side scripting with JavaScript?

- ✔ `Cookies`: Does it support Cookies?

The inside story: How the Browser Capabilities Component works its magic

You may expect that this useful component pulls the information from mysterious, invisible HTTP headers that tell you everything you'd ever want to know about the client's browser. Unfortunately, the only thing sent in the HTTP headers is the name and version of the browser. So how does the Browser Capabilities Component do it? Answer: It cheats.

The Browser Capabilities Component keeps track of all the browsers it knows about through the use of a simple `.ini` file that is stored in your computer. The `Browscap.ini` file is stored in the same place as the `Browscap.dll` file that has the Browser Capabilities Component code.

If you are running Windows NT, the file is stored in

```
WinNT\System32\InetSrv\Asp\Cmpnts
```

Or if you are using NT Workstation, you may find the file in

```
WINNT\System32\InetSrv
```

Finally, if you are running Windows 95/98, the file is stored in

```
Windows\System\Inetsrv
```

The `Browscap.ini` file has a list of all the browsers available and what their capabilities are. Then, after a browser connects to your site, it sends the name and version of the browser in the HTTP header. The Browser Capabilities Component just looks up the browser and reads its capabilities.

This is what a typical `Browscap.ini` file looks like. Well, part of one, at least. They are typically very long. I've cut some parts out of the middle and replaced them with a ... so that you know when some sections are missing.

```
;;;;;;;;;;;;;;;;;;;;;;;;;;;;
;;; Microsoft Browsers ;;;
;;;;;;;;;;;;;;;;;;;;;;;;;;;;
[Microsoft Internet Explorer/4.40.308 (Windows 95)*]
browser=IE
version=1.0
majorver=#1
minorver=#0
frames=FALSE
tables=FALSE
cookies=FALSE
backgroundsounds=FALSE
vbscript=FALSE
javascript=FALSE
javaapplets=FALSE
platform=Windows95
[IE 1.5]
browser=IE
version=1.5
majorver=#1
minorver=#5
frames=FALSE
tables=TRUE
cookies=TRUE
backgroundsounds=FALSE
vbscript=FALSE
javascript=FALSE
javaapplets=FALSE
beta=False
Win16=False
[Mozilla/1.22 (compatible; MSIE 1.5; Windows)*]
parent=IE 1.5
platform=Unknown
...
;;;;;;;;;;;;;;;;;;;;;;;;;;;;
;;; Netscape Browsers ;;;
;;;;;;;;;;;;;;;;;;;;;;;;;;;;
;;Netscape 4.0
[Netscape 4.0]
browser=Netscape
version=4.0
majorver=#4
minorver=#0
```

```
frames=TRUE
tables=TRUE
cookies=TRUE
backgroundsounds=FALSE
vbscript=FALSE
javascript=TRUE
javaapplets=TRUE
ActiveXControls=FALSE
beta=False
[Mozilla/4.0 * (WinNT; I)]
parent=Netscape 4.0
platform=WinNT
...
;;;;;;;;;;;;;;;;;;;;;;;;;;
;;;   Lynx   ;;;
;;;;;;;;;;;;;;;;;;;;;;;;;;
[Lynx/2.6 libwww-FM/2.14*]
browser=Lynx
version=2.14
majorver=#2
minorver=#6
frames=False
tables=False
cookies=False
backgroundsounds=FALSE
vbscript=FALSE
javascript=FALSE
javaapplets=FALSE
platform=Unknown
...
```

Although this is a pretty simple way of solving the problem of figuring out the capabilities of each browser, it is also a pretty flexible way. When Microsoft comes out with an upgrade of Internet Explorer or Netscape comes out with an upgrade for Navigator, all you have to do to update your Browscap.ini file is follow these steps:

1. **Make a new entry to your** .ini **file.**

2. **Copy all the information from the previous entry to the new version's entry.**

3. **Update any properties that have changed in the new version of the browser.**

In addition, you can add new properties to the Browser Capabilities Component by adding new entries into the Browscap.ini file. So, if a new capability becomes available, you just add the entry in the appropriate section of your Browscap.ini file, and then you can start checking for it in your pages.

What a pain in the ASP!

You may be thinking that keeping your Browscap.ini file up-to-date for every new release of every new browser would be a pain. You'd be right, if you had to do it yourself. But you don't. Check out this Web site:

www.cyscape.com/browscap

This is the address for CyScape. It keeps a Browscap.ini file up-to-date all the time. You can go there and download its Browscap.ini file, and you're in business. They also offer a product called BrowserHawk, which replaces the Browscap.ini file. BrowserHawk offers more capabilities and is always kept up-to-date automatically.

Just What the World Needs: More Advertising

The Advertisement Rotator is a completely different kind of ActiveX Server Component. But it is every bit as useful as the Browser Capabilities Component, if you're lucky enough to have paying advertisers supporting your site.

Suppose that you have a very popular site and a very popular page on that site. You obviously want to sell an advertisement on that popular page. But why sell only one advertisement, if you can sell two or three or four? Well, because your users will get pretty ticked off if your advertisements are making it difficult, if not impossible, for them to find the content on your page!

The Ad Rotator makes it possible, though, to sell advertising for the *same space* several times. You do this by rotating through your ads — each time a new user pulls up a page, the ad is different.

How do you go about creating this kind of advertisement? Well, you can create or use an existing ActiveX control and embed the control in the Web page instead of the graphic. Then the control can go out and get a different image each time the page is refreshed. That solution works, but only if their browsers support ActiveX controls. What about the users whose browsers *don't* support ActiveX controls?

The Advertisement Rotator Component solves this problem on the server side so that you don't have to worry about what capabilities their browsers have.

The rotator schedule file

In order to use the Ad Rotator Component, you need to create a *rotator schedule file*. A rotator schedule file is a text file that can have any name you like. The following listing shows a typical schedule file:

```
REDIRECT /adscript/redir.asp
WIDTH 500
HEIGHT 50
BORDER 0
*
http://ads/bastrix.gif
http://www.bastrix.com/
Bastrix Has Your Needs Covered
10
http://bitbix/wk1.gif
-
BitBix Is Your News Source
30
http://ads/condor.gif
http://www.condorPC.com/
Condor PC is the place for systems
40
http://ads/flowr.gif
http://www.flowr.com/
Flowr me with love - - Flowr, Inc.
20
```

The first line identifies a file that you create that is executed after the user clicks on the ad box to go to the ad's home page. This redirection file ultimately sends the user to the home page, but it allows you to do other things first — such as count the number of times users have clicked on ads for each company. This is very useful information for you and the advertiser. If you leave the first line blank, no redirection file is used and the user is automatically taken to the ad's home page.

The next three lines of the rotator schedule file determine, in pixels, the width, height, and border size of the graphic. The default values are 440, 60, and 1, respectively.

One line, with a star in it, must always be between the *global parameters* (these first four lines) and the rest of the file.

You can choose to not specify any of these global parameters and go with the default values instead. If you do this, however, you must leave the line blank with only an asterisk in the first position. If you went with the defaults for all the global parameters, your file would simply start with five asterisks, each on a line by itself.

Now look at the rest of the file in the preceding listing. Each entry has four lines:

- ✔ The first line tells the server where the graphic to be displayed can be found. This graphic is usually on your server, but it doesn't have to be.

- ✔ The second line identifies the ad's home page. This is where the user is taken if he clicks on the ad. If no home page is associated with the ad, a dash can be placed on a line by itself to indicate that.

- ✔ The third line provides a text alternative for those who don't have graphical browsers or who have graphics turned off.

- ✔ The fourth line specifies a weight — a relative number that determines how often the ad comes up. In the example in the preceding rotator schedule file, the numbers add up to 100, so that the individual numbers can be seen as the percentage of time the ad appears. The numbers do not have to add up to 100, though. The server simply adds the numbers together and allots the correct portion of time to each ad.

Using the Ad Rotator Component

After the schedule file is created, using the component is a snap.

```
. . .
And now a word from our sponsor:
<% Set ad = Server.CreateObject("MSWC.AdRotator") %>
<% = ad.GetAdvertisement("/adscript/rotsched.txt") %>
Now back to our regularly scheduled program...
. . .
```

The first line creates the object and stores it in the variable ad. The second line calls the GetAdvertisement method of ad and passes the filename of the Rotator Schedule file. Because this line begins with an equal sign, whatever this function returns is placed into the final HTML file. What will that final HTML file be?

```
. . .
And now a word from our sponsor:
<A HREF="/adscript/redir.asp?url=http://www.bastrix.com/">
<IMG
SRC="http://ads/bastrix.gif"
ALT="Bastrix Has Your Needs Covered"
WIDTH=500 HEIGHT=50 BORDER=0>
</A>
Now back to our regularly scheduled program...
. . .
```

The anchor and image tags are returned from the GetAdvertisement function and are placed right in the code where they belong. Notice that the href on the anchor does not go directly to www.bastrix.com. Instead, it calls the redirection ASP page with the www.bastrix.com address as a query argument. You create the redirection page yourself and you can make it do anything you like. Here's what a simple redir.asp page may look like:

```
<%
Response.Buffer = True
Application("AdHits") = Application("AdHits") + 1
Response.Redirect(Request.QueryString("url"))
%>
```

The number of hits is tallied and the the user is sent to the advertising site's home page (which is passed as a query string variable named url).

That Fresh Site Feeling with the Content Rotator

Does your Web site ever have that not-so-fresh feeling? The Content Rotator Component can help.

The Content Rotator Component works in much the same way as the Ad Rotator Component. Instead of rotating graphics files, however, it rotates snippets of HTML. This rotation keeps your pages constantly changing every time the user comes to your site.

One simple use of the Content Rotator Component is to include a different quote or joke on the page every time it is visited. This is a fun option, and the Content Rotator makes it easy. But that's not all the Content Rotator can do.

Because the Content Rotator displays HTML, you can use it to rotate any kind of content you like: images, background music, ActiveX controls — anything!

The content schedule file

Here's how it works. Just like the Ad Rotator, the Content Rotator has a file that provides its agenda — in this case, a *content schedule file*. The content schedule file is simpler than the rotator schedule file.

```
%% #33 // This quote will appear one third of the time.
Experience is a comb which nature gives us when
we are bald.<p>
<i>Chinese proverb</i><p>
%% #33 // Comments can span two lines if both
%% // start with two % signs
Never explain. Your friends do not need it and
your enemies will not believe you anyway.<p>
<i>Elbert Hubbard</i><p>
%% #34 // Use images, background music or any other HTML
<IMG SRC="/images/zen.gif"><p>
Here's your moment of zen...<p>
```

The content schedule file can have any name you want to give it. It begins with %% followed by a pound sign (#) and then a *weight*. This weight is a number that determines how often this content appears. (See "The rotator schedule file" earlier in this chapter for more information on weight.)

After the weight come two slashes (//). These slashes indicate the beginning of a comment. You can put anything you want in the comment. You can even have a second line of comments if you like. Just begin with %% again and follow with //, as I do in the second entry in the preceding listing.

After the comments come the content. The content can span as many lines as you like. The content doesn't end until a new line begins with %%. Then the whole thing starts over again with another entry. You can have as many entries as you like. And if you want to keep your jokes fresh, you'd better have a lot of them!

Using the Content Rotator Component

Including the Content Rotator Component in your Web page is a piece of cake. Create the component and then call the ChooseContent method.

```
<%Set Quote = Server.CreateObject("MSWC.ContentRotator")%>
<%=Quote.ChooseContent("/quotes/quoterotator.txt")%>
```

The HTML from the entry chosen replaces the call to ChooseContent in your page.

Linking Your Content

It's funny: No matter how easy it is to link to a zillion different places from a single page, people still seem to want to read Web pages like they read a book — top to bottom, one page after another. And sometimes that's the best way to present your information. Especially if your site is an electronic version of a more traditional medium, like a newsletter, magazine, or book. It's exactly this kind of information that the Content Linking Component helps you organize.

First, you have to create your pages. Then you create a document that the Content Linking Component uses to access and maintain your pages. That document is called a *content linking list*. It may look like this:

```
newsltr1.asp    Lead stories
newsltr2.asp    Editorial
newsltr3.asp    Real estate
newsltr4.asp    Comic strips
newsltr5.asp    Entertainment
```

The page name and the description are separated by a tab. A return is at the end of each line. You can name the file whatever you like. The file must be stored in one of the server's virtual folders — probably the one where you store the pages.

The next step is to create a page that has the table of contents. The code to do that looks something like this:

```
<%
Dim PageNum, Count, NextLink
Set NextLink = Server.CreateObject ("MSWC.NextLink")
Count = NextLink.GetListCount ("/nextlink/nextlink.txt")
For PageNum = 1 To Count %>
<a href=
  " <%= NextLink.GetNthURL( _
  "/nextlink/nextlink.txt", PageNum) %> ">
<%=NextLink.GetNthDescription( _
  "/nextlink/nextlink.txt", PageNum)%>
</a> <p>
<% Next %>
```

After the `NextLink` component is created, I call the `GetListCount` method and pass the name of the content linking list. Actually, *every* time you call a `NextLink` method, you have to pass the content linking list. To have to do this is annoying, but it does make it possible for you to have several separate sets of pages that work like this in one application — you keep them straight by using two different content linking lists.

`GetListCount` returns the number of pages that are a part of this list. Then I loop through each of those pages, I get the URL and description, and use them to create a link to the page. In the end, all the descriptions are listed and you can click any one to go to the associated page.

The final step is to put `Previous` and `Next` links on each page so that your users can easily navigate through the pages. You probably want to use clever arrow graphics instead of the text I use here.

```
<%
Dim NextLink
Set NextLink = Server.CreateObject ("MSWC.NextLink")
If NextLink.GetListIndex( _
 "/nextlink/nextlink.txt") > 1 Then %>
<a href=
 " <%=NextLink.GetPreviousURL( _
 "/nextlink/nextlink.txt")%> ">
Previous Page</a>
<% End If %>
<%If NextLink.GetListIndex("/nextlink/nextlink.txt") < _
 NextLink.GetListCount("/nextlink/nextlink.txt") Then %>
<a href=
" <%=NextLink.GetNextURL ("/nextlink/nextlink.txt")%> ">
Next Page</a>
<% End If %>
```

Notice that I have to create the `NextLink` object again. When I created it the first time, I didn't put it into a session-level variable. I don't have to. All I have to do is create it each time I need it.

Then I check to see if the current page's index is greater than 1. If it is, I create a `Previous Page` link using the `GetPreviousURL` method. Likewise, if this isn't the last page, I use `GetNextURL` to create a `Next Page` link.

In addition to the `GetNextURL` and `GetPreviousURL`, a `GetNextDescription` and a `GetPreviousDescription` also exist. A `GetNthURL` and a `GetNthDescription` require you to pass a number, and they return the URL or description associated with that index's page.

The Tools of the Trade

The Tools Component does nothing more than collect a few methods together. A list of the important methods and what they do follows:

- ✔ `FileExists`: After passing it a relative URL with a file name, `FileExists` returns true or false to indicate whether the file actually exists.

- ✔ `ProcessForm`: Takes the contents of a form submitted and writes it directly to a file. Optional features allow you to use a template for arranging the data and specify a location within an output file to begin.

- ✔ `Random`: Returns a random integer between -32768 and 32767. Provides an alternative to the VBScript and JavaScript random functions.

If you are using PWS on Windows 95/98, a Tools object is already declared for you in the Global.asa file. Because of this, you don't need to declare your own and you can simply use the Tools object as if it were a built-in object.

Counting Page Hits

The Page Counter Component does just what you expect — it keeps track of the number of hits for a particular page. To make the component track hits on a particular page, create the component on the page like this:

```
Set HitCount = Server.CreateObject("MSWC.PageCounter")
```

The number of hits is periodically saved in a text file called a *hit count data file* so that in case the server abruptly loses power or some other such emergency occurs, the information is saved. But don't worry, you don't ever have to mess with that file — the Page Counter Component takes care of it for you.

To display the hit count for the current page, use the Hits method.

```
Hits: <%=HitCount.Hits%><p>
```

You can also pass a URL and filename to Hits to get the hit count for a different page.

To reset the hit count for a page, use the Page Counter Component's Reset method.

Counting Other Things

The Counters Component allows you to create any number of counters that can be used to keep track of any application-wide counts you need in your Web application. For example, you can use a counter to keep track of the number of hits on a page.

Now hold on just a second. Isn't that what the Page Counter Component is designed for? Yup! It seems that, for some reason, Microsoft has included two different mechanisms for doing pretty much the same thing. That's what you get when you design by committee!

I don't suggest that you use the Counters Component for counting the hits to a page, because the Page Counter Component is specifically designed to do that. But that doesn't mean the Counters Component is useless. You can think of it as a place to store numbers of any kind on an application level.

You only need one Counters Component for your entire application because one component can track any number of individual counters you want to create. So it's a good idea to create the component in the Global.asa file, rather than in any particular script.

```
<object runat=Server scope=Application id=Counter
progid="MSWC.Counters">
</OBJECT>
```

 If you're using PWS on Windows 95/98, a Counters object is already declared for you in the Global.asa file. You don't need to declare your own and you can simply use the Counters object as if it were a built-in object.

After the object is created, you can use the Set method to create new individual counters.

```
<% Counter.Set("score", 100) %>
```

Set accepts a counter name and a value as arguments. If a counter with the name you specified doesn't exist, a new counter with that name is created. The value passed is assigned to the counter.

And where there's a Set, there's always a Get.

```
Your Score Is <%=Counter.Get("score")%>!<p>
```

Get returns the value of the counter passed. Two other Counters Component methods are available. Like Set and Get, they both accept the counter name as an argument.

- ✔ Increment: Adds one to the value of the counter.
- ✔ Remove: Destroys the counter.

Remembering Who You Are with MyInfo

The MyInfo Component is a very simple component. It has no methods. It is designed to hold information about the server, the company or the organization that runs the server, and the Webmaster of the server in its many properties. You can fill in or display these properties from any script. The values are automatically stored in a text file named MyInfo.xml to hold onto them permanently. (Again, this is a file you don't ever need to mess with.)

This component is one that is best created in the Global.asa file. You only need one copy of it and its scope should always be Application.

```
<object runat=Server scope=Application id=MyInfo
progid="MSWC.MyInfo">
</OBJECT>
```

TIP

If you are using PWS on Windows 95/98, a MyInfo object is already declared for you in the Global.asa file. You don't need to declare your own and you can simply use it as if it were a built-in object.

A tremendous number of property values exist for you to specify. And whole groups of properties certainly exist that don't even apply to you. Here's a list of some of the common property values you can set or display, organized by the type of server that would use them:

- **For personal web servers:** PersonalName, PersonalAddress, PersonalPhone, PersonalMail

- **For company-owned web servers:** CompanyName, CompanyAddress, CompanyPhone, CompanyDepartment

- **For school-owned web servers:** SchoolName, SchoolAddress, SchoolPhone, SchoolDepartment

- **For web servers owned by other organizations:** OrganizationName, OrganizationAddress, OrganizationPhone

You can also create your own properties simply by assigning values to them.

```
<%
MyInfo.WifeName = "Melanie"
MyInfo.CatName = "Tiger"
%>
```

Sending E-Mail

E-mail has become the communications medium of choice for most big companies these days. People can send you messages from anywhere — and by the number of e-mails you get everyday, it looks like they are!

So, of course, it wasn't long before someone came up with the idea of computers sending e-mail, too. That's right — your ASP pages can fire off their own e-mails to anyone on the Internet.

Sending e-mail creates a whole world of possibilities available to your Web applications. You can let Purchasing know when a new Purchase Order has been entered. You can notify the purchaser of your e-commerce products how long it will take to ship their item. The only limit is your imagination!

So how do you do it? With a group of objects called the Collaboration Data Objects (CDO). There are actually two different sets of CDO objects:

✔ CDO for NT Server is the simpler of these two choices and provides simple e-mail sending and receiving capabilities.

✔ CDO for Exchange is more complex and supports the full range of the Microsoft Exchange capabilities.

Both of these object collections require that you be using NT Server and IIS. You can't use either with PWS.

So how does it work? Here's a simple example showing how you can create an e-mail and fire it off to someone.

```
<%
Set objNewMail = CreateObject("CDONTS.NewMail")
MsgFrom = "billhatfield@edgequest.com"
MsgTo = "melaniehatfield@edgequest.com"
MsgSubject = "The Cats"
MsgMessage = "Don't forget to feed the cats before you leave
            today!"
MsgImportance = 0 ' Low Importance
objNewMail.Send(MsgFrom, MsgTo, MsgSubject, _
    MsgMessage, MsgImportance)
%>
```

The NewMail object is created. NewMail is an object that is only included in the NT Server version of CDO (not in the Exchange version). NewMail is intended to simplify the process of quickly creating and sending a message. As demonstrated here, all you have to do is use the Send method and pass the from, to, subject, message, and level of importance.

A Whole World of Server Components

In this chapter I summarize the components that come with IIS and PWS. This description provides not only information on using these specific components but also an overview of the variety of components out there and how they can integrate with your ASP script.

But you don't have to stop there. A whole world of components is available:

✔ Microsoft offers free components on its Web site as do many other ASP sites on the Web.

✔ All the time, more and more companies are offering server components for sale.

✔ And, of course, you can always create your own components using Microsoft Visual Basic or Microsoft Visual C++.

Get in the habit of looking for components to do all the hard work on your Web pages. Any time you run into a problem that you think someone else has probably run into before, check to see if there's a component out there. For more information on the best places to look for server components, see Chapter 16.

By letting the components do most of the work, you minimize your scripting code. And less scripting code has three *big* advantages:

✔ You spend less time developing new applications.

✔ You spend less time debugging your applications.

✔ You have less code to maintain as things change.

And less time spent with your ASP scripts means more time for the stuff in life that's really important — like golf!

Part IV
Accessing the Database

The 5th Wave   By Rich Tennant

"Do you want me to help you name your Open Database Connectivity DSN, or do you have your own idea of what to call it?"

In this part . . .

Databases are very important to your Web applications. Why? Because that's where all the interesting information is! Fortunately, accessing the database, retrieving information, and displaying it on a Web page is pretty easy. After you've mastered that, you go on to discover how to add new records and edit existing records in the database using HTML forms. Finally, you find out how to delete records that are no longer needed.

Chapter 10

Accessing a Database from ASP

· ·

In This Chapter

▶ Creating a database

▶ Identifying a data source

▶ Understanding the ActiveX Data Objects (ADO)

▶ Connecting to a database

▶ Retrieving records from a database table

▶ Displaying the results of a query on a Web page

▶ Fine-tuning your queries to get exactly the information you want

· ·

Connecting web servers to databases is one of the hottest topics in Web development today. Why? Because most of the interesting information is located in databases. And, if you can create Web pages that pull their content primarily from a database, then those Web pages are automatically updated whenever the database is updated.

In this chapter, I show you how to create a simple database application that plays an important role in your company's intranet — while clueing you in on what the cafeteria is serving today. This intranet tool helps you make that key corporate decision you have to make every single day — to eat out or not to eat out.

For database virgins: This chapter assumes that you have a *basic* understanding of how relational databases work. If you have never worked with relational databases of any kind, don't sweat it. I include a quick crash course in database basics in Appendix B. It tells you everything you need to know to get by in just a few short pages. So, if you need to brush up on databases, you may want to flip through the appendix before continuing with this chapter.

Creating a New Database and Table

Before you can access data from tables in a database, you need to have a database with tables and data, right? How do you get a database? Well, you have several options:

- ✔ You can take the easy way out and just steal the menu.mdb file from the CD-ROM included with this book. That file is an Access database that already has a table with data in it for use with this chapter.

- ✔ If you know Microsoft Access, you can be adventurous and create your own Access database, table, and data. I give you all the information you need in the next section.

- ✔ If you don't know Access, you can still create your own database. I include step-by-step directions in Appendix C, which tell you exactly what to do. By doing it this way, you discover enough about Access to begin to create databases and tables for your own pages.

- ✔ If you are using another Database Management System (DBMS) — like Microsoft SQL Server, Oracle, or Sybase SQL Server — and you're familiar with the way that system works, you can create tables and add records using your own DBMS. Just read the instructions in the next section, use the information as a basis for creating your own database, and access it there.

Why Access?

I demonstrate ASP database capabilities using Microsoft Access, versus other systems, for a number of reasons:

- ✔ Access is very easy to use for those who've never worked with databases before.

- ✔ It's inexpensive to purchase.

- ✔ Because it is created by Microsoft, it works very well with ASP and IIS.

- ✔ Regardless of the database you use, the methods for accessing it in ASP are very similar.

And if you are creating an Internet site or an intranet site that won't be doing heavy database activity and won't have high volumes of people on it, Microsoft Access is a good choice.

However, if you are working on a site that *will* require lots of database access and have a high volume of hits, then you probably want to consider a more powerful *client/server* database. Client/server databases are designed to perform well, even with heavy use, and to provide the security measures needed to keep sensitive corporate data. They also cost a lot of money.

If you are the one who gets to choose which client/server database to buy, your best bet is Microsoft SQL Server. It is optimized to work very well with IIS and ASP. If not, you can also access Oracle, Sybase SQL Server, and any other client/server database that has an ODBC driver. (For more on ODBC, see "YAMA: Yet Another Mysterious Acronym — Creating an ODBC DSN" later in this chapter.)

For the Do-It-Yourselfer

Congratulations! You are one of the few, the proud, the bold — you have decided to create your own database, either in Access or in some other DBMS. Here are the steps you need to take:

1. **Create a new database and name it** menu.mdb.

2. **Create a table called** Menu **inside that database. The table should have the following fields:**

Field Name	Data Type	Description
Date	Date/Time	The date this food will be served
MainCourse	Text	Main course of the meal
Fruit	Text	Fruit served with the meal
Vegetable	Text	Vegetable served with the meal
Dessert	Text	Dessert after the meal

3. **Make** Date **the primary key.**

4. **Now add several records of data to the table. Use meals you're most fond of. For the** Date **field, use today's date for the first record, and work forward from there.**

Now, if you have trouble with any of these steps, and you are working with Access, skim through the detailed steps in Appendix C until you find the answer to what's tripping you up. Another great resource is *Access 2000 For Windows For Dummies* by John Kaufeld (IDG Books Worldwide, Inc.).

If you have trouble with one of these steps and you are *not* using Access, then your best bet is to find someone who knows about the database you're working with and ask them for help. If you have no one to turn to, you can try looking it up in your manual, finding a book on the topic, or making a call to technical support.

YAMA: Yet Another Mysterious Acronym — Creating an ODBC DSN

After you have a database with one or more tables and data to fill the tables, you need to identify the database so that your ASP pages can find it. You do that by creating an *ODBC Data Source Name (DSN)*.

What's ODBC?

ODBC stands for Open Database Connectivity. It is a piece of software created by Microsoft that allows programs to access lots of different kinds of databases in almost exactly the same way. ODBC makes it easier to work with different kinds of databases without having to learn from scratch how to use each one. But, in order for a particular database to work with ODBC, that database must have an ODBC *driver*. Almost every popular database out there has an ODBC driver these days.

All the objects you use to access the database from your ASP pages ultimately go through ODBC to access the database.

What's an ODBC Data Source Name?

An ODBC *Data Source Name (DSN)* is a system name that is given to a database. Why does the database need another name? Good question.

Usually, if you want to connect to a database, you have to send a whole bunch of arguments to get the connection going. It's tedious to spell out this information again and again every time you connect to the database, especially because the information never changes. DSNs were created to fix this problem. A DSN lets you store in one place all that information you normally have and give it a name — the Data Source Name. Then, whenever you want to connect to a database, instead of spelling out all that stuff, you simply use the DSN, and it gets all the information automatically.

How do I create a DSN?

In order to add a System DSN on Windows NT, you must be a member of the Administrators group. In Windows 95/98, anyone can do it.

To create a new ODBC Data Source Name:

1. **Open the Control Panel.**
2. **Double-click the icon labeled** ODBC 32 **or** 32bit ODBC, ODBC Data Sources **or just** ODBC.

    The ODBC Data Source Administrator dialog box is displayed.
3. **Click the System DSN tab (see Figure 10-1).**
4. **Click the Add button.**

    The Create New Data Source dialog box appears (see Figure 10-2).

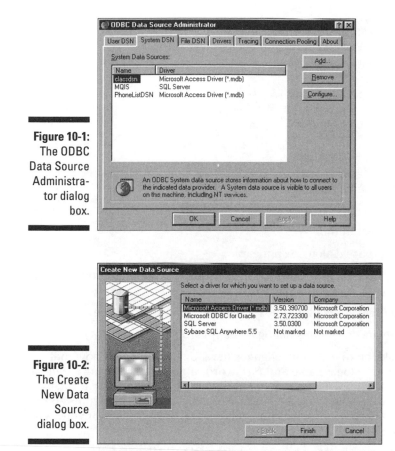

Figure 10-1:
The ODBC
Data Source
Administra-
tor dialog
box.

Figure 10-2:
The Create
New Data
Source
dialog box.

5. **Scroll down and click the name of the driver that goes with your database. In the case of Microsoft Access, click the entry that looks like this:**

```
Microsoft Access Driver (*.mdb)
```

6. **Click Finish.**

   The ODBC Microsoft Access Setup dialog box appears (see Figure 10-3). (If you are using a different DBMS, the dialog box appropriate to your DBMS appears.)

7. **Type the name you want to give this database in Data Source Name. For this project, type** Menu.

   You don't have to give the data source the same name you gave the database after you created it. But doing so can help you keep them all straight.

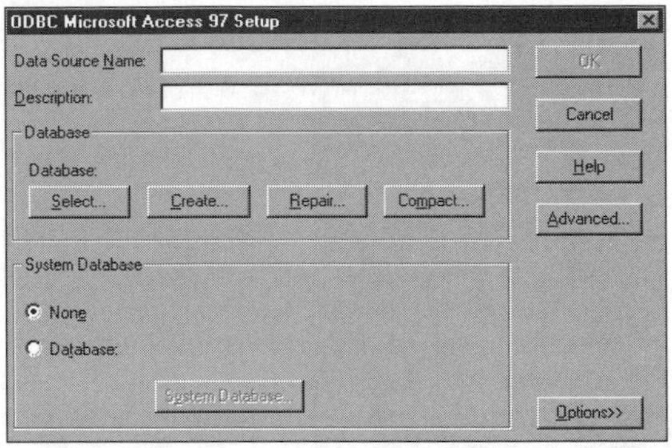

Figure 10-3: The ODBC Microsoft Access Setup dialog box.

8. **Click the Select button.**

   A Select Database dialog box appears.

9. **Rummage through your directories and find the database you created. Click OK.**

10. **Before you leave this dialog box, click the Advanced button.**

    The Set Advanced Options dialog box appears (see Figure 10-4).

    I do not ask you to make any changes here, but you should know that you can enter a login name and password, if you like. Entering a login name and password allows you to automatically provide this information to the database when you use this DSN. This is a very handy time-saver, but remember that it provides immediate database access to anyone who can use this DSN.

11. **Click the Cancel button to go back to the ODBC Microsoft Access Setup dialog box.**

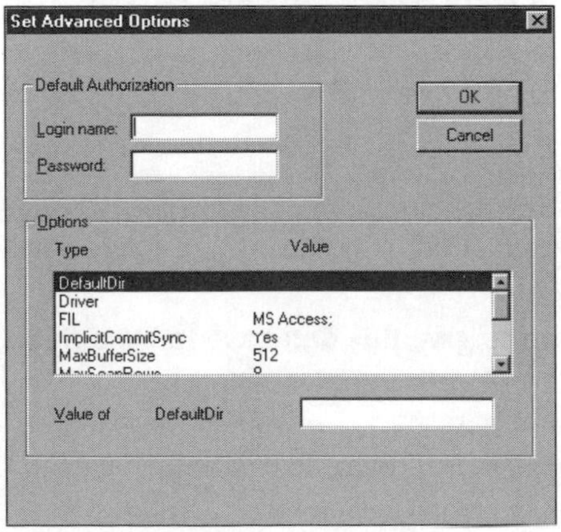

Figure 10-4: The Set Advanced Options dialog box.

12. **Click OK in the ODBC Microsoft Access Setup dialog box.**

13. **Find the new DSN you just created (they're in alphabetical order). Click OK.**

You now have a database, a table with data, and a DSN to identify it. All you have to do now is create the pages to access your information.

SMMA: Still More Mysterious Acronyms — Using the DAC to Get to Your ADO

The Database Access Component is a server component just like the Browser Capabilities and Advertisement Rotator Components I discuss in Chapter 9. But the Database Access Component provides a lot more capabilities than any of the other server components provided with your web server software. Through the Database Access Component, you access the *ActiveX Data Objects (ADO)*.

The ADO are a set of objects that you can use to access databases. Why do you want to access databases? Because most modern computer applications store their data in databases. Storing the information in a database is much easier, more convenient, and faster than putting it in a text file to read it back later.

DSNs on hosted Web sites

If you have your own web server, then you can follow the process above to create a DSN on that server. But if you have your site on a hosting provider company, then you don't have access to their web server to make these changes. What do you do?

Many hosting services that provide ASP scripting as one of their features also allow you to use Access databases. You have to inform them that

you need a new DSN, give them the DSN name you want to use, and the name and location of your Access file on their server. As soon as they have all this information, they can set up the DSN for you.

Also note that many hosting services also offer, usually for an additional charge, a database on their SQL Server.

Including ADO Constants

You can use the #include directive to read another page in and make it part of the current page. This directive is handy if you want to use a common function in lots of different places or if you have a common set of constants that you want to use on many pages. I discuss the #include directive in a section called "Server-Side Includes" in Chapter 7.

Because ADO includes many interrelated objects that have lots of methods and properties, Microsoft created two include files — one for VBScript and one for JScript — to specify a set of common constants to use with these methods and properties.

Including the appropriate constants file on any page you use in ADO is a good idea. For VBScript, the file's name is adovbs.inc and for JScript, it's adojavas.inc. By default, the file is placed in C:\Program Files\ Common Files\System\ADO\. You can simply copy the file into your current Web application folder and then include this line in all of your pages that use it:

```
<!- - #include file="adovbs.inc" - ->
```

A better solution may be to create a folder under wwwroot called common. Then you can put these two ADO include files in this folder along with any other include files you create. All the include files can then be easily shared among many Web applications. If you decide to organize your include files with a common folder, your #include line looks more like this:

```
<!- - #include virtual="common/adovbs.inc" - ->
```

Connecting to a Database

The first ADO object is the Connection object. It represents your connection to the database.

```
<%
Dim Connect
Set Connect = Server.CreateObject("ADODB.Connection")
Connect.Open "Menu"
%>
```

Just as you do with all server components, you call Server.CreateObject to create an object and use Set to associate the object with a variable. Then that variable can be used to access the properties and methods of that object. Notice that I pass "ADODB.Connection" to the CreateObject method. All ADO objects begin with ADODB.

TECHNICAL STUFF

To close or not to close. . . .

After you're finished working with a database, you can use the `Close` method to close the connection.

```
<% Connect.Close %>
```

This method closes the connection, but it does not make the `Connection` object go away. In order to make the `Connection` object go away, you have to execute a line like this:

```
<% Set Connect = Nothing %>
```

`Nothing` is a special value that you can assign to an object. This value actually releases the memory that the object held.

The really, really good news is that you don't have to do *any* of this stuff. After your page ends, the connection is automatically closed and the memory for the object is freed up. All you have to do is create the connection and use it — then let VBScript clean up when you're done.

In this case, I create a `Connection` object, and then I call the `Open` method of that object. I pass the ODBC Data Source Name (DSN) to the `Open` method to identify the database I want to use (see "YAMA: Yet Another Mysterious Acronym — Creating an ODBC DSN" earlier in this chapter).

You can also pass a user ID and a password as arguments to `Open` after the DSN. The user ID and password are necessary if DSN doesn't automatically provide them and they're required by the database. For more information on automatically providing the user ID and password through the DSN, see "YAMA: Yet Another Mysterious Acronym — Creating an ODBC DSN" earlier in this chapter.

From the Database to the Web Page

To retrieve information from the database, you must use a `Recordset` object. The `Recordset` object is the most important object in the ADO. It makes possible retrieving a whole bunch of records at once and then accessing them, one at a time. The `Recordset` object also allows you to easily update and delete existing records.

In this section, I show you how to use the `Connection` object together with the `Recordset` object to retrieve all the menu information from the database and display it in your Web page.

Executing SQL

The first question is this: How do you execute a SELECT statement on the database? You can do it in several ways, but one of the easiest is to use the Execute method of the Connection object. (If you are unfamiliar with the SQL SELECT statement, see Appendix B. There I cover all the basics of working with a database, including the SQL SELECT statement.)

```
<%
Dim Connect, OnMenu
Set Connect = Server.CreateObject("ADODB.Connection")
Connect.Open "Menu"
Set OnMenu = Connect.Execute("SELECT * FROM Menu")
%>
```

Execute takes the string that is passed and sends it to the database as a SQL command. You can send SQL commands to update data, delete records, and manipulate information any way you like. In this case, I'm executing a SELECT statement to retrieve data from the database.

But where does the data go after it's retrieved? As you may guess from looking at the code, the data goes into the OnMenu variable. Actually, the Execute method returns a Recordset object that contains the results of the query. The results of the query are what OnMenu receives.

Displaying the results

So, to display the results on your Web page, you have to retrieve them from the OnMenu Recordset.

```
<% Option Explicit %>
<HTML>
<BODY>
<h1>The Cafeteria Menu</h1>
<%
Dim Connect, OnMenu
Set Connect = Server.CreateObject("ADODB.Connection")
Connect.Open "Menu"
Set OnMenu = Connect.Execute(_
  "SELECT * FROM Menu ORDER BY Date")
do until OnMenu.EOF %>
<font size=5><%=OnMenu("Date")%></font><br>
Main Course: <%=OnMenu("MainCourse")%><br>
Fruit: <%=OnMenu("Fruit")%><br>
Vegetables: <%=OnMenu("Vegetable")%><br>
Dessert: <%=OnMenu("Dessert")%><p>
```

```
<% OnMenu.MoveNext
loop %>
</BODY>
</HTML>
```

You can see the results in Figure 10-5.

The Recordset object contains a collection of Field objects. The Field objects are identified by the field (or column) names from the database. In this case, there are four fields: MainCourse, Fruit, Vegetable and Dessert. Usually, you see them listed first in the SELECT statement, but in this case I've done a SELECT *, which simply pulls all the fields in the Menu table.

I can display the values in each field, but displaying the values in each field doesn't display all the information retrieved. It only displays one record. So, in order to display all the values, I create a loop and the very last thing I do in the body of the loop is called the MoveNext method. The MoveNext causes the Recordset to move to the next record and allows me to display those field values.

Notice that the loop goes until the OnMenu's EOF property contains true. Doing a MoveNext takes you beyond the last record, and the EOF property is set to true. If you try to do another MoveNext when EOF is set to true, you get an error.

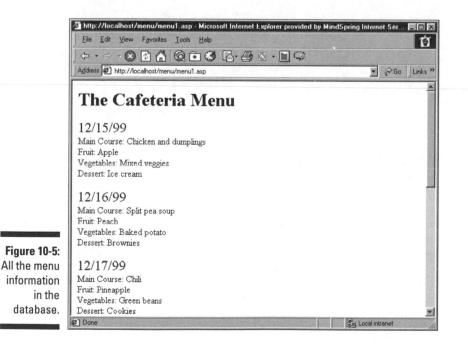

Figure 10-5:
All the menu information in the database.

Getting Exactly the Information You Want

The example in the last section gives you a good feel for how data is retrieved and displayed on a Web page. But you don't want to simply retrieve *everything* from a table too often. Usually, your queries are more specific than that.

Today's menu

In the case of the Cafeteria Menu, you probably want to be sure you don't display menus for yesterday or the day before. No one cares about those menus. They only care about today and maybe the rest of the week.

To narrow the search, you have to create the SELECT statement more carefully and add a WHERE clause to the end.

```
<% Option Explicit %>
<HTML>
<BODY>
<h1>The Cafeteria Menu</h1>
<%
Dim Connect, OnMenu, ThisDay, Query
Set Connect = Server.CreateObject("ADODB.Connection")
Connect.Open "Menu"
ThisDay = CStr(Date)
Query = "SELECT * FROM Menu WHERE Date=#" & ThisDay & "#"
Set OnMenu = Connect.Execute(Query)
%>
<font size=5>Today: <%=OnMenu("Date")%></font><br>
Main Course: <%=OnMenu("MainCourse")%><br>
Fruit: <%=OnMenu("Fruit")%><br>
Vegetables: <%=OnMenu("Vegetable")%><br>
Dessert: <%=OnMenu("Dessert")%><p>
</BODY>
</HTML>
```

You can see the result in Figure 10-6.

The difference here is that the date is obtained with the Date function and converted to a string and then added to the end of the WHERE clause. Because the date is the primary key of the table, you can be sure that you only retrieve one record. That record is then displayed.

Notice that the pound signs (#) are required to surround the date literal in the SELECT statement. These work just like quotation marks that surround string literals.

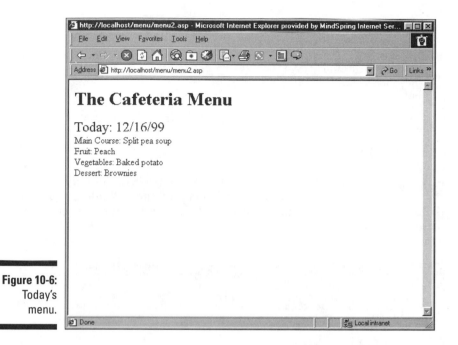

Figure 10-6:
Today's
menu.

Planning for the next few days

To get a head start on planning your week, you may also want to query for today and the next three days or so. This query works the same way.

```
<% Option Explicit %>
<HTML>
<BODY>
<h1>The Cafeteria Menu</h1>
<%
Dim Connect, OnMenu, ThisDay, Query, DayNum
Set Connect = Server.CreateObject("ADODB.Connection")
Connect.Open "Menu"
ThisDay = CStr(Date)
Query = _
  "SELECT * FROM Menu WHERE Date >= #" & _
  ThisDay & "# ORDER BY Date"
Set OnMenu = Connect.Execute(Query)
DayNum = 1
do until OnMenu.EOF Or DayNum > 4
%>
<font size=5><%=OnMenu("Date")%></font><br>
Main Course: <%=OnMenu("MainCourse")%><br>
Fruit: <%=OnMenu("Fruit")%><br>
```

```
Vegetables: <%=OnMenu("Vegetable")%><br>
Dessert: <%=OnMenu("Dessert")%><p>
<%
   DayNum = DayNum + 1
   OnMenu.MoveNext
loop %>
</BODY>
</HTML>
```

Figure 10-7 shows the result.

Now any date greater than or equal to today is retrieved. But only today and the next three days are displayed. I still included the `OnMenu.EOF` as part of the `Until` condition, though, just in case the cafeteria hadn't yet entered the menu three days ahead.

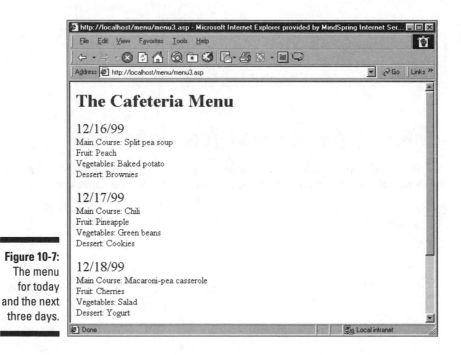

Figure 10-7:
The menu
for today
and the next
three days.

Chapter 11

Updating the Database

● ●

● ●

*I*n this chapter you go beyond the basic retrieve-and-display-in-table-type database applications I demonstrate in Chapter 10. You discover how to create really flexible Recordset objects that you can move around in, remember a record's location so that you can come back to it, and figure out how to temporarily filter out data from a Recordset that doesn't meet your criteria. These new capabilities allow you to create even more flexible Web pages based on, and automatically updated by, database records.

Finally, no matter how flashy your page and no matter how many ways you can slice and dice data, it is only useful if you can also update the information in the database. In the second half of this chapter, I show you how to add new records as well as update and delete existing records — right from your Web pages.

Diving Deeper with the Connection and Recordset Objects

The Connection object literally represents your connection to the database. But after that connection is made, the Recordset is the single most important object in all the ADO. I introduce the Connection and Recordset objects in Chapter 10. In this chapter I show you more of their capabilities, such as moving freely throughout the entire Recordset, using bookmarks to keep your place, and using filters to control the records displayed.

Opening a Connection *and a* Recordset — *revisited*

In Chapter 10, I demonstrate a simple way of connecting to the database and then executing a SELECT statement to create a Recordset. The code to connect and execute a SELECT statement looks like this:

```
<%
Dim Connect, OnMenu
Set Connect = Server.CreateObject("ADODB.Connection")
Connect.Open "Menu"
Set OnMenu = Connect.Execute(_
"SELECT * FROM Menu ORDER BY Date")
%>
```

In this example, Connect holds the Connection object and OnMenu holds the Recordset object. You don't actually have to create the Recordset object using a Server.CreateObject, as you do with the Connection object, because the Execute method creates and returns a Recordset for you, automatically.

But often, creating your own Recordset object can give you more flexibility. The code for opening a connection, creating your own Recordset, and then retrieving records from the database looks like this:

```
<%
Dim Connect, OnMenu
Set Connect = Server.CreateObject("ADODB.Connection")
Connect.Open "Menu"
Set OnMenu = Server.CreateObject("ADODB.Recordset")
OnMenu.Open "SELECT * FROM Menu ORDER BY Date", Connect
%>
```

This code doesn't look much different and, in fact, it does exactly the same thing as the first listing in this section. First a Connection object is created and then opened. Then a Recordset object is created and the Recordset's Open method is called. The Open method for the Recordset is different from the Open method for the Connection.

The Open for a Recordset executes the SQL you send it and fills the Recordset with the results of that SQL — much as the Connection object's Execute method did in the first listing in this section. The second argument you send the Recordset's Open method is the Connection object you want to use with this Recordset.

So if you can do it either way, why switch now? The Recordset object's Open method has a number of optional arguments you can send to change the way the Recordset works. This provides a lot of flexibility that you wouldn't have if you didn't create the `Recordset` object yourself. I explore some of those optional arguments in the next section.

Connect, disconnect, connect, disconnect — is this really a good idea?

You may be wondering, as you begin to create ADO Web pages, if connecting at the top of every page is the right thing to do. In Chapter 10, I say that the connection is automatically closed at the end of the page, so that it has to be opened again on each new page.

Wouldn't it make more sense to make the `Connection` object a session-level thing, open it once, and leave it open? You'd think so.

But, in fact, both PWS and IIS have a capability built-in called *connection pooling*. If connection pooling is on, the server doesn't automatically close your connection to the database if the `Connection` object goes out of scope. Instead, it waits for a while to see if you will need access to the database again in the near future.

It also shares your connection to the database with *other* sessions that need one, especially if you're not using yours right now. The end result is that even though there are, say, five sessions, all with their own connection to the database, the server may have only created one or two *actual* connections, and then it manages the sharing of those connections among the different processes.

But don't worry. All this connection pooling happens behind the scenes. You don't have to worry about it at all. And it's optimized so that if you simply connect to the database at the top of every page, it handles the actual database connections in an optimal way. You don't need to create a session-level connection — in fact, if you do, it will probably throw off the connection pooling.

There's just one catch to all of this. Connection pooling is not turned on by default. You have to tell your web server to use it. Depending on your operating system and its version, you may be able to make this change using the ODBC configuration utility. Simply go into Control Panel and double-click on the ODBC icon. If there is a Connection Pooling tab in the dialog box, you can enable pooling for your DSN.

If you don't have a Connection Pooling tab, you have to make the change the hard way. You have to use the Windows 95 or Windows NT registry editor to go in and physically change the registry. I give you the step-by-step directions you need to make that change.

But before I give you these directions, I have to tell you one very important thing: Be very, very careful with the registry. The registry is the heart and soul of your system. Actually, it's probably more accurate to call it the DNA of your system. All the information the system holds about itself and the programs it runs is here. And the Registry Editor gives you willy-nilly access to it all. If you mess it up, your system can be toast. Be very careful to follow these steps closely and don't fool around with other stuff in the registry unless you're sure of what you're doing.

1. **Choose Start⇨Run.**

2. **Type** RegEdit **into the edit box and click OK.**

   You see a window that looks like Figure 11-1.

3. **Click the plus sign beside HKEY_LOCAL_MACHINE, the plus beside System, the plus beside CurrentControlSet, and the plus beside Services.**

   You see a long list of folders under Services.

4. **Click the plus beside W3SVC. Then click the plus beside ASP.**

5. **Click the folder labeled Parameters.**

   Look at the pane on the right. You may or may not see an entry called StartConnectionPool.

6. **If you see the StartConnectionPool entry, jump to Step 8. If you *don't* see the StartConnectionPool entry, choose Edit⇨New⇨DWORD Value.**

   A new entry with its name highlighted appears in the pane on the right.

7. **Type the new name for this entry:** StartConnectionPool.

8. **Double-click the StartConnectionPool entry.**

9. **In the Edit DWORD Value dialog box, change the Value data from 0 to 1. Click OK. Close the Registry window.**

Now connection pooling works for you behind-the-scenes, and you won't ever have to worry about it again.

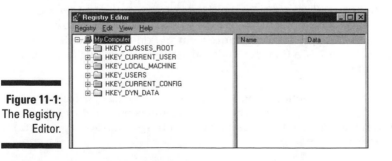

Figure 11-1:
The Registry
Editor.

Cursors and other people with soapy mouths

You are probably familiar with the term *cursor*. It's used to identify the little flashing line or box that indicates where your next character will be typed. Sometimes the cursor also refers to the pointer you use to point and click on things in Windows.

In this section you discover a new meaning for the word cursor. And it has virtually *nothing* to do with any of the other meanings of the word you already know.

A *database cursor* is a place in memory where records are placed after they are retrieved from a database. The cursor then allows you to access the records row-by-row so that you can display or manipulate them however you want.

Isn't that exactly what a Recordset does? Yes — a Recordset is simply a way of providing access to a database cursor.

Cursors come in a variety of different types. The most important ones follow:

- **Static:** The SELECT statement is executed and the results are returned. If someone else working with the same database changes the records while you are looking at your Static cursor, you do not see the changes. You're looking at the records as they appeared *after you ran the query*.

- **Forward Only:** Exactly like Static, except that it is limited so that you can only go forward one row at a time, starting with the first one, then the second, and so on, all the way to the end. You cannot look back or move around within the cursor, as you can with Static.

- **Dynamic:** After you receive your results from the query, the records are constantly updated so that any changes someone else makes to the records you're looking at are immediately visible. This cursor is the most flexible, but also requires the most overhead and resources.

The default cursor type is also the most restrictive — Forward Only. And, in Chapter 10, that's the cursor I use. And that's really all I need to display the contents of the Menu. I start at the beginning and go forward using the MoveNext method until I get to the end.

```
<%
do until OnMenu.EOF %>
<font size=5><%=OnMenu("Date")%></font><br>
Main Course: <%=OnMenu("MainCourse")%><br>
Fruit: <%=OnMenu("Fruit")%><br>
Vegetables: <%=OnMenu("Vegetable")%><br>
Dessert: <%=OnMenu("Dessert")%><p>
<% OnMenu.MoveNext
loop %>
```

If you want to move more freely within the Recordset, you must specifically identify which cursor type you want to use after you call the Recordset object's Open method.

```
<%
Dim Connect, OnMenu, Query
Set Connect = Server.CreateObject("ADODB.Connection")
Connect.Open "Menu"
Set OnMenu = Server.CreateObject("ADODB.Recordset")
Query = "SELECT * FROM Menu ORDER BY Date"
OnMenu.Open Query, Connect, adOpenStatic
%>
```

The adOpenStatic is a constant that is defined in adovbs.inc. You need to include this file at the top of every page that uses ADO. For more information on including adovbs.inc, see "Including ADO Constants" in Chapter 10.

The three options for this third argument to the Recordset object's Open method are these:

- ✔ adOpenStatic
- ✔ adOpenForwardOnly
- ✔ adOpenDynamic

As you may have guessed, these three options correspond directly to the three kinds of cursors I mentioned previously. The adOpenStatic in the previous code indicates that a Static cursor needs to be used. The cafeteria menu database isn't one that's likely to have lots of changes all the time, so that using a Dynamic cursor is overkill. But using adOpenStatic instead of the default adOpenForwardOnly enables you to use several new methods in the Recordset object, which I discuss in the next section.

Freely moving around a Recordset

The Recordset object has more than just a MoveNext method. If you've specified a static or dynamic cursor, as I describe in the last section, you can use any of these Move methods.

- ✔ MoveFirst: Makes the first row in the Recordset the current row.
- ✔ MoveLast: Makes the last row in the Recordset the current row.
- ✔ MoveNext: Makes the next row the current row.
- ✔ MovePrevious: Makes the previous row the current row.
- ✔ Move: Moves a specified number of records forward or backward.

The first four methods are pretty straightforward. They don't take any arguments and you just call them and they do their thing. The Move method is a little more complicated than the other four, but a lot more flexible.

The Move *method*

You pass two arguments to Move — a *starting position* and the *number of records to move* from the starting position. Actually, you pass the *number of records to move* first.

This line moves to the third record after the first record in the Recordset. So, the current record ends up being the fourth row.

```
Move 3, adBookmarkFirst
```

This line moves to the current record five records after the current record. If I'm on record 10, this would move me to record 15.

```
Move 5, adBookmarkCurrent
```

This line moves the current record back two records from the current record. If I'm on record 10, I end up on record 8.

```
Move -2, adBookmarkCurrent
```

This line moves the current record seven records back from the last record.

```
Move -7, adBookmarkLast
```

Different DBMSs — different capabilities

Not every DBMS supports all the cursor types I discuss here. For example, some may not support the Dynamic cursor so that you are forced to always use Static.

Keep this in mind not only for cursors, but for many of the features I discuss in this chapter. Not every DBMS supports every feature. You can check out your DBMS's documentation to see which ones it does support.

Another option is the Recordset object's Supports method. If you pass it a constant, such as one of the following, it returns true or false, indicating whether the DBMS the Recordset is connected to supports that feature: adAddNew, adApproxPosition, adBookmark, adDelete, adHoldRecords, adMovePrevious, adResync, adUpdate, adUpdateBatch. See your web server's documentation for more details on the Supports method.

Both Microsoft Access and Microsoft SQL Server support all the features discussed in this chapter.

You can get by without specifying a starting position. If you do that, adBookmarkCurrent is the default.

This line moves the current record three records forward from the current record.

```
Move 3
```

Bumping into walls

You only have to be careful of one thing when you are doing all this moving about in the Recordset. You have to make sure you don't bump into the beginning or the end. To make this easier to figure out, the Recordset has two properties: BOF and EOF. I used EOF in Chapter 10 to see when I had reached the end of the records in the Recordset. BOF works the same way when you are walking backward through the Recordset — it lets you know when you've hit the beginning.

Actually BOF and EOF work like separate records themselves. For example, if you have three records in your Recordset and the current record is the first one, the Recordset actually looks like Figure 11-2.

Now just because you are on record 1, this does not mean that BOF is true. It is *not*. If you execute a MovePrevious, the Recordset looks like Figure 11-3.

Now if you check BOF, it is true. But it is important to realize that you are *not on a real record*. If you try to display the data for the current record, you get an error. And if you try another MovePrevious, you also get an error.

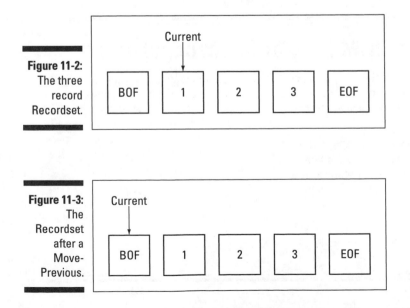

Figure 11-2:
The three record Recordset.

Figure 11-3:
The Recordset after a Move-Previous.

The same is true for EOF — it is not set to true until you go *past* the final record. And after you're there, you cannot access any data in the EOF non-record.

This setup may seem odd, but it makes it very easy to write loops, as I did in this loop from Chapter 10.

```
<%
do until OnMenu.EOF %>
<font size=5><%=OnMenu("Date")%></font><br>
Main Course: <%=OnMenu("MainCourse")%><br>
Fruit: <%=OnMenu("Fruit")%><br>
Vegetables: <%=OnMenu("Vegetable")%><br>
Dessert: <%=OnMenu("Dessert")%><p>
<% OnMenu.MoveNext
loop %>
```

Holding your place with bookmarks

Just as you use bookmarks to keep track of your place in a book, you can use the Bookmark property of the Recordset object to keep track of a particular record.

After a Recordset is first filled with records, each record is given a unique Bookmark value. If you want to save your place on a particular row, you can simply put the Recordset object's Bookmark property value into a variable.

```
<%
Dim FavoriteMeal
...
If OnMenu("MainCourse") = "Steak" Then
FavoriteMeal = OnMenu.Bookmark
End If
%>
```

Then, later, if you want to jump back to that record you bookmarked, all you have to do is assign the value you saved back to the Bookmark property.

```
<%
OnMenu.Bookmark = FavoriteMeal
%>
```

The current record is immediately changed.

This clever implementation means that you can keep any number of bookmarks in your own variables. You could even create an array of bookmarks to keep track of certain records you want to remember.

Change your data filters at least twice a year

A filter is a way of taking all the records in a Recordset and dividing them up into those that meet a certain criteria and those that don't. Those that meet the criteria continue to be a part of the Recordset, while the rest of the records temporarily disappear. I say *temporarily* because even though they don't appear in the current Recordset, the records are still in memory and can be brought back later.

Filtering records based on a columns value

Suppose you have a Recordset called PhoneList that contains (surprise!) a phone list. The fields are FirstName, LastName, and Phone. If a lot of records are in the Recordset and you want to find someone with the last name Smith, you could filter out all the other records in the Recordset by doing this:

```
<% PhoneList.Filter = "LastName = 'Smith'" %>
```

If there were only five people on the list with the last name Smith, only those five appear in the Recordset now.

Getting all the records back again

To get all of the records back you can simply assign an empty string to the Filter property.

```
<% PhoneList.Filter = "" %>
```

Or you can assign a special constant, which does the same thing.

```
<% PhoneList.Filter = adFilterNone %>
```

Filtering using the Like keyword

Now suppose you want to find someone's name that begins with a K, but you can't remember the rest. Using the Like keyword inside a filter string makes it possible to specify wildcards.

```
<% PhoneList.Filter = "LastName Like 'K*'" %>
```

The * is a wildcard meaning zero or more of any character.

Filtering with an array of bookmarks

You can filter records in one additional way — by passing the `Filter` method an array of bookmarks.

```
<%
Dim FavRecs(5)
...
FavRec(1) = PhoneList.Bookmark
...
' FavRec(2) to FavRec(5) are also filled in
...
PhoneList.Filter = FavRec
%>
```

After this code, only the five records identified by the five bookmarks appear in the `Recordset`.

Other Recordset *properties and methods*

A couple of useful `Recordset` properties and a couple of handy methods are left that didn't fit neatly into any other category. Here are the properties:

- ✔ `RecordCount`: Gives you the number of records in the `Recordset`.

- ✔ `MaxRecords`: You can set this property before the `Recordset` is opened to specify the maximum number of records you want to read in from the database. Sometimes you may be unsure of how many records are returned, and a large database could return more than your machine has the memory to handle. `MaxRecords` is a convenient way of setting an upper limit, if you are concerned about it.

And here are the methods:

- ✔ `Requery`: Executes the query again and re-retrieves the records into the `Recordset`.

- ✔ `Resync`: Gets the current information from the database for all the records in the `Recordset`. It does not re-execute the query as `Requery` does. `Resync` simply refreshes the records that are in the `Recordset`, which is convenient if you are using a Forward Only or a Static cursor, which aren't automatically updated.

The difference between `Requery` and `Resync` can be tough to see at first. Imagine this:

1. You do a query that retrieved three records.

2. Someone else modifies the first record you retrieved in the database.

3. Another person adds a new record, which also matches your query.

Now if you do a `Resync`, you see the change that happened in Step 2, but you won't see the new record added in Step 3. `Resync` only updates the information for the records *currently* in the `Recordset`.

If you did a `Requery`, on the other hand, you would see both the change and the newly added record.

Updating the Database

Displaying database information is a very important capability. But it is limiting if you can't also add information to a database as well as update and delete existing records. In this section I show you how to do all of those functions with ADO's easy-to-use methods.

Putting your records in a headlock

Whenever you have more than one person accessing and potentially changing the same data in the database, the chance for trouble always exists. For example, imagine that two people retrieve a record at the same time, both make updates, and one of them saves. The data has been updated with the information of that person. But then suppose the other person saves. Now the second person has overwritten the first person's information without ever knowing what it was.

This kind of tricky problem, along with others like it, may seem unlikely. But a Web site that gets lots of hits and does lots of database updating can run upon all kinds of strange situations.

Fortunately, most DBMSs handle these situations for you through a mechanism called *record locking*. If someone is about to change information in a record, that record is locked so that no one else can access it. Then the updates are made safely, without interference from others. Finally, the record is unlocked and others can access it.

Again record locking generally happens automatically in the database. I'm describing it to you here for two reasons. First, it's good to have some idea how this works if you work with databases. Second, and most importantly, you have to choose *how* you want the database to do its locking. Here's what the code to open a Guest Book database and `Recordset` to edit looks like:

```
<%
Dim Connect, GuestBookRS, Query
Set Connect = Server.CreateObject("ADODB.Connection")
Connect.Open "GB"
Set GuestBookRS = Server.CreateObject("ADODB.Recordset")
Query = "SELECT * FROM GuestBook"
GuestBookRS.Open Query, Connect, adOpenStatic, _
adLockOptimistic
%>
```

The primary difference here is the addition of the fourth argument, adLockOptimistic, to the Recordset object's Open method. This argument specifies the *lock type* you want the database to use. In this case, you are suggesting *optimistic* locking. And, yes, one of the other alternatives is *pessimistic* locking. You don't want me to go into all the details of how optimistic and pessimistic locking work, trust me. You'd be dozing before the second paragraph. But take my word for it, pessimistic locking is usually not the best way to go.

So what are the best lock types to use? Well, you can only use two all the time:

- ✔ adLockReadOnly: Use this lock type if you will only be retrieving data and not adding, editing, or deleting. This is the default, which is assumed if you leave off the third argument of the Open method.

- ✔ adLockOptimistic: Use this if you will be adding, editing, or deleting information in the database. It is the preferred locking method for most databases.

Editing and updating records

Before you can make changes to a Recordset, you must make sure you do two things first:

- ✔ Open the Recordset object with the adOpenStatic or adOpenDynamic cursor, and specify in the second argument of the Recordset object's Open method.

- ✔ Use adLockOptimistic for the lock type, the third argument of the Recordset object's Open method.

Now you're ready to edit the Recordset. And it's pretty straightforward.

1. **Navigate to the record you want to edit.**

2. **Set the values for the** Recordset **variables.**

3. **Call the** Recordset **object's** Update **method.**

Suppose you have a Guest Book application that saves its information in the database and you want to update Carmen Moore's record so that it has a new age and e-mail address. You already know how to accomplish Step 1 using the methods MoveNext, MovePrevious, Move, and so on. Steps 2 and 3 look like this:

```
<%
...
GuestBookRS("Age") = "32"
GuestBookRS("Email") = "carmen@aol.com"
GuestBookRS.Update
%>
```

You change her age and e-mail address and then call the Update method. Update changes to database so that it matches what is in the Recordset for the current record.

Adding new records

Adding a new row in the Guest Book is very similar to changing a row, except for the addition of one new method — AddNew.

```
<%
GuestBookRS.AddNew
GuestBookRS("FirstName") = "Barbara"
GuestBookRS("LastName") = "Hatfield"
GuestBookRS("Gender") = "Female"
GuestBookRS("Age") = "45"
GuestBookRS("Email") = "barbhatfield@aol.com"
GuestBookRS.Update
%>
```

AddNew creates a new, blank row in the Recordset and automatically positions itself on that new row. So all you have to do is fill in all the fields (or at least all the required fields) and then call Update. Update creates the new record in the database to match the new one you just created in the Recordset.

Deleting records

To delete an existing record, all you have to do is navigate to that record and call one function — Delete.

```
<%
...
GuestBookRS.Delete
%>
```

This deletes the current record in the database immediately. You don't have to call the Update function after the Delete.

After you've deleted the current record, you probably expect that the current record changes to the record before or the record after the one that was deleted. Unfortunately, that's not true. After you delete a record, that record is still the current record. But if you try to do anything with it, you get an error because the record is not valid. A common solution is to do a MoveFirst or something like it after the Delete to make sure the current record is a valid one.

You can also pass an argument to the Delete method to delete more than one record at a time.

```
<%
GuestBookRS.Filter = "VisitDate < #1/1/1999#"
GuestBookRS.Delete adAffectGroup
GuestBookRS.Filter = ""
%>
```

Passing adAffectGroup to Delete tells it to delete all the records that meet the current filter criteria. In the preceding example, all those that had a VisitDate before January 1, 1999, are deleted. By setting the Filter property to the empty string at the end, the filter is removed.

By the way, if you already know SQL, you can also do your adds, edits, and deletes by building the appropriate INSERT, UPDATE, and DELETE statements in a string and then using the Connection object's Execute method to send the SQL to the database.

Catching Database Errors

Whenever you are working with another application outside your own — which is exactly what the DBMS is — you should always be especially careful. A user can cause a huge variety of errors,and you can never anticipate them all. But you certainly can *handle* them, if you trap them first. By trapping them, you stop them from crashing your application and you're given the chance to recover, if possible. You trap database errors just as you trap any VBScript errors — using the On Error Resume Next and the Err object. Both of these are described in the section "To err is human. . . ." in Chapter 6.

But sometimes the Err object just isn't enough. The Err object is designed to hold information about one error. But sometimes one database operation can produce multiple errors or warnings. To solve this problem, the ADO Connection object has a collection called Errors. Errors is intended to *extend* the Err object to provide information about multiple errors, when they occur.

If a statement sent to the database causes an error, a new Error object is created in the Errors collection. If the statement sent to the database causes more than one error, then all the errors caused are each placed in their own Error object in the Errors collection. The Error objects stay there until another database operation causes an error. At that time, the old Error objects are cleared out and new ones are created for the new operation.

You can access this collection and its associated objects to find all the errors that a statement caused.

The Errors *collection*

The Errors collection is itself a property of the Connection object, so that you must preface it with the name of your Connection object. The collection has one important method and one important property:

- ✔ Clear **method:** Manually clears the contents of the Errors collection, destroying all the Error objects.
- ✔ Count **property:** Holds the number of Error objects in the Errors collection.

The Error *object*

The Error object itself has no methods. The most important Error object properties follow:

- ✔ Number: The error number that ODBC assigns to this error.
- ✔ NativeError: The error number that the DBMS itself assigns to the error. If you are going to look up this error in your SQL Server or Oracle documentation, you use this number.
- ✔ Description: A description of the error that occurred.

Error handling tips

I have a number of quick tips for you to think about when handling errors for database applications:

- ✔ You can continue to use the Err object to identify database errors. If a database statement produces one error, that error appears in the Err object as well as in a single Error object in the Errors collection. The only time you have to use the Errors collection is if you want to see additional errors that may have been produced by the same database statement.

✔ Sometimes the database produces warnings to give you information about something you've done. These warnings aren't errors and they should be completely expected, but they do appear in the Errors collection. You can easily distinguish between real errors and warnings, though — the Number property of a real error is always negative. The Number property of a warning is positive.

✔ If you are trapping database errors with On Error Resume Next, always check after each database operation to be sure that no errors are triggered. You can do this by checking the Err.Number to see if its something other than 0, or you can check the Errors collection's Count property to see if it's greater than zero.

✔ But after you check to see if the last operation caused an error, make sure you aren't looking at old information! It's not a bad idea to use the Clear method of the Err object or the Clear method of the Errors collection (depending on how you check for errors) after you have completely handled an error or warning. Calling the Clear method before your operation assures that any information in the Err object after your operation is there because of your operation.

Here's an example of database error handling in action:

```
<%
Dim e
' Execute a database command
If Connect.Errors.Count = 1 Then %>
Error #<%=Err.Number%>:
<%=Err.Description%><br>
<%
Else
For e = 0 To Connect.Errors.Count -1 %>
<% If Connect.Errors(e) < 0 Then %>
Error #
<% Else %>
Warning #
<% End If %>
<%=Connect.Errors(e).Number%>:
<%=Connect.Errors(e).Description%><br>
<% Next %>
<% End IF %>
```

If only one error exists, then the Err object is used to display the error number and description. Otherwise, a For loop goes through each object in the Errors collection. First, it determines whether the Error object holds an error or a warning and displays the appropriate text. Then the number and description are displayed.

This chapter explores many, many database techniques. If you are eager to see some of these techniques in action, take a look at Chapter 13. There you can find an application called Classy Classifieds. It neatly displays lists of classifieds that the application retrieves from a classifieds database. It even allows users to add, edit, and delete classifieds on the database through various Web pages. This application not only demonstrates these techniques at work, it also provides a good foundation for almost any other kind of Web database application you want to create.

Part V
Really Cool ASP Applications

The 5th Wave   By Rich Tennant

"It happened around the time we started creating that
real-time chat room using ASP."

In this part . . .

This is the fun part! Here I walk you through the process of creating two complete, full-blown ASP applications. The first is the Café — a real-time chat room. The second is Classy Classifieds — a complete solution for presenting classified ads to your visitors and allowing them to post and maintain new ads. To create these applications, you put everything you've discovered so far to use, and you find out a few new things along the way.

Chapter 12

The Café: Creating a Real-Time Chat Room

Chat rooms are to people in the '90s what diners were to people in the '50s — a place to socialize, a place to meet new people and talk with old friends about everything from world affairs and politics to music and pop culture. Today, chat rooms allow people from all over the world to meet in the same place to discuss topics that interest them with people they've never met before. When you enter a chat room, you use a nickname — most people never use their real names. These nicknames provide anonymity, which, in turn, tends to make people feel free to loosen up and have a good time, without worrying about how they look or sound. Ironically, nicknames, and the anonymity that goes along with them, don't stop people from getting to know each other and developing long-term relationships. In fact, hearing about a newlywed couple who met online is not at all unusual these days.

Chat rooms were first introduced to the general public by online services, such as America Online and CompuServe. But with the tremendous increase in the popularity of the Internet and the World Wide Web, chat rooms inevitably came to be a part of these growing technologies. Originally, Internet Relay Chat (IRC), which required a special server and a special program to access it, was the only form of chatting available on the Internet. But in the last few years, various HTML, CGI, Java, and ActiveX chatting solutions have been created to make chatting easier and more available on the Internet.

In this chapter, I show you how to create your very own chat room that you can put on your Web site. You can use it as a meeting place to discuss topics of interest or as a forum to introduce experts of whom visitors can ask questions. This chat room can be accessed by any browser that supports frames, and the user doesn't need to download or install anything. The chat room is created using only HTML and ASP — and a few clever tricks.

The Blueprint for the Café

I dub the chat room application I create in this chapter, the Café. It's designed to be a simple way to implement a chat room on your Web site. Before getting into the actual ASP pages, I want to first cover some of the sticky design problems you may encounter yourself while putting together an ASP chat room.

Sharing information between visitors

The heart and soul of a chat room is the dialog being shared simultaneously among a group of people. A chat room isn't like a Web page, where the same information is shown to everyone. And it isn't like a newsgroup or discussion forum, where you see postings made over the last several days by visitors to the site. The dialog is real-time, and it is shared.

Fortunately, ASP provides an easy solution to sharing data across several sessions — application-level variables. You just have to create an application-level variable called, for example, `conversation`. Then, whenever anyone submits text to the chat room, you just append it to the `conversation` variable. The variable then holds the shared, ongoing conversation.

Updating the browsers with new information

Although an application-level variable allows you to *share* the information, it doesn't solve the problem of how to *display* the information. The `conversation` variable changes and grows all the time. How does each browser get a new copy of the `conversation` variable on a regular basis?

This problem goes to the core of the way the World Wide Web is designed. Unlike online services and other networks, HTTP, the networking communication language used by the World Wide Web, is *stateless*. That means that instead of logging in and having an open, ongoing channel of conversation between the client and the server, HTTP depends on the client (the browser) to request what it needs. The server then meets that need by sending requested data back, and then the transaction is over. If the browser wants something else, it simply makes a new request. Each request is separate and individual. The server, by default, makes no distinction between a second request from you and a request from a completely different person.

Because each request is separate and individual, nothing on the World Wide Web happens, for the most part, until the browser makes a request. This process works very well for Web browsing. But for many other applications, it would be better if the server had more control. A couple of strategies have been designed to fix this problem.

Push! Push!

The first strategy is *server-push*. You may have heard all the hype about push technology and how it is going to change the way things work on the Internet. Like most new Internet ideas, the benefits of push technology have been exaggerated. But that doesn't mean it isn't still a very interesting idea. The basic concept of push technology is this: Instead of the browser simply making a single request and receiving the results, the browser makes a request and then keeps the channel open. This puts the server in control, rather than the client. Now the server can send information continually or whenever new information is received. This technology, or variations on it, is used to send all kinds of up-to-the-minute information directly to your desktop. You can find out about stock prices, sports scores, news, weather, and anything else you need to know.

If you are interested in learning more about server-push technologies, check out *Push Technology For Dummies* by Bud Smith and *Web Channel Development For Dummies* by Damon Dean (both from IDG Books Worldwide, Inc.).

Pull! Pull!

You can also put the ball back into the server's court and give the server more control by using regularly timed *client-pull*. Instead of holding a channel open to the server, the browser is timed to check with the server to see if it has anything new to send. The browser can make these checks once a minute, once an hour, or once a day, depending on the kind of information involved and the timeliness required.

The Café solution

Client-pull is the technology I use to implement the Café. Using an HTML tag called `meta`, I tell the Web page to refresh itself every ten seconds or so (you can adjust this however you like). Then when the server receives the request to refresh the page, it simply displays the newest version of the `conversation` variable on the page. This technology enables the user to always see the most up-to-date version of the ongoing discussion possible.

Putting together the pieces

Now that the two biggest technical issues are out of the way, what will this application look like?

Well, every chat room I've ever visited requires you to at least enter the nickname you want to use in the room. So the `Default.asp` page has to be a login page. I call it the Café Entrance. After the user has entered a nickname, he can go to the Café's main page.

When I first created the main page for the Café, I put a button and an edit box at the top of the page where the user could type in text and push the button to submit it. I then displayed the `conversation` variable below. However, if you make the page automatically refresh itself every ten seconds or so, you may interrupt the user as she is typing a message in the edit. A problem occurs when the page is refreshed and any text in the edit is cleared. This can be frustrating, to say the least.

The best (and only) solution I can think of is to use frames. You can put the edit and the submit button in a small frame at the top and then display the contents of the `discussion` variable on another page in the lower frame. The page in the lower frame can then refresh itself every ten seconds without disturbing the upper frame, where the user types.

The capabilities I've described so far are enough for a very simple chat room. But one more feature is usually a part of the chat room equation. That feature is a list of the nicknames of all those who are currently in the room. The frame holding these nicknames can be dropped in as a narrow frame down the right-hand side of the window.

But implementing a frame that will hold the nicknames of everyone in the room brings up another problem. You can count someone as logged in to the room when they log in using `Default.asp`. But how do you tell when the users have logged *off* the chat room so that their nicknames can be removed from the frame? You could wait until their session expires, but by default that's 20 minutes! If you wait until the session of a user ends, you could have people trying to carry on a conversation with someone who left 15 minutes ago. That won't work. The nickname list has to be much more timely than that.

You can use the same solution for this problem that I use to solve the problem of keeping the conversation updated. If a person is in the chat room, then the chat room page is automatically refreshing approximately every ten seconds. So to see if a person has logged off, simply log the exact time of the last refresh. Then go through that list every now and then and look for people whose last refresh was more than 20 seconds ago. If a user has gone more than 20 seconds without refreshing, then he isn't on the chat room page anymore. He can then be counted as logged off.

Building the Café, Brick-by-Brick

After all the design issues have been ironed out, the actual ASP pages should go smoothly. In the coming sections, I show you each page as it is executed and describe exactly how it works. I begin with the login page, which will collect the user's nickname and then go on to the Café itself. Three frames divide up the window in the Café — the place where the user can type what he wants to say at the top, the conversation at the bottom, and the list of nicknames of people in the room along the right side.

If you are building this application as you read, now is the time to create a new virtual directory on your web server. Name it Café. You may also want to throw in a blank global.asa file.

Then, as I walk through the pages in the following sections, you can either create them in that directory or pull them over from the CD-ROM included with this book.

The login page: `Default.asp`

The login page is the first page that the users see when they begin this application. It prompts them to enter a nickname to be used in the chat room (see Figure 12-1).

Cafe Entrance - Microsoft Internet Explorer

File   Edit   View   Go   Favorites   Help

Address http://www.edgequest.com/cafe/

Welcome to the Cafe

The Cafe is a casual gathering place to meet new friends and chat with old ones.

To enter the Cafe, type the name you wish to use below and click the button.

Your Name: [   ]

[Take Me To The Cafe]

Internet zone

This is the code that makes it happen.

```
<% Option Explicit %>
<% Response.Buffer = true %>
<HTML>
<head>
<title>Cafe Entrance</title>
</head>
<body bgcolor="#FFFFFF">
<% If trim(Request.Form("name")) = "" Then %>
<h1>Welcome to the Cafe</h1>
The Cafe is a casual gathering place to meet
new friends and chat with old ones.<p>
To enter the Cafe, type the name you wish to use below and
click the button.<p>
<form action="default.asp" method="POST">
<p>Your Name: <input type="text" size="20" name="Name"></p>
<p><input type="submit" name="Submit"
value="Take Me To The Cafe"></p>
</form>
<%
Else
   Dim users, refresh
   Session("name") = Request.Form("name")

   If Application("NumUsers") = 0 Then
      ' Initialize (or re-initialize) the user list
      ' and the conversation
      ReDim temp1(50)
      ReDim temp2(50)
      Application("users") = temp1
      Application("refresh") = temp2
   End If

   ' Retrieve the application arrays
   users = Application("users")
   refresh = Application("refresh")

   ' Find an empty spot and add the new user
   Dim i
   For i = 1 To 50
      If users(i) = "" Then
         users(i) = Session("name")
         refresh(i) = time
         Application.Lock
         Application("NumUsers") = Application("NumUsers") +
            1
         Application.Unlock
         Exit For
      End If
```

```
      Next
      If i = 51 Then Response.Redirect "toomany.asp"

      ' Put the arrays back in the application vars
      Application.Lock
      Application("users") = users
      Application("refresh") = refresh
      Application.Unlock

      If not IsEmpty(Application("conversation")) Then
          Application.Lock
          Application("conversation") = "<b><i>" &
            Session("name") & _
            " Enters The Room</b></i><br>" &
          Application("conversation")
          Application.Unlock
      End If

      Response.Redirect "cafe.asp"
End If
%>
</body>
</HTML>
```

This listing actually combines a form and the response to the form in one page. It could easily be divided into two pages, if you prefer. But for small forms and small response pages, putting them together helps keep the number of pages in your application small.

I combine the form and its response page by putting almost the entire contents of the page inside one long If..Then..Else statement. The first VBScript code on the page checks to see if Request.Form("name") has anything in it. The first time this page loads, of course, it doesn't — so the form is displayed.

The form's action attribute refers to *this* page. So when the form is submitted, this page is loaded to handle it. But the second time it is loaded, Request.Form ("name") *does* have a value. This causes the Else part of the If..Then..Else statement to execute where the form is handled.

The nickname entered on the form is stored in a new Session variable called name.

The application variable NumUsers is checked. This variable holds the number of users logged into the chat room currently. If it is 0, then either this is the first time someone has joined the room or people came and left and this is the first person who has entered the room since the last person left.

Whatever the situation, when there aren't any other users in the room, I take the opportunity to initialize (or re-initialize) the two application-level arrays that I use in this application: users and refresh. Here's how these arrays work:

- ✔ The users array holds the user's name of everybody currently in the room.
- ✔ The refresh array holds the user's last refresh time. The refresh array is also used in another page to make sure that each user is still logged in.

You may have noticed that I've created two local arrays, temp1 and temp2, and then assigned them to the application variables. This is the only way to initialize an application-level array. Why? Because you can't use Dim or ReDim directly with an application-level variable. Like Session variables, you create them automatically just by referring to them.

Next, even if you haven't just initialized the application arrays, the arrays are dumped into two local variables: users and refresh. You can't really use application-level arrays directly. Something like this just wouldn't work:

```
Application("users")(27) = "fred" ' Won't work
```

So I put the values into local variables and then use the local variables. But if you make changes, don't forget to put the local variables back into the application-level variables when you're done (as I do later in this page).

Next, the array searches for an empty spot (users(i) = ""). As soon as one is found, the new user's name is stored at that location in the array and the current time is stored in the same location in the refresh array.

The If...Then after the loop catches it in case all 50 spots in the array are full. If that's the case, then the room is considered full and the user is sent to the toomany.asp page to inform them of that. Finally, the local users and refresh array variables are assigned back to the application variables so that they can be accessed again on other pages.

Notice the Application.Lock and Application.Unlock. These lines of code are required whenever you change an Application variable's value. Using Lock and Unlock assures that only one session at a time changes an Application variable. You don't need to use Lock and Unlock when you simply access the value in an application variable – only when you change it.

If the conversation variable already exists, that indicates that people are probably already in the chat room. If this is the case, then you add this message to the beginning of the conversation string:

```
Nickname Enters The Room
```

The nickname the user entered appears in place of Nickname. This lets everyone in the room know that a new person has entered and tells them what his or her nickname is.

If the conversation variable doesn't exist yet, you can be sure that no one is in the room, so that these lines are skipped.

Finally, control is passed to cafe.asp, which is the page that identifies how the frames are set up.

The frames page: café.asp

The main page for the Café is divided into three separate frames, each with its own ASP page inside. cafe.asp just identifies how big the frames are, where they are located, and which pages fill each frame.

```
<HTML>
<frameset ROWS="10%,90%">
<frame SRC="say.asp" NAME="cafe_top"
MARGINWIDTH="1" MARGINHEIGHT="1" SCROLLING="no">
<frameset COLS="75%,25%">
<frame SRC="cafeconvo.asp" NAME="cafe_convo">
<frame SRC="users.asp" NAME="cafe_users">
</frameset>
<noframes>
<body>
This Web page uses frames, but your browser
doesn't support them.<p>
</body>
</noframes>
</frameset>
</HTML>
```

This page is straight HTML. Notice that I did name it cafe.asp, though, just in case I decide to add ASP scripting to it in the future.

A frame that is only 10 percent high is located at the top of the page. The other 90 percent of the page is divided vertically so that the frame on the left is 75 percent wide and the frame on the right has the remaining 25 percent. When the other pages that fit into the frames are created, the final Café page will look like Figure 12-2.

The page at the top is called say.asp. It has a button and an edit box. When the user wants to say something in the room, she types the text into the edit box and then clicks the button to send it off.

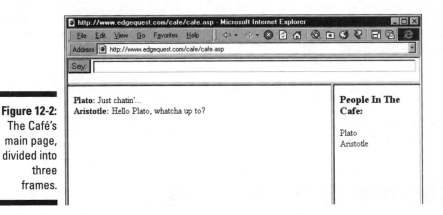

Figure 12-2:
The Café's
main page,
divided into
three
frames.

The actual conversation appears on the big page on the left, `cafeconvo.asp`.
The narrow frame on the right, `users.asp`, shows the list of people currently
in the room.

Saying something: `Say.asp`

`Say.asp` is a simple form with a long edit and a submit button. This form
allows the user to say something that appears in the chat room.

```
<HTML>
<body bgcolor="#FFFFFF"
onload="document.form1.Say.focus()">
<%
If trim(Request.Form("say")) <> "" Then
Application.Lock
Application("conversation") = "<b>" & _
Session("name") & ": </b>" & _
Request.Form("say") & "<br>" & _
Application("conversation")
Application.Unlock
End If
%>
<form action="say.asp" method="POST" name="form1">
<input type="submit" name="Submit" value="Say:">
<input type="text" size="80" name="Say">
</form>
</body>
</HTML>
```

Again, I put both the form and the page that responds to the form together on
the same page. But this time, it looks a bit different — no `Else` clause is present.
The first time through, the `If` condition fails, the `Then` portion is skipped, and
the form is displayed. When the form is submitted, the `If` condition succeeds,

the Then portion is executed, and the form is again displayed. No Else is in this If..Then clause because, on this page, you want to continue to redisplay the form every time, whether this is the first time the page is processed or the twentieth.

 When I first created Say.asp, I wanted the cursor to always appear in the edit every time the form was displayed. Otherwise, the user would always have to click in the edit before they could enter text — which would become a pain after a while. In many development environments, you have what is called a *tab-order,* which determines the order in which you move through the controls as you click the tab key. You can use the tab-order to determine where the cursor appears when a window first opens. HTML forms don't have this tab-order feature, and I racked my brain trying to find a way to determine the cursor's placement. Finally, I settled on using a tiny, tiny bit of client-side script. In the body tag, notice that a value is specified for the onload attribute. This value is a single line of JavaScript code which executes on the client every time this page loads. The code places the focus in the form called form1 and on the control called Say. And it works like a charm!

I begin the scripting on this page by checking to see if the user entered anything in the form field, this time called say. When the user submits the form, the code inside the If..Then is executed. The user's nickname, followed by the line the user entered in the edit, is attached to the *top* of the conversation variable. Notice how this works. Every time someone says something, the text appears at the top of the window. This may seem a bit backwards, but it keeps the current conversation at the top of the window and lets the old stuff scroll off the bottom. It also makes it possible for you to read the conversation from top to bottom — from most recent comments to older comments.

You should notice one more thing about this page: The conversation frame is *not* automatically refreshed when the user enters a line of text and clicks submit. So after new text is submitted, the text may not immediately appear as a part of the conversation. I intentionally chose to do it this way to keep the application simple. Remember that the conversation frame refreshes itself automatically every ten seconds anyway. So the next time it refreshes, the user will see what she typed, along with anything anyone else typed within that time. She'll wait, on average, about five seconds before the other user's newly entered text appears.

Displaying the conversation: cafeconvo.asp

The biggest frame in the window is the conversation frame. This is where the user sees what she types and what everyone else has typed. Now that all the groundwork is laid, this page is pretty short.

```
<HTML>
<head>
<meta http-equiv="refresh" content="5">
</head>
<body bgcolor="#FFFFFF">
<%
Dim convo
convo = Application("conversation")
If Len(convo) > 2000 Then
convo = Left(convo, 2000)
Application.Lock
Application("conversation") = convo
Application.Unlock
End If
Response.Write convo
%>
</body>
</HTML>
```

Look at the meta tag at the top of the page. The meta tag is a relatively obscure tag that is usually used to hold information about the page and its contents. For example, search engines often use the information in meta tags to find keywords that identify the page's contents or to provide a concise summary of the page.

But the meta tag can be put to a couple of other uses, too. The first use is what I do in this application. You can use the meta tag to cause this page to continually refresh again and again, if you specify the attribute http-equiv, set it to "refresh", and then set the content attribute to the number of seconds it should wait before refreshing the page. This page refreshes itself every ten seconds.

Another neat trick you can do with the meta tag is use it to display the contents of a page, and then automatically load a new page after a specified number of seconds. Here's an example:

```
<meta http-equiv="refresh"
content="10;http://www.newpage.com">
```

With this line at the top, the page is displayed and waits ten seconds. After the time is up, the page automatically redirects the browser to the URL specified after the semicolon in content. This technique is often used if a site has been moved from one URL to another. In this case, the owners of the site may want to inform the user that he has navigated to the old URL and should update his Favorites or Bookmarks entry.

This technique can also be used to display a series of Web pages one after the other, in sequence. Combine this with graphics, audio narration, and maybe even background music, and you've created a multimedia slide show.

Who's here? Find out with `users.asp`

The last feature I include in this little application is the ability to see who is in the room right now. It's tough to carry on a conversation if the person you're talking to has left the room!

```
<html>
<head>
<meta http-equiv="refresh" content="10">
</head>
<body bgcolor="#FFFFFF">
<%
Dim Userlist, Datelist, i, num, users, refresh

' Retrieve application arrays
users = Application("users")
refresh = Application("refresh")

' Find current user and update his refresh time
For i = 1 To 50
    If users(i) = Session("name") Then
        refresh(i) = Time
        Exit For
    End If
Next

' Has ANYONE been gone more than 20 seconds?
For i = 1 To 50
    If users(i) <> "" Then
        If DateDiff("s",refresh(i), Time) > 20 Then
            Application("conversation") = "<b><i>" & _
                users(i) & " Leaves The Room</b></i><br>" & _
                Application("conversation")
            users(i) = ""
            Application("NumUsers") = _
                Application("NumUsers") - 1
        End If
    End If
Next
Application.Lock
Application("users") = users
Application("refresh") = refresh
Application.Unlock
%>
<h3>People In The Cafe:</h3>
<%
For i = 1 To 50
    If users(i)<> "" Then
        Response.Write users(i) & "<br>"
    End If
Next
%>
</body>
</html>
```

The first thing I do here is get the users and refresh arrays out of the application variables and into the local variables users and refresh. Then I use a For loop to find the current users and update their last-refreshed time in the refresh array.

Next, I go through the arrays to see if anyone has failed to refresh in the last 20 seconds. If they have, I append a message to the conversation in the room, indicating that the person has gone and set the user's nickname to " ", which removes the user from the list.

After the loop is complete, I update the application variables from the local arrays. Then I write the current number of people in the chat room and list their user names in this frame.

Playing in the Café

After you implement the Café on your site, call up some friends and invite them to your Café to chat. It can be a lot of fun, and there's no better way to find the bugs, annoyances, and inconsistencies in your application than by inviting friends to pound on it and offer friendly criticism. You may notice that you can actually use HTML tags when you type a message. For instance, if you type this

```
I <b>really</b> like your Cafe.
```

it appears in the conversation frame like this

```
I really like your Cafe.
```

This is a really fun feature to play with. Virtually any tag you want to try out will work. And tags make it possible to be very expressive. However, if you aren't expecting it, this feature can sometimes be annoying. For example, if you sent this text normally:

```
He is funny <g>
```

it would end up displaying like this

```
He is funny
```

If you type <g>, you probably intend to indicate that you are grinning. But the <g> is interpreted as an unknown tag and is simply ignored by the browser. If you decide you'd rather not allow HTML tags to work and you simply want to display exactly what the user types, you can do it by using the HTMLEncode method of the Server object. This method takes whatever text you pass as an argument and turns it into HTML that will display looking exactly like the text you sent. For more information on the HTMLEncode method, see "HTMLEncode — the Web master" in Chapter 7.

Making It Better

The Café is a simple, HTML and ASP solution for a versatile chat room. But it has lots of room for enhancements. Here are some of my ideas.

- **At the time of login, allow users to choose URL filenames that contain a small graphic to represent them when they speak, and have the graphic appear beside their nicknames.**

- **Assign users different colors for their text after they enter the room so that it's easier to distinguish who said what.**

- **Add multiple chat rooms.** Provide a list that shows each chat room name and how many people are in it.

- **Give users the ability to create and name their own chat rooms.** Then provide a list of the currently available rooms and how many people are in each.

Chapter 13

Classy Classifieds

● ●

In This Chapter

▶ Planning Classy Classifieds

▶ Placing a new ad

▶ Displaying ads by category

▶ Updating and deleting ads

▶ Searching for ads

▶ Extending Classy Classifieds

● ●

*C*lassified ads are a way to reach large audiences inexpensively. The costs of classifieds on the Internet are even lower than they used to be because nearly the entire process can be automated. In fact, many sites on the Web allow you to place *free* classified ads.

Why do you want classifieds on your site? Well, you may want to become the next big classifieds-central for a broad variety of topics. Or perhaps you have a site that specializes in a particular area, such as music. You may want to offer visitors to your site a free classifieds section where they can buy and sell musical instruments or sheet music. Providing specialized classified ads on a topic related to your Web site is a great way to stir up interest and draw people back to your site again and again.

In this chapter, I show you how to create a completely automated classifieds Web application. Everything from browsing ads to placing new ads to maintaining and deleting existing ads can be handled automatically using the power of ASP.

Planning to Create Classy Classifieds

In this section, I show you how I went about planning to create Classy Classifieds. You can use the same process when you create your own ASP applications or when you begin to extend Classy Classifieds.

The first thing I did when planning Classy Classifieds was to go to a Web search engine and search for "classifieds." You can find links to many sites that offer both pay and free classified ads. Explore both big and small sites to see how they accept new ads, how they are organized, what categories they use, and how they allow you to search.

Learning from what others have done is not cheating. It's research! If someone else has devised a clever solution to a problem, why not borrow it? Of course, you can't steal code or copyrighted text or graphics, but you can get a lot of good ideas on layout, presentation, and user-interface organization by looking at the work of others.

What classified ad categories should I use?

After you conduct your research, decide which categories you want to use to organize your classifieds. I chose five: Vehicles, Real Estate, Computers & Software, Collectibles, and General Merchandise. But depending upon the topic and purpose of your Web site, you may want entirely different categories. The home page of your Web site will list these categories and link visitors to pages containing all the classifieds that belong to that category.

In addition, you may want to create a header that appears at the top of every page. In my application, the header displays the name "Classy Classifieds" and provides links to each category. From the header, you could also link to pages where the user can place an ad and do a general search.

What pages do I need?

If you want to create a classifieds application, what pages do you need to create? Well, I've hinted at several already. I chose the following:

- ✔ A home page with a menu
- ✔ An include file with a page header
- ✔ A page to list classifieds by category
- ✔ A search page and a page to display the results of the search
- ✔ A page that allows the user to place a new ad
- ✔ A page to allow the user to edit an ad
- ✔ A page to allow the user to delete an ad

You may choose to organize the application differently. Here are some suggestions:

> ✔ Use separate form and form-response pages after an ad is edited or deleted. I chose to put them together in this application.
>
> ✔ Create a page footer or even a sidebar to go down the left of the page to provide links to key pages on the site.

A whole world of options is out there, so don't feel confined to what I've done here. It's only one solution among many.

What technical issues are left?

After you've done some research to discover what others have done and you've organized your application into pages, you have to look for any other technical problems that may stand in your way. These problems could be specific functionality that you don't know how to do or simply a tough task that you think is going to require some time to work out. When I got to this point, there were only a couple of things I was concerned about. The first was using the database and the second was authentication.

Using the database

I use Microsoft Access for the database for this application because Access is the DBMS, I discuss in Chapters 10 and 11. Also, Access is readily available, inexpensive, and easy to learn.

Access is not, however, designed for heavy-duty volume. If you are expecting many visitors to your Web site, you probably want to consider a more serious DBMS, Microsoft SQL Server. How many visitors is too many for Access? That's a very complicated question. The answer depends upon many variables, such as the number of people accessing your site over time, the largest number to access your site at any given time, the amount of database access being done, and whether the database access consists mostly of simple queries or lots of records being added and updated.

The good news is that you can start with Microsoft Access and watch your site to see what the response time is. If the response time is acceptable, you're set. If not, you can upgrade to Microsoft SQL Server very easily. In fact, there's an Upsizing Wizard that makes moving from Access to SQL Server pretty simple. And the code to interface with SQL Server from your Web pages is almost exactly the same code you use with Access.

The actual database work I do in this application is pretty straightforward. The database includes only one table, called "Items," which has the following columns:

- **ItemNum:** The primary key of the table. It is what Access calls an AutoNumber, which means that when you create a new record, Access automatically generates a unique value for this field. This is a *surrogate key,* which means that the field doesn't hold any important data itself and won't be entered or viewed by the users. It is just used to uniquely identify each ad.

- **Item:** The name of the item.

- **Category:** A string holding the name of the category this item is associated with.

- **Description:** A memo field which means that it can, theoretically at least, hold up to 65,000 characters — far more than the capacity of any one classified, I would hope!

- **Price:** The amount the user wants for the item.

- **Phone:** The user's phone number, including area code.

- **Email:** The user's e-mail address.

- **State:** The state the user lives in (for geographical searches).

- **Posted:** The date the ad was posted.

- **Password:** Used to verify who originally created the ad. (I discuss this field more in the next section.)

If you are creating this application as you read through this chapter, you'll probably want to at least pull the database itself off the CD-ROM. It is called `classdb.mdb`. You can create the database easily enough yourself, but I've entered six or eight bogus ads for each category to get you started. So save yourself some typing time and just use my database.

If you want to make the categories more specific, you could choose to use a different set of fields for each category and then store the data for each category in a different table. I've chosen to use one set of fields and store them in one table to keep it simple.

Who are you? Are you sure?

Authentication is one of those words that Internet programming nerds like to sling around to scare everyone else. It really means something very simple — making sure you *are* who you *say* you are. In this application, you want to allow only the person who placed an ad to later edit or delete it. So how do you confirm that the person who is trying to edit an ad is the same person who created it?

You could require all people who use the system to log in with their own user IDs and passwords. But that's a bit drastic. If you just want to browse ads, you shouldn't have to put in that much effort. Besides, you want to make it as easy as possible to browse so that you encourage a lot of people to do it.

Another option would be to require only those who want to *place* ads to get an account with a user ID and password. This solution works and is probably necessary if you are creating an online auction or some other kind of site where you're likely to have a lot of interaction with those who sign up.

But this application is very simple. Most people who use the classifieds application will be placing ads and never touching them again. So why make them go through a process of signing up and getting an account?

My solution to this problem is to make the password something that you enter when you place an ad. You just enter the password along with the rest of the ad information, and then the password is saved with the ad itself. There's very little extra trouble involved (except you have to remember the password), and you don't have to go through a separate process of signing up for an account or logging in each time you want to access the system. If you want to edit or delete a record, you simply have to type in the password you used when you created it.

You have a downside to this solution, though. This is not a very secure system — not by a long shot. The password itself is sent over the Internet as plain text and is even stored in the database as plain text. With the right equipment, someone can, theoretically, intercept the password as it is sent over the Internet. And if someone had access to the database on the server, he would have easy access to all the passwords.

But let's be honest — these aren't government secrets or the encryption codes for nuclear weapons. They are just classified ads. It isn't worth anyone's time or effort to use intense authentication techniques.

 If you're concerned about security and authentication, weigh the intrusiveness, the sensitivity of the data, and the likelihood of theft and then use the solution that is the most appropriate for the application.

Kicking Off the Site Development

As soon as you've thought your site through and addressed all the issues you think you may run into in the course of developing the site, you can get started.

If you are developing this site as you read, now is a good time to create a virtual directory on your web server. Name it `Classy`. You may want to throw the `classdb.mdb` Access database in the new directory, too.

In addition, create another virtual directory on your web server named
`common`. Inside that directory, put the file `adovbs.inc`. You can find it on
your web server in one of these two directories:

```
C:\Program Files\Common Files\System\Ado
C:\Inetpub\wwwroot\ASPSamp\Samples
```

If you don't find it there, you can download it from my Web site for this book at:

```
www.edgequest.com/ASPDummies/
```

As I discuss each page on the site, you can either create it yourself or pull it
off the CD that came with this book.

The Home Page: `Default.asp`

The home page is the simplest to understand of all the pages.

```
<HTML>
<BODY bgcolor="#FFFFFF" vlink=red>
<!-- #include file="header.inc" -->
<% ShowHeader "Home" %>
Welcome to Classy Classifieds. We make it easy to
turn your stuff into cash and to get other
people's stuff cheap.<p>
<font size=4>The Categories:</font><p>
<table width=100%>
<tr>
<td><a href=category.asp?Category=VEHICLES>
Vehicles</a><p></td>
<td><a href=category.asp?Category=COMPUTERS>
Computers & Software</a><p></td>
</tr><tr>
<td><a href=category.asp?Category=REALESTATE>
Real Estate</a><p></td>
<td><a href=category.asp?Category=COLLECTIBLES>
Collectibles</a><p></td>
</tr><tr>
<td><a href=category.asp?Category=GENERAL>
General Merchandise</a><p></td>
<td><a href=search.asp>Search</a><p></td>
</tr>
</table>
</BODY>
</HTML>
```

At the top of the page I set the background color to white and the *VLink* color
(the color for visited links) to red. I choose these colors in all the pages. The
default link color is blue, so that the primary colors are red and blue, with

most of the text appearing black on a white background. I didn't hire a graphic designer (obviously), but I realized that coming up with something that looks pleasant and standardizing is always a good idea because it gives your application a more cohesive look and feel.

I use a #include at the top of the page to include the header.inc file, which I discuss in the next section. I then call the ShowHeader subroutine, which is inside header.inc. This displays the header for this home page and for every page throughout the application (see Figure 13-1).

Finally, I create a table to organize the links to the various categories into two columns. Notice that all the categories link to the same page — category.asp. The page knows which category to display because when I link to it, I pass the category after a question mark. In the category.asp page, I access the information passed using the Request object's QueryString collection, as I discuss in the section later in this chapter titled "The Category Listing: Category.asp."

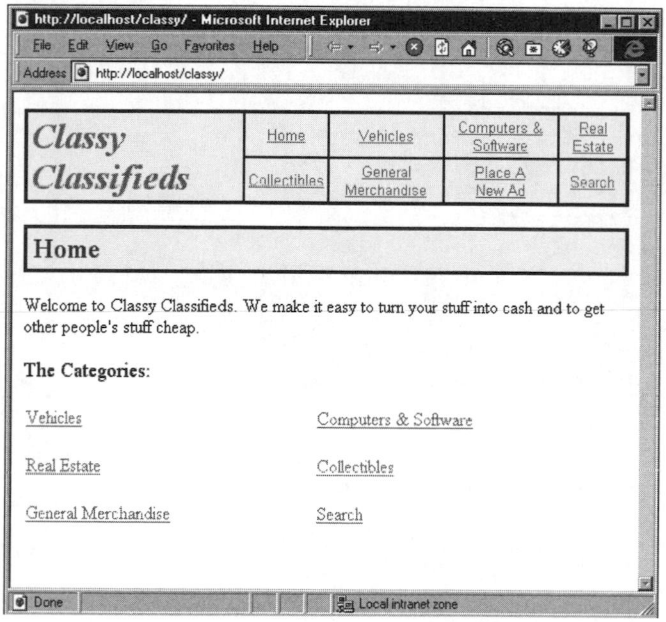

Figure 13-1:
The Classy
Classifieds
home page.

The Header Include File: Header.inc

Include files allow you to place the same HTML or scripting code into multiple pages. This strategy makes reusing common formatting or certain functions or subroutines easy. In this application, I decided to give the application a cohesive look and feel across all of its pages by creating a header include file that would show a neatly formatted header that presented the name of the application and links to its most important pages.

My original idea was to create a header using only HTML and then include it right where I wanted the header to appear on every page.

Then I decided that I wanted not only an application header, but also a page header to give a title to the current page. But that title would be different for each page. How can you send an argument to a header file? Answer: You can't. But you *can* create a subroutine inside the header file and send an argument to the subroutine. So that's what I did.

```
<% Sub ShowHeader(PageName) %>
<table border=2 cellspacing=0 cellpadding=3
width=100% bordercolor=Black bgcolor=yellow>
<tr><td rowspan=2>
<font size=6 color=Red><b><i>
Classy Classifieds</b></i></font>
</td>
<td align=center valign=center>
<a href=default.asp>
<font face="Arial,Helvetica" size=2>
Home</font></a></td>
<td align=center valign=center>
<a href=category.asp?Category=VEHICLES>
<font face="Arial,Helvetica" size=2>
Vehicles</font></a></td>
<td align=center valign=center>
<a href=category.asp?Category=COMPUTERS>
<font face="Arial,Helvetica" size=2>
Computers & Software</font></td>
<td align=center valign=center>
<a href=category.asp?Category=REALESTATE>
<font face="Arial,Helvetica" size=2>
Real Estate</font></td>
</tr><tr>
<td align=center valign=center>
<a href=category.asp?Category=COLLECTIBLES>
<font face="Arial,Helvetica" size=2>
Collectibles</font></td>
<td align=center valign=center>
<a href=category.asp?Category=GENERAL>
<font face="Arial,Helvetica" size=2>
General Merchandise</font></td>
<td align=center valign=center>
<a href=placead.asp>
<font face="Arial,Helvetica" size=2>
Place A<br>New Ad</font></td>
<td align=center valign=center>
<a href=search.asp>
```

```
<font face="Arial,Helvetica" size=2>
Search</font></td>
</tr>
</table><br>
<table border=2 bgcolor=yellow width=100%
bordercolor=Black cellspacing=0 cellpadding=5>
<td>
<font size=5 color=Blue><b>
<%=PageName%></b></font></td>
</table><p>
<% End Sub %>
<% Sub ShowItem(Item,Description,Price,Phone,_
  Email,State,Posted) %>
<table border=1 width=100% bordercolor=Black
cellspacing=0 cellpadding=2 bgcolor=Lime>
<tr><td bgcolor=yellow colspan=2>
<font size=4><b><%=Item%></b></font>
</td></tr>
<tr><td width=25% valign=top>
Description:</td><td><%=Description%></td></tr>
<tr><td width=25%>Price:</td><td>$<%=Price%></td></tr>
<tr><td width=25%>Phone:</td><td><%=Phone%></td></tr>
<tr><td width=25%>Email:</td>
<td><a href="mailto:<%=Email%>">
<%=Email%></a></td></tr>
<tr><td width=25%>Location:</td>
<td><%=State%></td></tr>
<tr><td width=25%>Posted Date:</td>
<td><%=Posted%></td></tr>
</table><p>
<% End Sub %>
```

The first subroutine, ShowHeader, accepts PageName as an argument and then displays the application header and the page header one after another. Everything in ShowHeader is HTML.

I found putting the ShowHeader HTML into a subroutine is beneficial for a couple of reasons:

✔ Not only does it give me the chance to pass an argument, but it also gives me the flexibility to call the subroutine more than once on a page.

You may ask why I would display the header more than once on a page. If I use the same page to present and respond to a form, often I need a header in both instances. Instead of including the same Header.inc twice, as I would if I were using HTML alone, I just include it once and call the ShowHeader subroutine twice. Look at PlaceAd, EditAd, and DelAd to see examples of this.

✔ Putting the `ShowHeader` HTML in a subroutine also gives me the opportunity to include *other* subroutines in this include file that I may need elsewhere, for example, a subroutine to neatly and conveniently display a classified ad.

`ShowItem` accepts all the fields of an ad as arguments and then displays them in a fancy box. I use it in `EditAd`, `DelAd`, and `Detail`. I could have broken this subroutine out into a separate include file and only included it in the pages where I use it, but it was easier just to drop it into the file that was included everywhere.

I use a yellow background for the header and a yellow/green background for the `ShowItem`. These colors may not be *your* favorites, but that's the beauty of HTML — it's easy to change!

Adding an Ad: `PlaceAd.asp`

`PlaceAd` is pretty straightforward. The form is displayed, the user enters all the information, and then the user submits the information. The same page is used to respond to the form.

```
<% Option Explicit %>
<!-- #include virtual="common/adovbs.inc" -->
<HTML>
<BODY bgcolor="#FFFFFF" vlink=red>
<!-- #include file="header.inc" --><p>
<%
' The first time this page is retrieved and any time it is
' submitted without being completely filled out, the form
' is displayed. If it is submitted and completely
' filled out the form is processed in the Else clause.
If Request("Item")="" Or Request("Description")="" Or _
 Request("Price")="" Or Request("Phone")="" Or _
 Request("Email")="" Or Request("State")="" Then
%>
<% ShowHeader "Place A New Ad" %>
Please fill in all of these fields below. Be sure to
choose an appropriate Category for your item.<p>
Be careful when entering a Password and be sure to
remember what you type. You will be required to enter
the password later to identify you if you need to edit
or delete this ad.<p>
When you are finished, click the Place Ad button.<p>
<form method="POST" action="placead.asp">
<table>
<tr><td>Item:</td>
<td><input type="text" size="50" name="Item"></td></tr>
<td valign=top>Description:</td>
```

```
<td><textarea name="Description" rows="6"
          cols="50"></textarea></td></tr>
<tr><td>Category:</td>
<td> <select name="Category" size="1">
<option selected value="VEHICLES">Vehicles</option>
<option value="COMPUTERS">Computers/Software</option>
<option value="REALESTATE">Real Estate</option>
<option value="COLLECTIBLES">Collectibles</option>
<option value="GENERAL">General Merchandise</option>
</select></td></tr>
<tr><td>Price:</td>
<td><input type="text" size="10" name="Price">
</td>
</tr>
<tr><td>Phone</td>
<td><input type="text" size="15" name="Phone">
</td>
</tr>
<tr><td>Email:</td>
<td><input type="text" size="50" name="Email">
</td>
</tr>
<tr><td>State:</td>
<td><input type="text" size="2" name="State">
</td>
</tr>
<tr><td>Password:</td>
<td><input type="password" size="50" name="Password">
</td>
</tr>
<tr><td><input type="submit" value="Place Ad"></td></tr>
</table>
</form>
<% Else %>
<%
Dim Query, Connect, Classifieds, Place
ShowHeader "Place A New Ad"
On Error Resume Next
%>
<font size=5><b>CATEGORY: <%=Request("Category")%>
</b></font>
<%
ShowItem Request("Item"),Request("Description"),_
 Request("Price"),Request("Phone"),Request("Email"),_
 Request("State"),Date
Set Connect = Server.CreateObject("ADODB.Connection")
Connect.Open "ClassDSN"
Set Classifieds = Server.CreateObject("ADODB.Recordset")
Classifieds.Open _
 "SELECT * FROM Items WHERE Category='" & _
```

```
  Request("Category") & "'",_
  Connect,adOpenDynamic,adLockOptimistic
Classifieds.AddNew
Classifieds ("Item") = Request("Item")
Classifieds ("Category") = Request("Category")
Classifieds ("Description") = Request("Description")
Classifieds ("Price") = Request("Price")
Classifieds ("Phone") = Request("Phone")
Classifieds ("Email") = Request("Email")
Classifieds ("State") = Request("State")
Classifieds ("Posted") = Date
Classifieds ("Password") = Request("Password")
Classifieds.Update
If Err.Number = 0 Then %>
<font size=5><i>Your classified ad has been
           placed.</i></font><p>
<a href="default.asp">Home</a><p>
<% Else %>
There was an error placing your ad.<p>
Error #<%=Err.Number%>: <%=Err.Description%><p>
<% End If %>
<% End If %>
</BODY>
</HTML>
```

The `If..Then` statement at the beginning of the page divides the page into
the form part and the form-handler part. The `If..Then` statement's condition
is met after all the fields in the form have information filled in. If any of the
form's information is not filled in, the form is redisplayed (see Figure 13-2).

If all the information is filled in, a `Recordset` is opened using `adOpenDynamic`
and `adLockOptimistic`. This allows the `Recordset` to be fully updateable. I
call `AddNew` to create a new record in the `Recordset` and then I fill in all the
fields with the information from the form. Finally, I call `Update` to send the
new record to the database. For more information on `adOpenDynamic` and
`adLockOptimistic`, see "Cursors and other people with soapy mouths" and
"Putting your records in a headlock" in Chapter 11. For more information on
adding records to the database, see "Adding new records" in Chapter 11.

Because I use `On Error Resume Next` for this part of the code, I check the
`Err.Number` at the bottom to make sure everything went okay and I display
an error message if it didn't (see Figure 13-3).

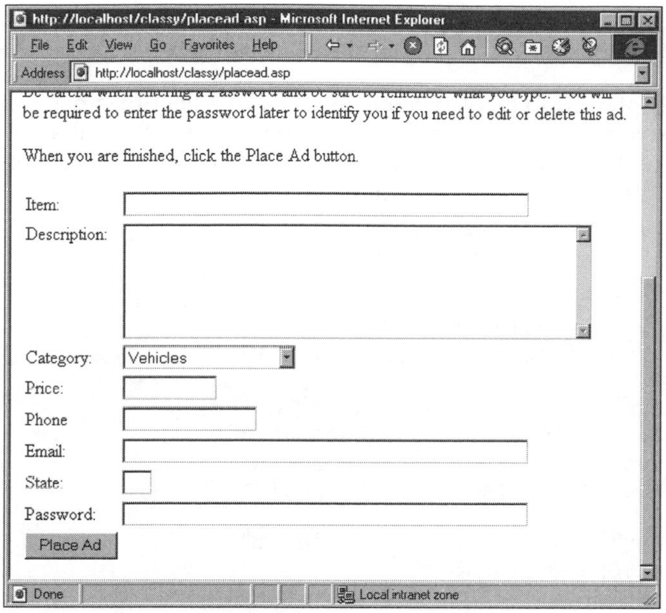

Figure 13-2:
The
PlaceAd
form.

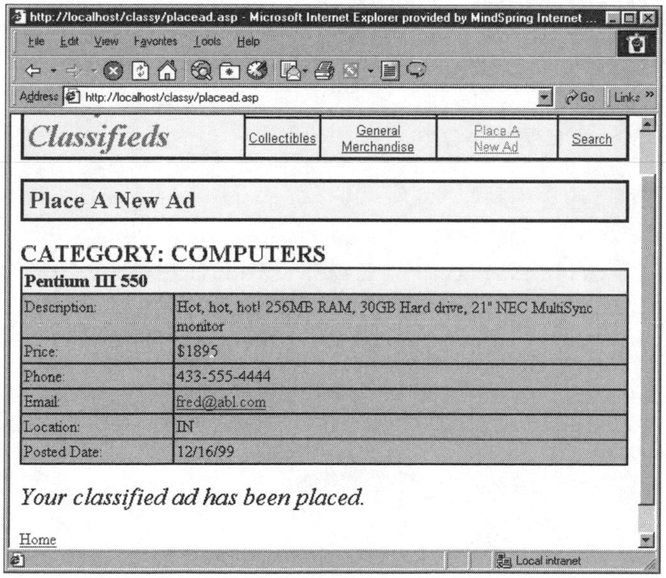

Figure 13-3:
The
PlaceAd
page after
the ad is
successfully
placed.

The Category Listing: `Category.asp`

I originally started to create a Vehicles page, a Collectibles page, and so forth to list the items in each category. I realized very quickly that all of these pages were going to look very, very similar. So I collapsed them together into one page that accepts an argument on the URL line.

```
<!-- #include virtual="common/adovbs.inc" -->
<HTML>
<BODY bgcolor="#FFFFFF" vlink=red>
<!-- #include file="header.inc" -->
<% ShowHeader("List by Category") %>
<%
Dim Connect, Classifieds, Query, Category
Category = Trim(Request("Category"))
If Category = "" Then
 Response.Write "No Category specified.<p>"
Else
 Set Connect = Server.CreateObject("ADODB.Connection")
 Connect.Open "ClassDSN"
 Query = "SELECT ItemNum,Item,Price,State FROM Items "
 Query = Query & "WHERE Category='" & Category & "'"
 Set Classifieds = Connect.Execute(Query)
%>
<font size=4><b><%=Category%>:</b></font>
<table border=1 bgcolor=yellow width=100%
bordercolor=Black cellspacing=0 cellpadding=5>
<tr><th align=left>Item</th>
<th align=left>Cost</th>
<th align=left>State</th></tr>
<%
 Do While Not Classifieds.EOF %>
<tr>
<td>
<a href=detail.asp?item=<%=Classifieds("ItemNum")%>>
<%=Classifieds("Item")%></a></td>
<td><%=Classifieds("Price")%></td>
<td><%=Classifieds("State")%></td>
</tr>
<%
 Classifieds.MoveNext
 Loop
End If
%>
</table>
</HTML>
</BODY>
```

The links to this page on the home page look like this:

```
<a href=category.asp?Category=COMPUTERS>
Computers & Software</a>
```

These links not only refer to the page but also pass an argument to the page on the URL line after a question mark. After the page is displayed, it looks like Figure 13-4.

Notice the Address line in the browser for this page. It looks like this:

```
http://localhost/classy/category.asp?Category=COMPUTERS
```

The information passed appears right on the URL, starting with the question mark. You access this information by using the Request object's QueryString collection. I discuss the QueryString collection in Chapter 7 in a section titled "Querying with QueryString". This page is a good example of passing and using QueryString arguments. Another alternative would have been creating a Session variable in one page, filling it with a value, and then accessing it from this page. I prefer using QueryString in situations like this for the same reason I prefer passing arguments to a function rather than simply accessing a global variable from each place. Passing arguments to a function is easier to keep track of, and you don't create more variables than you need.

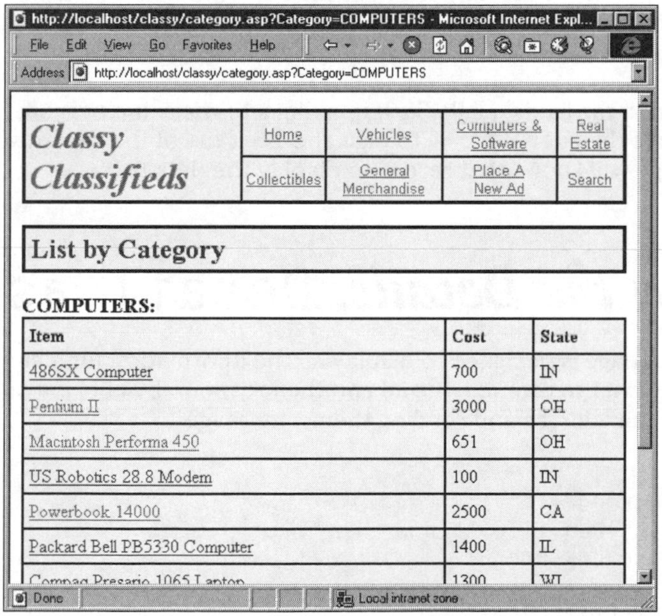

Figure 13-4: The Categories page listing Computers & Software ads.

But you may be confused at how the QueryString is accessed in the previous example because I don't even mention QueryString. You can access the elements of QueryString by using their names with the Request object, like this:

```
Category = Trim(Request("Category"))
```

You can also access information sent from a form in this way. As long as data isn't in both the QueryString and the Form collections that have the same name, you won't have a problem. If you do have a conflict, you must refer to each collection specifically to get the information you want.

After I identify the category (and make sure that one was, in fact, specified), I open the database. For this application to work, you must have a DSN named ClassDSN created that points to the database named classdb.mdb, included on the CD-ROM in the back of this book, or at least a database that has an Items table and the same fields I have in my Items table. For more information on creating a DSN, see the section titled "YAMA: Yet Another Mysterious Acronym — Creating an ODBC DSN" in Chapter 10. For more information on connecting to a database, see "Connecting to a Database" in Chapter 10.

Finally, I create a SELECT statement that pulls the information I need from the database and then I display it in a table.

This view isn't intended to display all the information for each ad. It just gives the visitor enough to interest them in getting more. You may choose to display different fields here for your application. You may, for instance, want to actually show whatever portion of the description fits on a line. For more information on retrieving data into a Recordset and displaying it in a table, see "From the Database to the Web Page" in Chapter 10.

Each item in the list is a link. Each item links to the same page: Detail.asp. Again, I use the QueryString to pass the ItemNum of the record so that the Detail page will know what record to display the details for.

Displaying the Details: Detail.asp

The Detail page is designed to display all the information for a single ad. This allows the user to examine the ad and then respond by clicking on the advertiser's e-mail address and sending them a message.

```
<HTML>
<BODY bgcolor="#FFFFFF" vlink=red>
<!-- #include file="header.inc" -->
<% ShowHeader("Detail") %>
<%
Dim Connect, Classifieds, ItemNum
Set Connect = Server.CreateObject("ADODB.Connection")
Connect.Open "ClassDSN"
ItemNum = Trim(Request("Item"))
```

```
If ItemNum = "" Then
 Response.Write "No Item Number was sent.<p>"
Else
 Set Classifieds = Connect.Execute(_
 "SELECT * FROM Items WHERE ItemNum=" & ItemNum)
 ShowItem Classifieds("Item"),Classifieds("Description"),_
  Classifieds("Price"),Classifieds("Phone"),_
  Classifieds("Email"),Classifieds("State"),_
  Classifieds("Posted")
%>
<i>To respond to this ad, just click on the email
address above and send a message.</i><p>
If you created this ad, you can...<br>
<a href="confirm.asp?
ItemNum=<%=Classifieds("ItemNum")%>&Operation=EDIT">
Edit it</a> or<br>
<a href="confirm.asp?
ItemNum=<%=Classifieds ("ItemNum")%>&Operation=DEL">
Delete it<p>
<% End If %>
</BODY>
</HTML>
```

After verifying that an `ItemNum` was sent, a query retrieves the record. The `ShowItem` subroutine in `Header.inc` is used to display the ad (see Figure 13-5).

I added links at the bottom of the page that allow the original creator of the ad to edit or delete the ad. These are the only links to the Edit and Delete pages in the application.

But notice that they don't actually link to the `EditAd.asp` and `DelAd.asp` pages. Instead, they link to a page called `Confirm.asp`. The Confirm page, which I discuss in the following section, is where I verify that the user is, in fact, the person who created this ad.

I pass the `ItemNum` to the Confirm page. In addition, I pass a variable called `Operation`, which I assign either the value `EDIT` or `DEL` depending on which the user wants to do. I use this `Operation` variable in `Confirm.asp` to determine which page to call next.

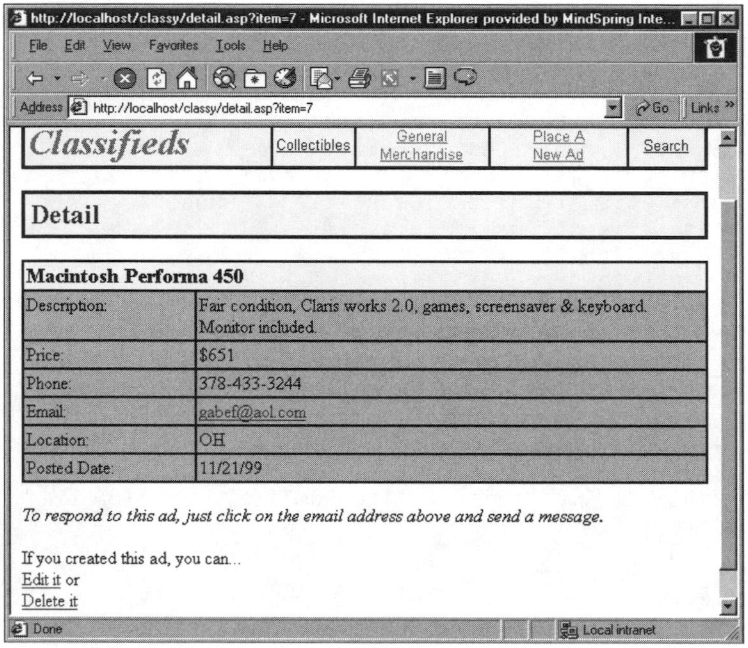

Figure 13-5:
The Ad
details.

Confirming the User: `Confirm.asp`

The user enters a password when he places an ad. Now, when he wants to edit or delete an ad, I have to confirm that he is the right person. The Confirm page asks the user to enter the password he used when he created the ad to prove who he is.

```
<% Option Explicit %>
<% Response.Buffer = True %>
<!-- #include virtual="common/adovbs.inc" -->
<HTML>
<body bgcolor="#FFFFFF" vlink=red>
<!-- #include file="header.inc" --><p>
<%
' The first time this page is retrieved and any time it is
' submitted without being completely filled out, the form
' is displayed. If it is submitted and completely
' filled out the form is processed in the Else clause.
If Request("Password")="" Then
%>
<% ShowHeader "Confirmation" %>
Please enter the password you used when you
created your ad.<p>
```

```
<form method="POST"
action="confirm.asp?ItemNum=<%=Request("ItemNum")%>&
Operation=<%=Request("Operation")%>">
<table>
<tr><td>Password:</td>
<td><input type="password" size="50" name="Password">
</td>
</tr>
<tr><td><input type="submit"
value="Enter Password"></td></tr>
</table>
</form>
<% Else %>
<%
Dim Query, Connect, Classifieds, Place
ShowHeader "Confirmation"
On Error Resume Next
Set Connect = Server.CreateObject("ADODB.Connection")
Connect.Open "ClassDSN"
Set Classifieds = Server.CreateObject("ADODB.Recordset")
Query = "SELECT ItemNum,Password FROM Items " & _
 "WHERE ItemNum=" & Request("ItemNum")
Classifieds.Open Query,Connect
If Classifieds ("Password") = Request("Password") Then
 If Request("Operation") = "EDIT" Then
 Response.Redirect "editad.asp?ItemNum=" & _
  Request("ItemNum")
 ElseIf Request("Operation") = "DEL" Then
 Response.Redirect "delad.asp?ItemNum=" & _
  Request("ItemNum")
 Else
 Response.Write(_
  "Internal Error. No valid Operation sent.<p>")
 End If
Else
 Response.Write(_
  "Invalid password. Click Back to try again.<p>")
End If
If Err.Number <> 0 Then %>
There was an error in confirmation.<p>
Error #<%=Err.Number%>: <%=Err.Description%><p>
<% End If %>
<% End If %>
</BODY>
</HTML>
```

A simple form gets the password from the user (see Figure 13-6).

The Recordset retrieves the password from the database and compares it to what the user entered. If the user entered something different, he is told to click Back and try again. I have not placed any limit on the number of times he can retry.

Figure 13-6:
The confirmation form.

If the passwords match, then Response.Redirect calls up either EditAd.asp or the DelAd.asp, depending on the value in Operation. Either way, the ItemNum of the record is passed.

TIP

By the way, if you want to edit or delete any of the records that are already in the database, the password for all the records is pickle.

Editing an Ad: EditAd.asp

The EditAd page looks very similar to the PlaceAd page. In fact, I used PlaceAd as my starting point for creating EditAd.

```
<% Option Explicit %>
<!-- #include virtual="common/adovbs.inc" -->
<HTML>
<BODY bgcolor="#FFFFFF" vlink=red>
<!-- #include file="header.inc"--><p>
```

```
<%
' The first time this page is retrieved and any time it is
' submitted without being completely filled out, the form
' is displayed. If it is submitted and completely filled
' out the form is processed in the Else clause.
If Request("Item")="" Or Request("Description")="" Or _
 Request("Price")="" Or Request("Phone")="" Or _
 Request("Email")="" Or Request("State")="" Then
Dim Connect,Classifieds
Set Connect = Server.CreateObject("ADODB.Connection")
Connect.Open "ClassDSN"
Set Classifieds = Connect.Execute(_
 "SELECT * FROM Items WHERE ItemNum=" & _
 Request("ItemNum"))
%>
<% ShowHeader "Edit An Ad" %>
Edit any of the entries you like. Make sure each entry
has a valid value before you click the Make
Changes button.<p>
<form method="POST"
action="editad.asp?ItemNum=<%=Request("ItemNum")%>">
<table>
<tr><td>Item:</td>
<td><input type="text" size="50" name="Item"
value="<%=Classifieds("Item")%>"></td></tr>
<tr>
<td valign=top>
Description:
</td>
<td>
<textarea name="Description" rows="6" cols="50">
<%=Classifieds("Description")%>
</textarea>
</td></tr>
<tr><td>Category:</td>
<% If Classifieds("Category") = "VEHICLES" Then %>
<td> <select name="Category" size="1">
<option selected value="VEHICLES">Vehicles</option>
<option value="COMPUTERS">Computers/Software</option>
<option value="REALESTATE">Real Estate</option>
<option value="COLLECTIBLES">Collectibles</option>
<option value="GENERAL">General Merchandise</option>
</select></td>
<% ElseIf Classifieds("Category") = "COMPUTERS" Then %>
<td> <select name="Category" size="1">
<option value="VEHICLES">Vehicles</option>
<option selected
value="COMPUTERS">Computers/Software</option>
<option value="REALESTATE">Real Estate</option>
<option value="COLLECTIBLES">Collectibles</option>
<option value="GENERAL">General Merchandise</option>
```

```
</select></td>
<% ElseIf Classifieds("Category") = "REALESTATE" Then %>
<td> <select name="Category" size="1">
<option value="VEHICLES">Vehicles</option>
<option value="COMPUTERS">Computers/Software</option>
<option selected value="REALESTATE">Real Estate</option>
<option value="COLLECTIBLES">Collectibles</option>
<option value="GENERAL">General Merchandise</option>
</select></td>
<% ElseIf Classifieds("Category") = "COLLECTIBLES" Then %>
<td> <select name="Category" size="1">
<option value="VEHICLES">Vehicles</option>
<option value="COMPUTERS">Computers/Software</option>
<option value="REALESTATE">Real Estate</option>
<option selected
value="COLLECTIBLES">Collectibles</option>
<option value="GENERAL">General Merchandise</option>
</select></td>
<% ElseIf Classifieds("Category") = "GENERAL" Then %>
<td> <select name="Category" size="1">
<option value="VEHICLES">Vehicles</option>
<option value="COMPUTERS">Computers/Software</option>
<option value="REALESTATE">Real Estate</option>
<option value="COLLECTIBLES">Collectibles</option>
<option selected value="GENERAL">
General Merchandise</option>
</select></td>
<% End If %>
</tr>
<tr><td>Price:</td>
<td><input type="text" size="10" name="Price"
value="<%=Classifieds("Price")%>">
</td>
</tr>
<tr><td>Phone</td>
<td><input type="text" size="15" name="Phone"
value="<%=Classifieds("Phone")%>">
</td>
</tr>
<tr><td>Email:</td>
<td><input type="text" size="50" name="Email"
value="<%=Classifieds("Email")%>">
</td>
</tr>
<tr><td>State:</td>
<td><input type="text" size="2" name="State"
value="<%=Classifieds("State")%>">
</td>
</tr>
<tr><td><input type="submit" value="Make
Changes"></td></tr>
```

```
</table>
</form>
<% Else %>
<%
Dim Query, Place
ShowHeader "Edit An Ad"
'On Error Resume Next
%>
<font size=5><b>CATEGORY: <%=Request("Category")%>
</b></font>
<%
ShowItem Request("Item"),Request("Description"),_
 Request("Price"),Request("Phone"),Request("Email"),_
 Request("State"),Date
Set Connect = Server.CreateObject("ADODB.Connection")
Connect.Open "ClassDSN"
Set Classifieds = Server.CreateObject("ADODB.Recordset")
Query = "SELECT * FROM Items WHERE ItemNum=" & _
 Request("ItemNum")
Classifieds.Open Query,Connect,adOpenDynamic,_
    adLockOptimistic
Classifieds("Item") = Request("Item")
Classifieds("Category") = Request("Category")
Classifieds("Description") = Request("Description")
Classifieds("Price") = Request("Price")
Classifieds("Phone") = Request("Phone")
Classifieds("Email") = Request("Email")
Classifieds("State") = Request("State")
Classifieds("Posted") = Date
Classifieds.Update
If Err.Number = 0 Then %>
<font size=5><i>Your classified ad has been
            updated.</i></font><p>
<a href="default.asp">Home</a><p>
<% Else %>
There was an error updating your ad.<p>
Error #<%=Err.Number%>: <%=Err.Description%><p>
<% End If %>
<% End If %>
</BODY>
</HTML>
```

Before the form is displayed, the record is retrieved so that the current values of the record can be defaulted into the form after it appears. Usually this is as simple as setting the value attribute of the input tag.

However, in the case of the select/option tags that are used to create the drop-down list box, I had to create a big If..Then..ElseIf structure and list out all the possibilities because the only way to specify the default value is to put the word selected in the option tag that you want to be the default (see Figure 13-7).

After the form is submitted, a `Recordset` holding only the one record is opened for updating and the information in the form is put into the record. `Update` then sends the changed record to the database. For more information on updating information in the database, see "Editing and updating rows" in Chapter 11.

The final error checking is the same as what I used in PlaceAd.

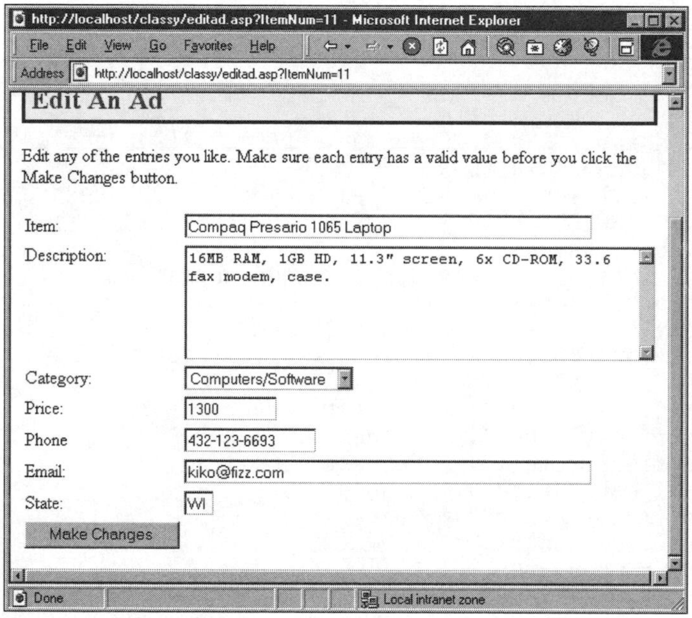

Figure 13-7:
The EditAd form with original ad's data defaulted in the form.

Deleting an Ad: `DelAd.asp`

Deleting an ad is much simpler than editing one.

```
<% Option Explicit %>
<!-- #include virtual="common/adovbs.inc" -->
<HTML>
<BODY bgcolor="#FFFFFF" vlink=red>
<!-- #include file="header.inc" --><p>
<%
' The first time this page is retrieved and any time it is
' submitted without being completely filled out, the form
' is displayed. If it is submitted and completely
' filled out the form is processed in the Else clause.
```

```
Dim Classifieds
If Trim(Request("Delete"))<>"DELETE" Then
 ShowHeader "Delete An Ad"
 Set Connect = Server.CreateObject("ADODB.Connection")
 Connect.Open "ClassDSN"
 Set Classifieds = Server.CreateObject("ADODB.Recordset")
 Classifieds.Open _
    "SELECT * FROM Items WHERE ItemNum=" & _
    Request("ItemNum"),Connect
 ShowItem Classifieds("Item"),Classifieds("Description"),_
    Classifieds("Price"),Classifieds("Phone"),_
    Classifieds("Email"),Classifieds("State"),_
    Classifieds("Posted")
%>
If you are sure you want to delete this record, type
the word DELETE in the edit below and click the Delete
Record button to confirm.<p>
<form method="POST"
action="delad.asp?ItemNum=<%=Request("ItemNum")%>">
<table>
<tr><td>Type DELETE:</td>
<td><input type="text" size="50" name="Delete"></td></tr>
</tr>
<tr><td><input type="submit"
value="Delete Record"></td></tr>
</table>
</form>
<% Else %>
<%
 Dim Query, Connect, Place
 ShowHeader "Delete An Ad"
 'On Error Resume Next
 Set Connect = Server.CreateObject("ADODB.Connection")
 Connect.Open "ClassDSN"
 Set Classifieds = Server.CreateObject("ADODB.Recordset")
 Query = "SELECT * FROM Items WHERE ItemNum=" & _
 Request("ItemNum")
 Classifieds.Open Query,Connect,adOpenDynamic,_
    adLockOptimistic
 Classifieds.Delete
 If Err.Number = 0 Then %>
<font size=5><i>Your classified ad has been
deleted.</i></font><p>
<a href="default.asp">Home</a><p>
<% Else %>
There was an error deleting your ad.<p>
Error #<%=Err.Number%>: <%=Err.Description%><p>
<% End If %>
<% End If %>
</BODY>
</HTML>
```

I do force the user to verify that he wants to delete the ad by actually typing the word DELETE into an edit before deleting the ad (see Figure 13-8).

This is done just to make it a bit more difficult to delete an ad. It makes the user think about it before he does it. If you think this step is excessive, you can just have users click a button that's labeled Yes, I'm Sure.

Just as I do in the EditAd page, a one-record, updateable Recordset is opened. Then the Delete method is called. For more information on deleting records, see "Deleting records" in Chapter 11.

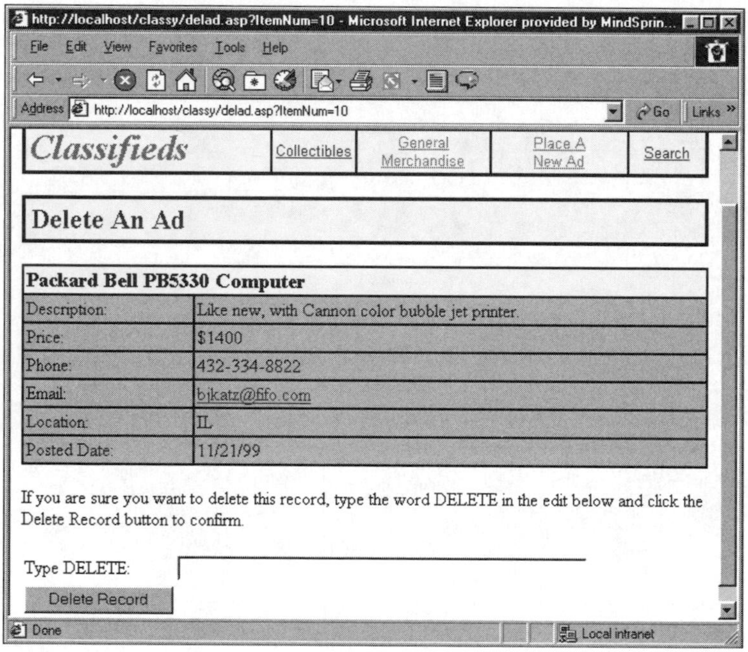

Figure 13-8:
The
DeleteAd
form
confirms
that the user
wants to
delete
the ad.

Searching for Ads: Search.asp

I didn't combine the form and the form-handler for the search page, although there's no reason I couldn't have. The form portion doesn't really present any surprises.

```
<HTML>
<BODY bgcolor="#FFFFFF" vlink=red>
<!-- #include file="header.inc" --><p>
<% ShowHeader "Search Page" %>
<form method="POST" action="results.asp">
<table>
<tr><td>Item:</td>
<td><input type="text" size="30" name="Item"></td></tr>
<td>Description:</td>
<td><input type="text" size="30"
name="Description"></td></tr>
<tr><td>Category:</td>
<td> <select name="Category" size="1">
<option selected value="">Any</option>
<option value="VEHICLES">Vehicles</option>
<option value="COMPUTERS">Computers/Software</option>
<option value="REALESTATE">Real Estate</option>
<option value="COLLECTIBLES">Collectibles</option>
<option value="GENERAL">General Merchandise</option>
</select></td></tr>
<td>State:</td>
<td><input type="text" size="2" name="State"></td></tr>
<tr><td>Price:</td>
<td>From:<input type="text" size="10" name="PriceFrom">
To:<input type="text" size="10" name="PriceTo"></td>
</tr>
<tr><td><input type="submit" value="Search"></td></tr>
</table>
</form>
</BODY>
</HTML>
```

I put the form in a table to line up the columns and make it look nice (see Figure 13-9).

Notice the addition of Any as an option for Category. A drop-down list box always forces you to choose one of the options or go with the default. You can't just leave it blank like you do with the other controls. So I added Any in case you didn't want Category to determine your search results.

Displaying the Results of a Search: Results.asp

The Results page is different from any of the other pages in this application. It is, however, a good template for a search results page in almost any database application.

```
<% Response.Buffer = True %>
<HTML>
<BODY bgcolor="#FFFFFF" vlink=red>
<!-- #include file="header.inc" -->
<% ShowHeader "Search Results" %>
<%
Dim Connect, Classifieds, WhereClause, Query, Item
Dim Descript, Category, State, PriceFrom, PriceTo
Dim NoResults
Set Connect = Server.CreateObject("ADODB.Connection")
Connect.Open "ClassDSN"
' Get the form information in local variables
Item = Trim(Request("Item"))
Descript = Trim(Request("Description"))
Category = Trim(Request("Category"))
State = Trim(Request("State"))
PriceFrom = Trim(Request("PriceFrom"))
```

```
PriceTo = Trim(Request("PriceTo"))
' If they only entered a category, go to the category page
If Item = "" And Descript = "" And Category <> "" And _
 State = "" And PriceFrom = "" And PriceTo = "" Then
 Response.Redirect "category.asp?Category=" & Category
End If
WhereClause = "WHERE "
If Item <> "" Then
 WhereClause = WhereClause & "InStr(Item,'" & _
 Item & "')>0 AND "
End If
If Descript <> "" Then
 WhereClause = WhereClause & "InStr(Description,'" & _
 Descript & "')>0 AND "
End If
If Category <> "" Then
 WhereClause = WhereClause & "Category = '" & _
 Category & "' AND "
End If
If State <> "" Then
 WhereClause = WhereClause & "State = '" &_
 State & "' AND "
End If
If PriceFrom = "" And PriceTo <> "" Then
 PriceFrom = "0"
ElseIf PriceFrom <> "" And PriceTo = "" Then
 PriceTo = "9999999"
End If
If PriceFrom <> "" And PriceTo <> "" Then
 WhereClause = WhereClause & "Price >= " & _
 PriceFrom & " AND Price <= " & _
 PriceTo & " AND "
End If
If Right(WhereClause,4) = "AND " Then
 WhereClause = Left(WhereClause, Len(WhereClause) -4)
 Query = "SELECT * FROM Items " & WhereClause
 Set Classifieds = Connect.Execute(Query) %>
<table border=1 bgcolor=yellow width=100%
bordercolor=Black cellspacing=0 cellpadding=5>
<%
NoResults = True
Do While Not Classifieds.EOF
 NoResults = False%>

<tr>
<td>
<a href=detail.asp?item=<%=Classifieds("ItemNum")%>
<%=Classifieds("Item")%></a></td>
<td><%=Classifieds("Price")%></td>
<td><%=Classifieds("State")%></td>
</tr>
```

```
<%
 Classifieds.MoveNext
Loop
%>
</table>
<%
 If NoResults = True Then %>
Sorry, no records in the database matched your
search parameters. Click Back and try again.<p>
<%
End If
Else
' They didn't enter any selection criteria
Response.Write "You didn't enter any search parameters. "
Response.Write "Please click the Back button and try "
Response.Write "again."
End If
%>
</BODY>
</HTML>
```

First I put all the information I receive from the form into local variables. This makes it easier to refer to them again and again in If..Then statements as I do on this page. The code also executes faster when working with local variables.

Next I check to see if any of the fields passed were empty. If so, I use Response.Redirect to display the forms page again.

The largest portion of this page is dedicated to If..Then statements that build the WHERE clause that I use in the SELECT statement at the bottom of the page. If they specified a value, I add that to the WHERE clause. If they didn't, I don't. The only one that works a little differently is Price. I allowed the user to specify a low and a high price and I use those values to search for something in between. If the user specified one but not the other, I assume 0 for the low value and I assume 9,999,999 for the high value. After I'm done adding to the WHERE clause, I check to be sure the last four characters are "AND ". If they aren't, that means nothing was added to the WHERE clause because nothing was specified. In theory, this should never happen because I check to make sure that they're not all empty at the top. Nonetheless, I display an error message if it happens. Assuming the last four characters are "AND ", the last four characters are removed and the final SELECT statement is created and then executed. The resulting Recordset records are displayed in a table (see Figure 13-10). I use the variable NoResults to be sure records were, in fact, displayed. If none were displayed, I display a message instead to let the user know that no records met his criteria.

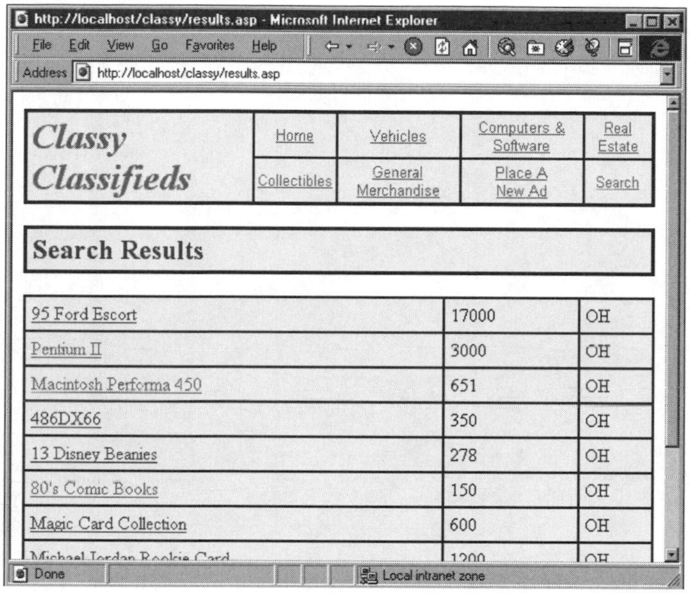

Figure 13-10:
The search
results.

As with the Category page, each item is a link to the Detail page which displays all the details about the item.

Making It Better

Classy Classifieds provides a great foundation for all sorts of interesting possibilities. Here are some of the thoughts I had for extending it:

- ✔ **Add error checking anywhere database operations are done.** Also, if information is passed using QueryString, always verify not only that you received information but that the information was valid (as much as you can). To keep the code simple, I didn't implement as much error checking as you will want to for your Web site.

- ✔ **Change the categories so that they are specialized for topics related to your Web site.**

- ✔ **Change the fields stored in the database so that they are more appropriate for your categories.** For example, a site for buying and selling automobiles may have fields like Make, Model, Year, and so on.

- ✔ **Change the fields stored as well as the look and feel of the site to create a Personals Web site where single people can place ads to meet others.**

- ✔ **Visit other classifieds Web sites to get more ideas.** Classifieds 2000 at www.classifieds2000.com is a great place to start.

Part VI
The Part of Tens

The 5th Wave By Rich Tennant

IF BOB DYLAN HAD PURSUED A CAREER IN COMPUTERS

"He's a genius integrating databases into his Active Server Pages, but don't ask him to explain it, you won't understand a word he says."

In this part . . .

Where do you go for help when you have a problem with an ASP page that you are creating? What if you just want to learn more about a particular topic? What does it take to be an ASP guru? All these questions and more are answered in these chapters. In addition, you discover ten new things server components can do to make your ASP development life easier and make you look like a hero!

Chapter 14

The Ten Best Places to Look When You Have a Question

. . . .

In This Chapter

▶ Books and manuals
▶ Magazines and newsletters
▶ List servers and newsgroups
▶ Tech support and other nerds

. . . .

*Y*ou've got a killer idea for a new Web application. You've designed your masterpiece and already started developing it. Then you hit a snag — a *big* one. You can't really go on until you get an answer to the problem that's tripped you up. Whom do you turn to? What do you do?

This chapter gives you ten answers to that question. Only one of them has to work to get you back on track. Good luck!

RTFM: Read the Flippin' Manual!

You may be surprised by all the information they've put in those books and help files that came with your web server. So *use* them!

Check the online help first. Searching for and finding the online help you need is easier and usually much faster than flipping through the index of a huge manual.

Both IIS and PWS come with a complete hierarchy of topics related to ASP, server components, VBScript, JScript, and ADO. Online help should always be your first stop if you have a question.

Books

In this book you get a good introduction to all the topics you need to get started with ASP. But no single book can cover everything. If you're looking for a book that hits some more advanced topics, check out *ASP: Active Server Pages* by Andrew M. Fedorchek and David K. Rensin (IDG Books Worldwide, Inc.). If you run into problems that aren't specifically ASP-related, a whole bunch of books are available that could help you. Among them are:

- ✔ *HTML 4 For Dummies,* by Ed Tittel and Stephen N. James
- ✔ *Java Programming For Dummies,* 3rd Edition, by Donald J. Koosis and David Koosis
- ✔ *VBScript For Dummies,* by John Walkenbach
- ✔ *Visual Basic 6 For Dummies,* by Wallace Wang

Magazines and Newsletters

An excellent resource of source code and articles on a broad variety of Microsoft Web development technologies is a technical journal called *ActiveWeb Developer*, published by Pinnacle Publishing. Edited by yours-truly, this journal picks up where this book leaves off and dives into real-world development with both feet. You can find out more information about it at

```
www.pinpub.com
```

Another periodical that focuses on Microsoft Web development is *Microsoft Internet Developer*. Although this magazine has the Microsoft name all over the front cover, it is not published by Microsoft. Instead, the magazine is put out by Fawcette Technical Publications and covers a variety of topics. The Cobb Group (which is now owned by Ziff-Davis) publishes a lot of newsletters on a variety of computer topics. Its *Active Server Developer's Journal* provides many introductory articles on Active Server Pages, VBScript, and database issues.

Newsgroups

Newsgroups are like bulletin boards where you can go and post a message and come back in a day or two to find replies and help from others around the world. They are a great peer-support option. To access newsgroups, you must have a newsgroup reader. The one that comes with Microsoft Internet Explorer is called Outlook Express. Microsoft hosts a number of newsgroups at the server.

```
news://msnews.microsoft.com
```

Point your news reader to that server and then subscribe to these newsgroups:

```
microsoft.public.inetserver.asp.components
microsoft.public.inetserver.asp.db
microsoft.public.inetserver.asp.general
microsoft.public.inetserver.iis
microsoft.public.jp.vinterdev
microsoft.public.scripting.jscript
microsoft.public.scripting.vbscript
microsoft.public.vi.debugging
microsoft.public.vi.dtc
microsoft.public.vi.general
microsoft.public.vi.setup
```

Another newsgroup server hosts the aspDeveloper newsgroup. Here's the address for that one:

```
news://news.extencia.com/aspDeveloper
```

List Servers

A List Server is similar to a newsgroup, but you don't use a special reader to access it. Instead, all the messages are sent via email to a central server that compiles them and then sends them back out again to everyone who is a member of the List Server. Some are set up so that you immediately receive a message whenever it is posted. Others compile the messages so that you receive one long email with all the messages in it for that day. Although a List Server is a little more primitive and a little more cumbersome to use, it is still very popular and a great way of getting and sharing information on a topic. Microsoft also supports one List Server on Active Server Pages. To join it, send e-mail to

```
LISTSERV@LISTSERV.15SECONDS.COM
```

Don't put anything in the Subject line. Put this text in the message:

```
SUBSCRIBE ActiveServerPages Your Name
```

Replace Your Name with your name.

Interested in finding more Listserv's? You can find a whole slew of them listed at this Web page:

```
www.asplists.com/asplists
```

Online Forums and Web Sites

You can get information, downloadable components, answers to common questions, and all kinds of other stuff from the online forums and Web sites that are available. CompuServe is a great resource for all sorts of developers. The forum that is most likely to cover topics like Active Server Pages, server components, and Visual InterDev is the Internet Publishing Forum. To get there, simply type:

```
Go INETPUB
```

See Chapter 15 for all the Web surfing information you need to get started.

Microsoft Web Technical Support

Microsoft provides online access to the same documents and source material that the telephone technical support people use. So, chances are, if you're persistent, you can get information using this Web site that's as helpful as you would if you called the telephone support line. And the Web site is free! Just go to

```
support.microsoft.com/support/c.asp
```

First you select the product your question is about from a drop-down list box. `Active Server Pages` is in the list, as are `ActiveX Data Objects (ADO)`, `Internet Explorer`, `Internet Information Server`, `Visual InterDev` and many, many more. Next, type in your question in plain English. It presents a list of articles that it thinks match your question. If you aren't getting any hits or you're getting hits for the wrong kind of thing, rewording the question or using different terms often helps.

Microsoft Telephone Support

Telephone support has a bad reputation — and for good reasons. Most people's experience with tech support includes busy signals or long periods of time spent listening to unpleasant music while waiting for someone to help. And even when you do get through to a real live human, they often don't know as much about the product as you do! So the best they can do is search their database and read to you off the screen what they found. This can be frustrating. But it's doubly frustrating if they turn around and charge you between $30 and $100 a call for the privilege! Having said all of that, I do have to say that my experience with Microsoft technical support has been much better than average. But it certainly isn't free. For issues associated with NT, IIS, or Web application development, you can expect a per-call charge in the $80 range. I'd recommend thoroughly checking into other options before choosing this one.

ASP Nerds

You often see them in their native habitat — surrounded by computers, computer parts, and books and manuals stacked to the ceiling. Programming nerds are hard to miss. If you have an ASP programming nerd near you, I strongly suggest that you strike up a relationship with this person. Your time will be well spent, because these ASP nerds can be your best resource for quick answers and explanations. If your nerd needs a little encouragement to share his prized information, you'll find that Jolt cola, pizza, and Chee-tos work best. But no matter how you add it up, it's cheaper than a call to telephone tech support.

User Groups

If you don't have your own nerd handy, you have to go where they hang out — user groups. A user group is a place where computer people who are into a particular technology can come together and share their knowledge. You may not find an ASP user group in your area, but you probably will find a Windows NT user group and maybe an Internet developer's group where you can meet people who can help.

Chapter 15

The Ten Coolest Web Sites for ASP Developers

*T*he Web is a great place to browse, but it isn't exactly the best place to go when you are looking for something specific — unless you already know where to look. Between wading through the random results you get from search engines and the recommended links on sites that you find, you eventually can tell the fool's gold from the real stuff. But that effort takes precious time you may not have.

I've included this chapter to save some of that time for you. I've already done all the footwork and come up with the best sites on the Web. Isn't it odd that I found exactly ten?

The EdgeQuest Active Web Site

This is my Web site. It has informative articles, examples, free downloads, links, and a complete site dedicated to this book. Check it out!

```
www.edgequest.com/ActiveWeb
```

ActiveServerPages.com

Links to articles on other sites organized by topic, news, and a very complete list of components available on other sites.

```
www.activeserverpages.com
```

15 Seconds

A Web-zine for developers working with IIS, ISAPI, and ASP. You can also sign up for an e-mail newsletter that is sent out periodically.

```
www.15seconds.com
```

The Official Microsoft SiteBuilder Network

This is the official site of Microsoft for Web developers using Microsoft technologies. Always a great resource for original, authoritative articles, new component downloads from Microsoft and other companies, plus a whole lot more.

```
www.msdn.microsoft.com/default.asp
```

The ASP Toolbox

This site contains literally hundreds of sample code and code snippets to solve your ASP problems! In addition, you find tutorials, tips, articles, and links.

```
www.tcp-ip.com
```

Windows NT ActiveX Server Bulletin Board

This site requires you to fill out some information about yourself before you log in the first time and then requires you to log in again each time you come back. In return for your trouble, you are given access to over a dozen newsgroup-like forums that work inside your web browser. Topics include ASP, ADO, IIS, commercial Web sites, VBScript, and Visual InterDev. Also included are several FAQs and links to other sites.

```
www.activexserver.com/BBS1/login.asp
```

The ASP Hole

Despite the unpleasant name, this site is well-designed and offers articles, book reviews, and rated downloads to support your ASP development efforts.

```
www.asphole.com/asphole/default.asp
```

The ASP Resource Index

An excellent resource for finding code examples, reviews, tutorials, and a lot more on the Web.

```
www.aspin.com/index/default.asp
```

ASP 101

A great site for tutorials, plus it has sample code and more.

```
www.asp101.com/home/home.asp
```

A Lot More Links

Looking for even more ASP sites? They're out there. Your resources on the Web are nearly endless. For more links check out the Links section on almost every single one of the pages listed above. A particularly good list of links appears here:

```
www.activeserverpages.com/genusa
```

Chapter 16

Ten Interesting Things That Server Components Can Do for You

In This Chapter

▶ Sending and receiving e-mail

▶ Implementing security

▶ Making money through Internet commerce

▶ Charting and reporting database information

Server components can be created to do anything you can imagine. In Chapter 9, I describe the components that come with IIS and PWS. But those components are just the beginning of the possibilities. In this chapter I reveal ten more really cool things server components can do for you, and then I tell you where you can find components that do those things. Many of the components are free or at least have free evaluation versions. Some of them are even included on the CD in the back of this book!

Make It Easy to Send and Receive E-Mail from ASP

Wouldn't it be great to notify visitors to your site by e-mail when new information is added to your Web site? Or let them know when you put an item on sale that they said they were interested in? You have many, many reasons to use e-mail with your ASP pages. E-mail can keep your users informed and a part of your Web community. And, as you may expect, a number of server components make it easy for you.

Zaks.Pop3

By: Simon Fell/Zak Solutions

Status: Freeware.

Written in Java. Reads Pop3 e-mail accounts. Version 2 supports MIME encoding, attachments, and better performance. For more information, see

```
www.zaks.demon.co.uk/code/cpts/pop/index.html
```

Mail Components

By: ServerObjects Inc.

Status: Evaluation versions. The cost of full versions vary with product and number of licenses purchased at once.

ServerObjects Inc. provides a number of powerful components to do a variety of e-mail tasks, including:

- ✔ **ASPMail:** Enables you to send SMTP e-mail from ASP. Supports: multiple attachments by using MIME and UUEncoding, PGP, priority, urgent, and custom mail headers, and much more. Used in more ASP installations than any other commercial or free product.
- ✔ **ASPQMail:** Queues e-mail messages so your ASP scripts don't have to wait for the mail to be sent before resuming execution.
- ✔ **ASPPOP3:** Lets you to retrieve mail from a POP3 server and delete messages.
- ✔ **ASPNNTP:** Sends and retrieves articles from a newsgroup server. Supports attachments and PGP.

For more information or to download evaluation versions of these components, see

```
www.serverobjects.com/products.htm
```

xPop3 and xSMTP

By: JE Software

Status: Evaluation version. Full versions cost $49 each.

xPop3 enables you to check and retrieve e-mail and xSMTP makes it possible to send new e-mail messages — all from your ASP scripts. Both handle ISO 8859-1 characters (Swedish characters for example) and are easy to use. For more information or to download an evaluation version, see

```
www.algonet.se/~jekman/components.htm
```

Security

Security is high on everyone's list of concerns on the Internet. But if you want to create a site that only allows certain people in or one that charges for admission, it's essential that you have some sure way to verify that someone is who he says he is. These components help you do just that.

ASPLogin

By: OceanTek

Status: Freeware. (ASP Login Pro adds additional features and costs $39.95)

Provides basic security for a set of ASP pages on your Web site. Does not use Windows NT user database, but stores its information in any ODBC data source. When a user tries to access a protected page, he is prompted for his user ID and password. If the user enters valid information, he can access all protected pages. Otherwise, he is locked out. Requires you to add a single server-side include at the top of each protected page. For more information or to download, see

```
www.oceantek.com/asplogin
```

AuthentiX

By: Flicks Software

Status: Evaluation version. Full version is $299.

Protects premium content directories or individual files by requiring users to enter a user ID and password. Does not use Windows NT password database. ODBC validation. For more information or to download an evaluation version see

```
www.flicks.com/flicks/authx.htm
```

Managing Files

File uploading and downloading is an essential part of a dynamic online community. These tools make that process easier.

SA-FileUp

By: Software Artisans

Status: Evaluation version. Purchase full version for $129.

Component designed to make it easy to upload files to the Web server from the user's browser through a form. Follows RFC 1876. Good documentation. Supports Secure Sockets Layer.

Seamless integration with Visual InterDev. For more information, see

www.softartisans.com/softartisans/saf.html

AspInet 2.0

By: ServerObjects, Inc.

Status: Freeware.

Lets you use FTP to remotely GET and PUT files from your ASP scripts. For more information or to download this component, see

www.serverobjects.com/products.htm#AspInet

Execute Applications from ASP

Execute Windows and DOS applications from your ASP pages!

ASPExec 3.0

By: ServerObjects Inc.

Status: Freeware.

Executes either DOS or Windows applications from your ASP scripts. You can receive the results of a DOS program that outputs to standard I/O as a string. An optional time-out setting can determine how long to wait for an application to complete. For more information, check out

```
www.serverobjects.com/products.htm#Aspexec
```

Make Money with Internet Commerce

Internet commerce is a fancy word that means selling stuff on the Web. They say there's a gold mine out there to be had, so now is the time to stake your claim! And these server components can get you started.

PCAuthorize

By: Tellan Software, Inc.

Status: Demo. Full version is $79.

Enables you to authorize credit transactions. Supports all major credit card types, batch transactions, detailed reporting and more. For information and an evaluation version of the Tellan Software PC Authorize, go to

```
www.tellan.com
```

A$PCharge

By: BlueSquirrel

Status: Demo. Full version is $299.95.

Enables you to accept credit card information for a service (like iBill, CyberCash, and so on) or acts as an interface to ICVerify, which is the software that allows you to accept credit cards yourself (in which case you must have a merchant account with each credit card you accept). Check out

```
www.bluesquirrel.com/products/asp/asp.html
```

Access Information on Your UNIX, AS/400, or Mainframe Computer

Aside from client/server databases, probably the biggest demand for information is from mini and mainframe computers. That's because they've been used for so many years to store and maintain information. These products will help you get that information to your intranet or the Internet to be viewed with a Web browser.

Cyberprise Developer Studio

By: Wall Data Incorporated

Status: For pricing, call 800-817-8001, x5605

Allows you to create a Web interface to access host data on the backend from AS/400 and IBM mainframe, VAX, and Unix applications. Integrates with Visual InterDev and Visual Basic. For more information, see

```
www.cyberprise.com
```

TeleSCOPE Elara

By: Metascybe Systems, Ltd.

Status: For pricing, call +44 (0)181-544 0100

Creates Web applications that can present data from mainframe or UNIX systems. Provides real-time access to legacy data and even creates Web applications that integrate data from a variety of data sources, including legacy systems. Integrates well with IIS and ASP. For more information, go to

```
www.metascybe.co.uk
```

Charting and Reporting

These tools make charting and reporting much easier.

Chart FX Internet Edition

By: Software FX, Inc.

Status: Trial version. Full version is $699.

Creates fully interactive charts by using both client and server-side component technology. Retrieves information by using ADO from any ODBC-compliant database to automated data population. For more information, see

```
www.softwarefx.com/cfxie/default.asp
```

Chili!Reports Enterprise Edition

By: Chili!Soft

Status: 30-day trial version. For pricing, call 888-290-8346, ext. 21.

This product allows you to design and deliver reports from any ODBC data source through an Internet or intranet Web page. Includes Visual InterDev design-time controls. For more information, go to

```
www.chilisoft.net
```

AspChart 2.0

By: ServerObjects Inc.

Status: Evaluation version. Full version is $69.95.

Professional looking charts are created on the fly in JPG or BMP formats and downloaded as a simple image. Supports 3-D charts, pie, bar, area graphs, and a variety of other charting features. For more information, go to

```
www.serverobjects.com/products.htm#AspChart
```

Accept Database Queries in English

What good is all that data in the database if the people who need it can't get to it? And why do you have to write a custom application to access the data for every question the user wants to ask of the database? With the English Wizard, you don't have to. Just give the user a line in which to type his question, and this Wizard turns the question into a complex SQL statement that returns just the information he wants to see. Now *this* is the information revolution!

English Wizard Web/Server

By: Linguistic Technology Corporation

Status: Demo. Call 800-425-8200 for pricing.

This tool allows users to request information from a database by using normal English sentences. It translates English questions into Structured Query Language (SQL), accesses any ODBC-compatible database, and dynamically formats results in HTML. For more information, see

```
jackson.englishwizard.com/engwiz98
```

Browsing from the Server

Give these tools a try!

xBrowser

By: JE Software

Status: Evaluation version. Purchase full versions for $49 each.

xBrowser is a minimal Web browser built as a server component. You can create content on your pages by using the content of pages you access through this browser. For more information, go to

```
www.algonet.se/~jekman/components.htm#xBrowser
```

ASPHTTP

By: ServerObjects, Inc.

Status: Evaluation version. Full version is $49.95.

Pass a URL and receive the page retrieved as a string. You can then use this string to customize the information on your ASP pages. For more information or to download an evaluation copy, see

```
www.serverobjects.com/products.htm#Asphttp
```

Other Interesting Stuff

There's really no end to the creative ideas for useful server components. Here are some of the interesting ones that didn't fit neatly into any other category.

AspBible Bible Component

By: ServerObjects Inc.

Status: Freeware.

Use this component to easily access specific Bible passages and then use them in your ASP pages. For more information or to download an evaluation copy, go to

```
www.serverobjects.com/products.htm#Bible
```

Strings Component

By: Tarsus

Status: 30-day evaluation version. Full version is $39.00.

Provides a tremendous number of string functions to supplement VBScript's and JScript's string handling capabilities. Supports filtering out HTML tags, filtering out specific text (such as profanity), and formatting strings for SQL or for use as dates, times, or numbers. Validates credit card numbers and e-mail addresses, converts numbers into words (for example, "one hundred fifty-two"), and much more. For more information, go to

```
www.tarsus.com/asp/ts
```

AspPager

By: ServerObjects, Inc.

Status: Evaluation version. Full version is $69.95.

Enables you to page and send alphabetic and numeric messages to someone. Uses the industry standard TAP protocol. For more information or to download an evaluation copy, see

```
www.serverobjects.com/products.htm#pager
```

Part VII
Appendixes

The 5th Wave   By Rich Tennant

"We're researching Active Server Page applications that move massive amounts of information across binary pathways that interact
with free-agent programs capable of making
decisions and performing logical tasks. We
see applications in really high-end doorbells."

In this part . . .

There are five appendixes:

Appendix A describes Visual InterDev, the Microsoft development environment for Web site developers. Visual InterDev brings together many of the tools you use to create Web applications into one cohesive environment.

Appendixes B and C are designed to be used with Chapter 10. If you haven't worked with a relational database before, Appendix B is a good place to start. It introduces you to the essential concepts and gives you a shove off in the right direction. Read this before you read Chapter 10. Appendix C provides step-by-step directions for using Access to create a new database, to create a new table, and to fill that table with records. Use this appendix if you want to walk through the process of creating your own database for the application described in Chapter 10.

Appendix D gives you tips and hints that help you troubleshoot common problems with your ASP pages. If you're feeling frustrated, this appendix may just help you out.

Appendix E tells you all about the great software included on the CD-ROM. Not only can you find all my applications from the book, but also some very cool applications, tools, components, and utilities to make ASP easier than ever!

Appendix A

Introducing Microsoft Visual InterDev

· ·

*A*ctive Server Pages is a technology that is built into both Internet Information Server and Personal Web Server. You can design ASP pages using anything from a high-end, expensive HTML editor, all the way down to the lowly Notepad. But if you want an editor designed for HTML, ASP scripting, server components, and all the rest, you'll have a tough time beating Microsoft Visual InterDev.

This appendix is a brief introduction to Microsoft Visual InterDev. Currently in version 6.0, this development environment is an integrated part of the Microsoft Visual Studio. Visual Studio is a single environment from which you can write Visual Basic, Visual C++, and Visual J++ applications in addition to Visual InterDev Web applications. You can purchase Visual InterDev separately or as a part of the complete Visual Studio.

If you're looking for a more in-depth guide to Visual InterDev, I happen to have just the book for you — *Visual InterDev For Dummies* by yours truly and published by IDG Books Worldwide, Inc., which is at your local bookstore just waiting for you to come in and pick it up.

Features of Visual InterDev and Why It Works So Well with ASP

Visual InterDev has the capability to create ASP pages that present information from the database, allow the user to change it, and then make the corresponding updates in the database — all automatically! I demonstrate exactly how that works in this chapter. This demonstration will give you a taste of what Visual InterDev can do. But, as impressive as Visual InterDev is, I only scratch the surface of what it has to offer.

If you are going to be a serious Active Server Pages programmer, you really owe it to yourself to give Visual InterDev a good look. Visual InterDev uses and adds to ASP's capabilities to create an environment where you can quickly create very powerful, dynamic, database-driven applications.

In addition to its support for ASP, Microsoft Visual InterDev provides tools for working with all kinds of exciting Microsoft client and server technologies. Here is a list of some of the many other technologies that Visual InterDev provides access to:

- Server-side database access through ADO and ODBC
- COM server components
- Client-side scripting
- ActiveX controls on the client

Visual InterDev offers a full-featured WYSIWYG HTML editor combined with a color-coded source-level editor and tools to make it easy to write both ASP and client-side scripts. But the strongest suit of Visual InterDev is its integration with any ODBC database. From high-power client/server DBMSs all the way down to Microsoft Access, the integration of database features is thorough and makes it easy to create a site that is completely data-driven and automatically updated as the information in the database changes.

How Visual InterDev Is Different from Microsoft FrontPage

Microsoft FrontPage is a user-level Web page development tool that Microsoft purchased and has been developing over the last year or two. It is a part of the Microsoft Office suite and is designed for the same audience as Microsoft Word and Excel.

Using Microsoft FrontPage, you can begin creating pages that include images, fonts, and colors — all without knowing any HTML. Even complex tables are a snap with its visual tools and wizards.

And although FrontPage allows you to go a long way toward creating a powerful Web site, it does have limitations. Although it allows access to the HTML tags and offers tools to help write ASP and client-side scripts, FrontPage isn't designed for creating large-scale, powerful, database-driven Web applications. That's where Visual InterDev comes in.

History of Visual InterDev

Visual InterDev began its life in the summer of 1995 (boy, weren't those the good ol' days?) in a very different form than it's in today, when Microsoft announced to everyone's astonishment that it would start its own dial-up computer service called The Microsoft Network (MSN). Immediately all the pundits started speculating that Microsoft may unceremoniously wipe out CompuServe and America Online in one fell swoop and dominate yet another segment of the computer industry. Was there no end to Bill Gates' lust for power, people wondered?

In retrospect, all that hype is pretty amusing. What made Bill Gates think he could topple two industry icons like CompuServe and America Online? Or that his online service would rival the Internet in popularity? The answer is simple: *dynamic content.* Bill Gates knew that if he could bring to online services the same sort of excitement and interactivity that people expected from the best in multimedia CD-ROM titles and games, he would have an extremely potent combination.

So, in addition to the dynamic content provided on MSN, Microsoft began a top-secret project code-named *Blackbird,* purported to be the development tool for the kind of online interactive multimedia content offered through MSN, and as the months rolled on, it became clearer and clearer that Microsoft was on the wrong track. It couldn't simply recreate the online world from the ground up with its own proprietary technologies — no matter how exciting they were. Even Bill Gates himself began to see the writing on the wall.

So it was at the end of 1995 and the beginning of 1996 that Bill Gates did his now-famous 180-degree turnaround. Microsoft would no longer work on proprietary technologies to compete with well-established Internet technologies. Instead, Microsoft would, in Gates' words "embrace and extend" the current Internet technology. But don't be confused — the vision never changed. The dream of online, interactive, multimedia content was still alive and well. Only the approach was different.

What happened to Blackbird? Well, the goal of the project changed, too. Instead of building on MSN's technology, the first release was a tool for developing Internet content. The code-name Blackbird was dropped at that point, and most in the industry referred to it from then until its release as "Internet Studio." Finally, it was dubbed *Microsoft Visual InterDev 1.0,* making it fit nicely into the Visual Studio family of development environments along with Visual Basic, Visual C++, and Visual J++.

In early 1999, when the latest release of Visual Studio came out, the Visual InterDev version number made a big leap — from 1.0 to 6.0. This was done to bring the version number of all the Visual Studio products in line. But with the big version number jump came a correspondingly large jump in functionality. Now designed to look, feel, and work much like Visual Basic, Visual InterDev has become a coherent, easy-to-use development tool with features that are tough to beat.

Visual InterDev offers most of the same features that FrontPage offers. But Visual InterDev is designed for the software developer. Visual InterDev has less hand-holding and requires more of a scripting/programming background than FrontPage does. But it also provides the tools for quickly creating much more powerful applications than FrontPage can.

So what's the difference? Although you can do many of the same things in both, FrontPage is designed for users with no programming or HTML background at all. Visual InterDev requires some programming background but offers a lot of power in return.

Come on Baby, Do the Local Mode-tion (Or the Master Mode)

You have two different modes to choose from when you set up:

- ✔ **Local mode:** If you're working on a development machine that accesses a web server on a different machine (a typical setup), then you should choose to work in Local mode.

  In Local mode, Visual InterDev creates a copy of the files for the project you're working on locally so that you can easily open and edit them. The server files are only updated when you request it.

- ✔ **Master mode:** If, however, you are working on the web server machine itself or are using Personal Web Server on your workstation, you may want to choose Master mode.

  In Master mode, you manipulate the files directly, and any changes you save are automatically made to the files on the web server itself.

You can work in Master mode even if your machine isn't the web server, but if you do, be very careful!

Projects can be created from scratch, which automatically creates the corresponding Web application on the web server. Projects can also be created to attach to an existing Web application. You define all this when you create a project. The New Project dialog box appears when you first launch Visual InterDev. You can access it anytime from within InterDev by choosing File➪New Project.

The Solution

You may have a variety of projects, but usually you tend to work on certain groups of them together because they are used together on your site. To make working on multiple projects at once easy, Visual InterDev uses the concept of a *solution*.

A solution is nothing more than a collection of projects you want to be able to work on at the same time. Although you can have only one solution open at a time, you can have any number of projects in your solution. And the same project can be a part of more than one solution.

Before You Start

If you own Visual InterDev, this quick step-by-step tutorial shows you how to get started creating applications with it. I walk you through the process of creating a Phone List and show you how to view database data in a Web page, modify the data, and even add new rows. Although I cover only a few of the many features of InterDev in this section, the following information should be enough to give you a sense of what's possible and how InterDev is structured.

- ✔ FrontPage Server Extensions
- ✔ Data Access Components
- ✔ Visual InterDev Server Components

These server components are on the Visual InterDev install CD.

Creating the Phone List Project and Solution

In this section, you create the project and solution for your phone list.

1. **Open Visual InterDev. The New Project dialog box immediately appears (see Figure A-1). (If the Visual InterDev primary window is displayed and the New Project dialog box doesn't appear, choose File⇨New Project to make it appear.)**

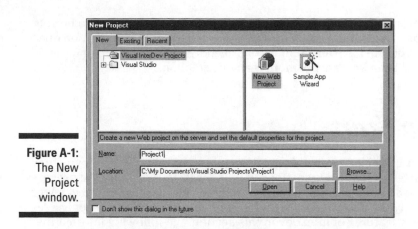

Figure A-1:
The New
Project
window.

2. **Enter the name** PhoneList **and click Open.**

3. **The Web Project Wizard Step 1 window appears (see Figure A-2).**

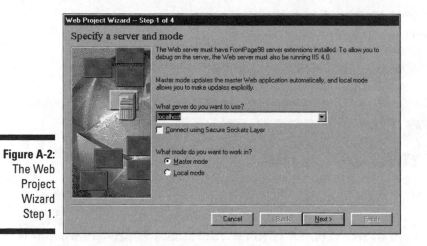

Figure A-2:
The Web
Project
Wizard
Step 1.

4. **The first question is** What server do you want to use? **If you're accessing a web server on your own machine, you can just enter** localhost. **If you're accessing a server on your network, enter that server's name. If you are accessing a server over the Internet, enter the Web address (without the** http://).

5. **For the mode, select** Local mode **unless the web server is running on your local machine.**

6. **Click Next.**

7. **A dialog box appears, indicating that Visual InterDev is attempting to contact the server. If it fails, make sure your server name is correct.**

8. **The Web Project Wizard Step 2 window appears (Figure A-3).**

9. **The first question you have to answer is whether you want to create a new Web application on the server or simply connect to an existing one. You want to create a new application, so select the first radio button.**

10. **The name for the new Web application defaults to the name you gave the project. Usually you want to keep it that way.**

11. **Click Next.**

12. **Web Project Wizard Step 3 and Step 4 enable you to pick a layout and a theme for your site. You can always add this later, so I recommend you usually choose ⟨none⟩ for both.**

13. **Click Next and then click Finish.**

14. **A dialog box indicates that Visual InterDev is Creating New Web Project and Copying Script Files among other things.**

15. **Finally, the main Visual InterDev screen is presented (see Figure A-4).**

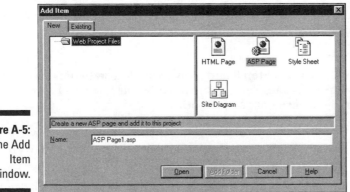

16. **From the primary menu at the top of the window, choose Project⇨Add Web Item⇨Active Server Page.**

17. **The Add Item dialog box appears (see Figure A-5).**

18. **Change the Name to** default.asp **and click Open.**

19. **The page opens in the center area of the primary window.**

Voilà, you're in! You've created a solution, a project, and a page to work on in your project.

Introducing the Visual InterDev User Interface

At first glance, the face Visual InterDev presents to the world is not necessarily so pretty. In fact, you may think it's downright intimidating. There are little windows and other doo-hickies everywhere. Makes you feel like a kid looking at the control panel of an airplane and being told, "Don't touch *anything*!"

But keep in mind that the interface was built for software developers. And people like that want to have every tool at their disposal right at their fingertips. Heaven forbid that they should have to click more than twice to get something done. So don't be overwhelmed. You don't have to fully understand how everything on the screen works to make use of the interface's tools. In fact, you can go along using Visual InterDev just fine for a long time without having any idea how some of its features work.

Just to help you keep your sanity, though, I take you on a brief tour of the highlights of the interface and at least describe some of the more important windows and doo-hickies as you see in Figure A-6:

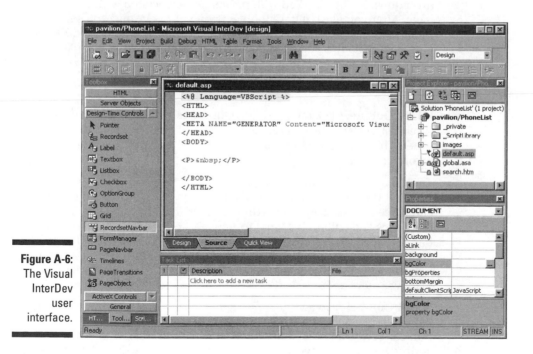

Figure A-6:
The Visual
InterDev
user
interface.

✔ **In the upper right corner you find the Project Explorer.**

The solution is at the top of the tree and each project in the solution appears below that. In this case, you have only one solution and one project, both named PhoneList.

Under the project are a series of folders and files that are a part of the project. Even though you haven't created anything yourself yet, you can see that Visual InterDev has created a _private folder, a _ScriptLibrary folder, and an images folder. You won't usually mess with the folders that have an underscore (_) at the beginning — these folders are for Visual InterDev to use. The images folder is just a place to put your image files so that they're out of the way.

In addition, a global.asa file and a search.htm page have also been generated. For more information about the global.asa file, see "The Global.asa File" in Chapter 7. The search.htm file is included to provide an easy way for users to search the pages in your site for the information they need. You don't have to use the page unless you want to.

✔ **Under the Project Explorer is the Properties window where you see a list of the properties and their values for the currently selected object.**

Right now the word DOCUMENT appears at the top of that list and the drop-down list box is filled with properties associated with the Web page. After you place different objects on your page and you select them, their properties will appear in the Properties dialog box. You can always scroll down and change whatever property value you like.

Down the left side of the window is a tabbed window — with the tabs at the bottom. The tabs are:

✔ **HTML Outline:** Click on the HTML Outline tab to see a detailed, structured list of all the tags in the document and how they relate to each other. This unique view of your HTML can often be helpful in identifying errors you've made.

✔ **Toolbox:** This is the tab you'll probably use most. It has several bars within it that allow you to choose all the different kinds of objects you can place on your page. Everything from HTML form objects (such as textboxes and Submit buttons) to ActiveX controls (such as a progress bar or calendar) to something called a Design-Time Control. Design-Time controls are very useful controls that come with Visual InterDev and make it easy to create database applications that you can update. You discover more about how they work later in this chapter.

✔ **Script Outline:** Also a very important tab, with Script Outline you find a list of all the client objects/events and scripts as well as the server objects/events and scripts. This view is used to track what objects and scripts are in your page already and it provides access to the objects' events so that you can write code to respond to them.

✔ **Task List:** Near the bottom of your screen, you may see a Task List. This is nothing more than a To Do list to help you remember all the programming tasks you need to do. The list can be quite handy. If you prefer to have the space to view your page, you can select the Task List and click the close box in the upper-right corner.

The Page Window

In the middle of all these little windows is the area where you edit your pages. You can have as many pages up as you like and each is represented by a different window. Each window has three tabs at the bottom:

✔ **Design:** This is the WYSIWYG view. If you add a table to your page, it looks in Design view much as it will in the final browser. But you can also modify how things look directly from this view. Design view is a very convenient place to work for visual thinkers.

✔ **Source:** Even visual thinkers have to drop down to the HTML tags and see what's *really* going on every now and then. Source view is a very handy color-coded editor that helps you understand what's going on.

✔ **QuickView:** This is nothing but the browser itself embedded in the window. You see exactly what your page will look like in the browser by using this view. If you prefer to *actually* see the page in a separate browser window, you can choose View⇨View in Browser. But keep in mind, if you are using ASP or server components in your page, none of those will appear in this view or in the separate browser window. These techniques simply open the page directly in the browser. I show you a bit later how to run your pages from the server so that your ASP code and server components can take part.

Using the Visual InterDev User Interface to Create a Phone List

To create the Phone List using theVisual InterDev user interface:

1. **Click the Design tab of the default.asp window.**

   A blank window appears.

2. **Click the Toolbox tab of the window along the left.**

3. **Click the Design-Time Controls bar in the Toolbox window.**

   You see a list of controls such as the ones shown in Figure A-7.

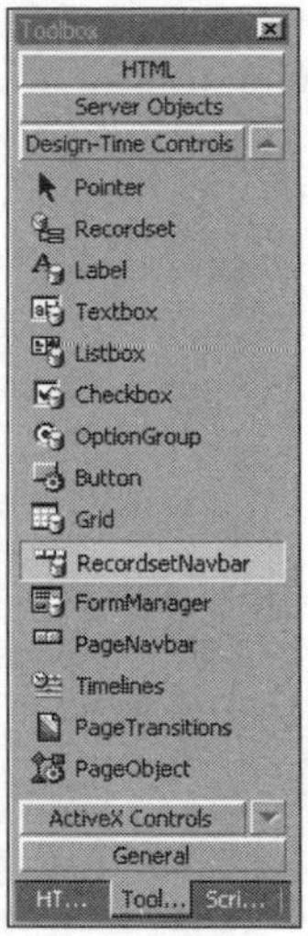

Figure A-7:
The Design-
Time
Controls
Toolbox.

4. Drag and drop a Label from the Toolbox into the upper-left corner of the window.

You see a dialog box such as the one shown in Figure A-8.

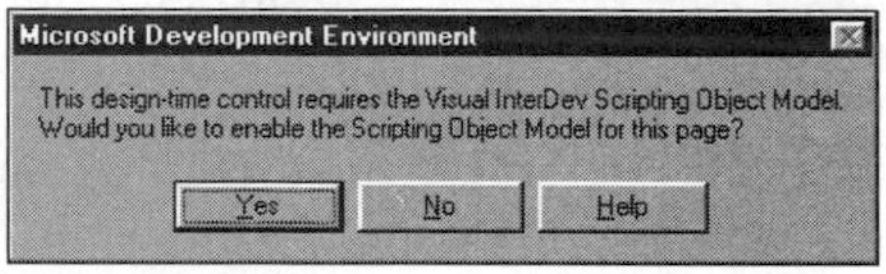

Figure A-8:
The
Scripting
Object
Model
dialog box.

The dialog box asks if you want to turn on the Scripting Object Model. The Scripting Object Model (SOM) is a technology built into Visual InterDev that makes these Design-Time Controls possible. But to use the controls, you must turn on SOM for the page.

5. Click Yes.

6. Click and drag a Textbox to the right of the Label (see Figure A-9).

7. Click to the right of the Textbox.

The cursor appears after it.

8. Press the Enter key a few times.

This creates some blank lines where you can put additional controls.

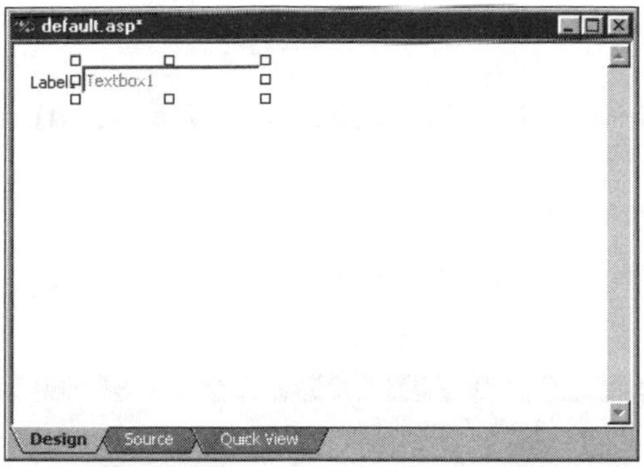

Figure A-9:
The Label
and the
Textbox.

9. **Drag another Label and Textbox under the first (see Figure A-10).**

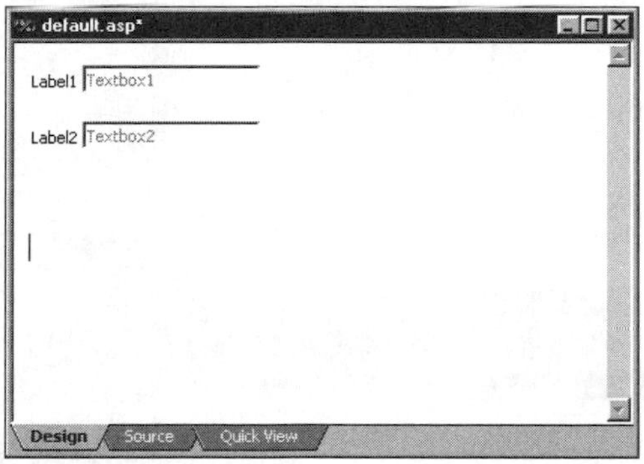

Figure A-10:
The second
Label and
the Textbox.

10. **Right-click on the top Label and choose Properties from the pop-up menu.**

   The Label Properties dialog box appears (see Figure A-11).

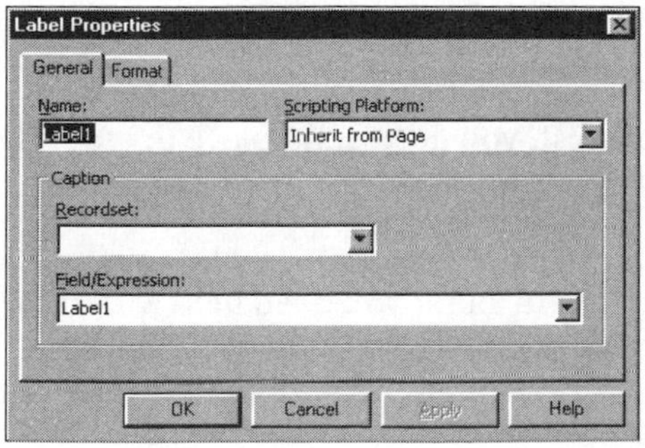

Figure A-11:
The Label
Properties
dialog box.

11. **In** `Field/Expression` **box at the bottom, first type** `Name:`, **and then click OK.**

12. **Right-click on the bottom Label and choose Properties from the pop-up menu.**

13. **Change Field/Expression to** `Phone:`

    Your page looks like Figure A-12 in the Design tab.

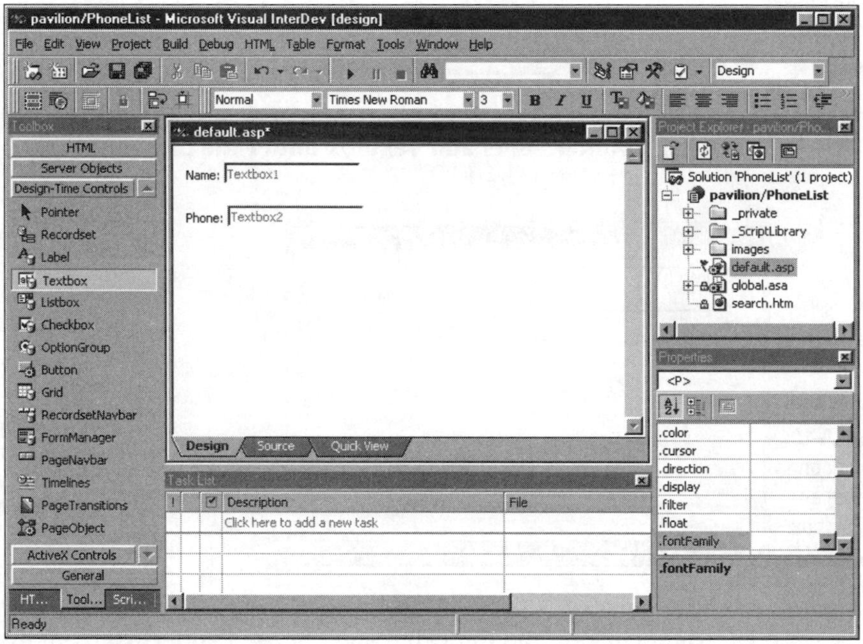

Figure A-12: Labels all filled in.

Creating a Database to Store Your Phone List

In order to create your phone list, you need someplace to store the names and numbers. A database is the easiest place to do that.

I'm not going to walk you through the detailed steps for creating a database and table in Microsoft Access here, but if you need help with these higher level steps, check out Appendix C, where all that cool stuff is covered.

To create a phone list using a database:

1. **Launch Microsoft Access.**

2. **Create a new database named** `phonelistdb.mdb` **and put it in a folder where you can find it again later.**

3. **Create a table with three columns: ID, which has an** *AutoNumber* **data type, Name, and Phone, which both have a** *Text* **data type.**

4. **Save the table and name it** `PhoneList`.

5. **Add at least three or four rows to the table including people you know and their phone numbers.**

Creating a DSN for Your Database

After the database is created and has some data stored, you're ready to tell Visual InterDev where to find it. First you create an ODBC DSN to hold the connection information. Then you create a Connection object in Visual InterDev to point your application in the right direction when it goes to find the data.

An ODBC DSN is a place where all the information needed to connect to your database is stored under a name. For more information on DSNs, see "YAMA: Yet Another Mysterious Acronym — Creating an ODBC DSN" in Chapter 10.

1. **Minimize Visual InterDev.**

2. **Click on the Start menu. Choose Settings⇨Control Panel and the Control Panel appears.**

3. **Double-click the ODBC icon (if you have more than one, click the 32-bit ODBC icon).**

4. **The ODBC Data Source Administrator dialog box appears.**

5. **Click the System DSN tab and then click the Add button.**

   The Create New Data Source dialog box appears (see Figure A-13).

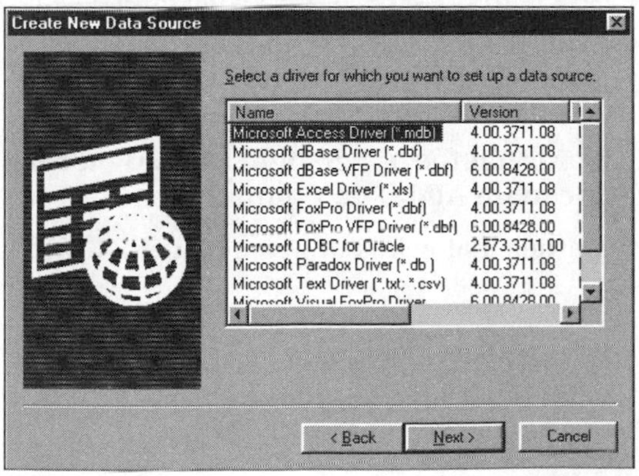

Figure A-13: Create New Data Source dialog box, with the Select a driver prompt.

6. **Choose the** Microsoft Access Driver (*.mdb) **from the drop-down list box and then click Finish.**

Now you're presented with the ODBC Microsoft Access Setup dialog box (see Figure A-14).

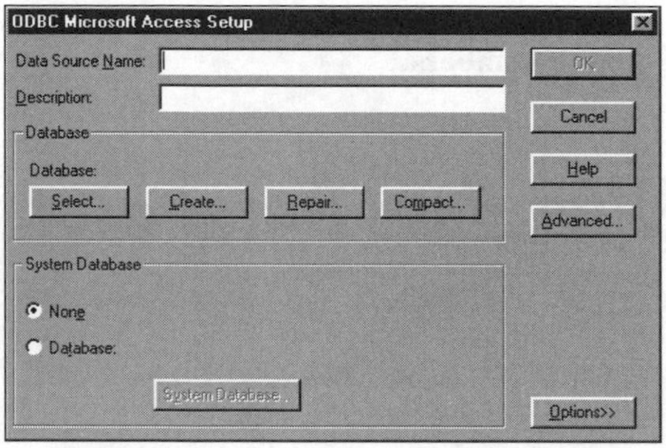

Figure A-14:
The ODBC
Microsoft
Access
Setup dialog
box.

7. **Click the Select button and then use the browse dialog box to find and select the .mdb file you created in the previous section.**

8. **Click in the Data Source Name textbox and type PhoneListDSN.**

9. **Click OK.**

The DSN is created for the database you chose and is given the name you specified.

Creating A Visual InterDev Connection Object

Now that you have a DSN created, you can tell Visual InterDev about it and then it can use the DSN whenever it needs to connect to the database.

1. **Restore Visual InterDev.**

2. **In the Project Explorer (on the upper-right side), right-click on the Global.asa file and choose Add Data Connection.**

The Data Link Properties dialog box appears (Figure A-15).

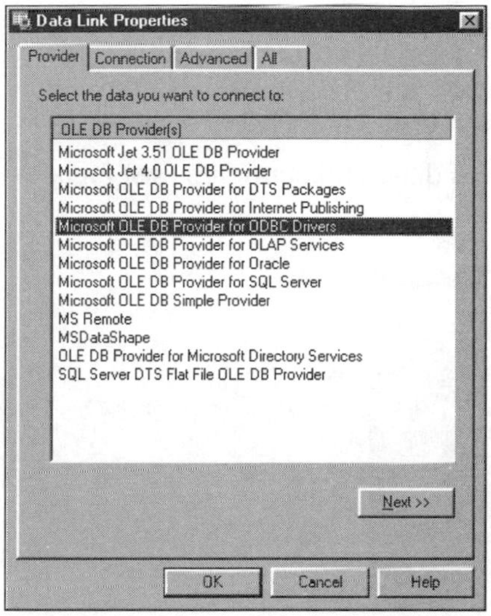

Figure A-15:
The Data
Link
Properties
dialog box.

3. **Select the provider named** Microsoft OLE DB Provider for ODBC Drivers **in the listbox. Click Next.**

   The Connection tab appears (Figure A-16).

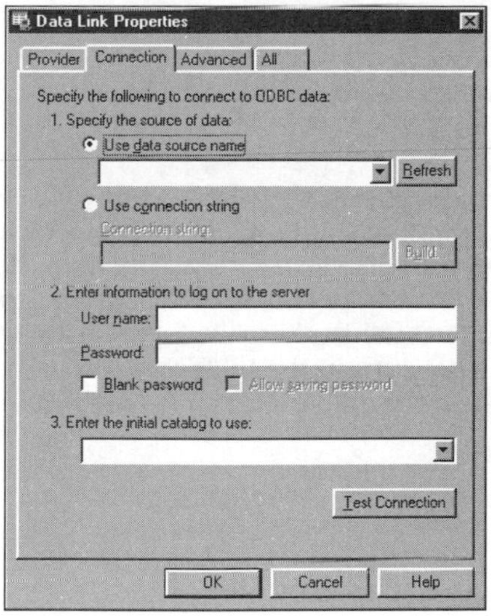

Figure A-16:
The
Connection
tab.

4. **The Use data source name radio button at the top of the dialog box should be selected. In the drop-down list box below, you should see the DSN it created in the last series of steps, with the name PhoneListDSN. Select it and then click OK.**

The Connection1 Properties dialog box appears (see Figure A-17).

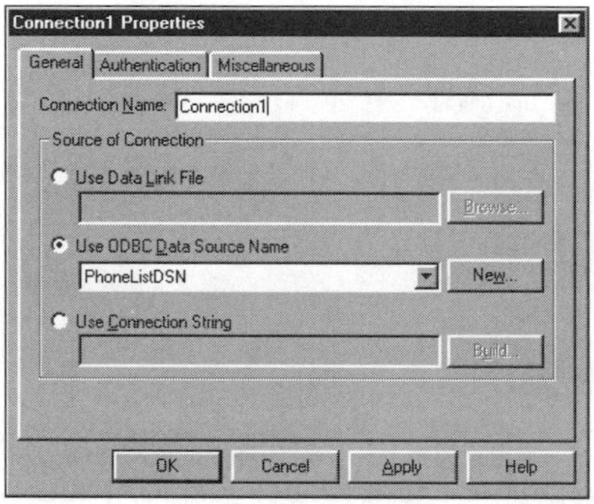

Figure A-17:
The
Connection1
Properties
dialog box.

5. **Type** `PhoneListCon` **in the Connection Name textbox at the top of the dialog box. Click OK.**

In the Project Explorer, under `global.asa`, you now have an entry named `DataEnvironment`. And under `DataEnvironment` is another entry named `PhoneListCon`. This is the connection object in Visual InterDev that points it to the right database.

If you look below the Project Explorer, you see a Data View window (instead of the Properties). This view shows the solution, all the projects, and all the data connections in each project. In this view, you can open up the `phonelistdb` and see two folders: `Tables` and `Views`. You can further open `Tables` to see the `PhoneList` table (shown in Figure A-18). You can open `PhoneList` to see the columns in the table and you can double-click on `PhoneList` to view and change the data in the table (see Figure A-19).

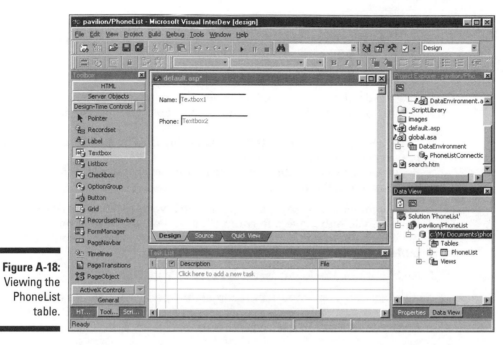

Figure A-18:
Viewing the
PhoneList
table.

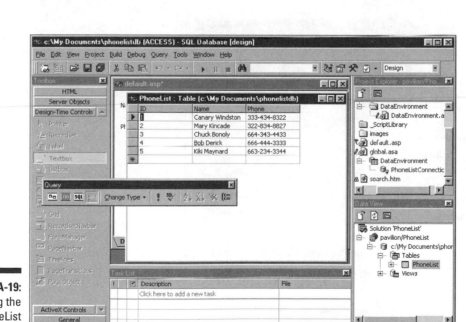

Figure A-19:
Opening the
PhoneList
table.

Connecting Your Database to Your Web Page

If you have a database, a DSN and a Connection object, and you have a page that is ready to display the data, all you have to do is connect them up!

1. **In the Design-Time Controls Toolbox (along the left side of the screen) the second item down is called a Recordset. Click and drag the Recordset on to the page (while leaving some space between the Textboxes and the Recordset).**

2. **The Recordset represents a query to retrieve data from the database. Because you only have one connection to a database with one table, the Recordset assumes that you want to pull information from that table. It fills in its properties automatically.**

3. **Right-click on the Recordset and choose Properties.**

   Although the most important recordset properties appear on the Recordset itself, additional properties are available from the Recordset Properties dialog box (see Figure A-20).

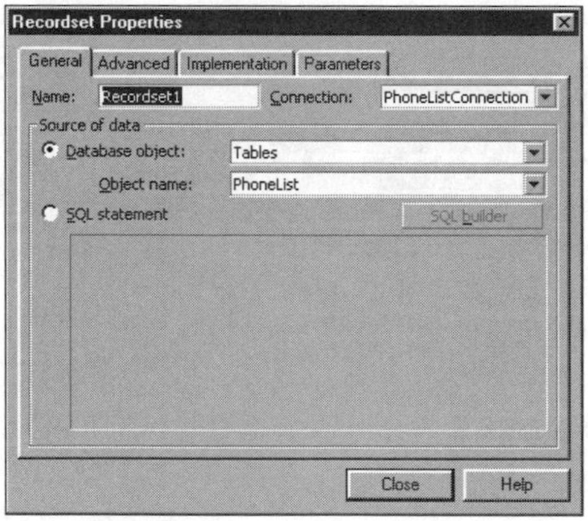

Figure A-20:
Recordset
Properties
dialog box.

4. **Look through the variety of properties available.**

   You don't need to understand them all, but it's handy to see what's there.

5. **Click Close without changing anything.**

6. **Right-click on the Textbox beside the Name label.**

7. **Choose Properties from the pop-up menu.**

8. **The Textbox Properties dialog box appears (see Figure A-21).**

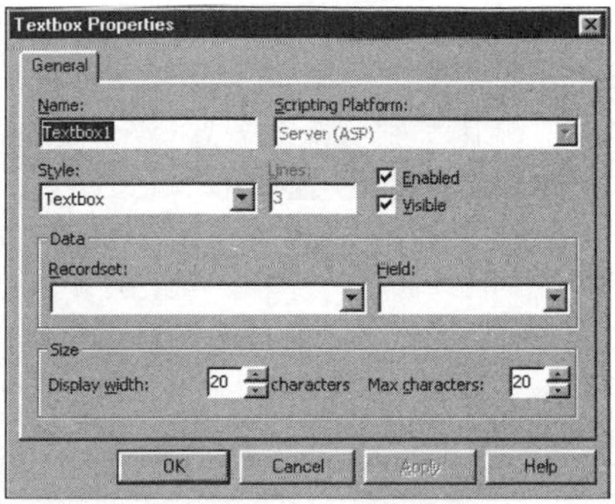

Figure A-21:
Textbox
Properties
dialog box.

9. **Use the Recordset drop-down list box to choose the only option —** Recordset1, **the name of the Recordset control you dropped on the page.**

10. **Use the Field drop-down list box to choose the Name field in the PhoneList table.**

11. **Click OK.**

12. **Right-click on the Textbox beside the Phone label and choose Properties from the pop-up menu. The Textbox Properties dialog box appears.**

13. **Use the Recordset drop-down list box again to choose the only option — Recordset1.**

14. **Use the Field drop-down list box to choose the Phone field in the PhoneList table.**

15. **Click OK.**

You just created a query in the form of a Recordset. It retrieves all the rows in the table PhoneList. Then you tied the Textbox controls to that Recordset and to a specific field in the query — the Name and Phone fields.

Now the page knows to display the name and phone data from the Recordset query in those Textboxes.

You have only one item left to add, a RecordsetNavbar:

1. **The Design-Time Control Toolbox, on the left side, has a control about halfway down the list named RecordsetNavbar. Click and drag the RecordsetNavbar control between the Textboxes and the Recordset control (see Figure A-22).**

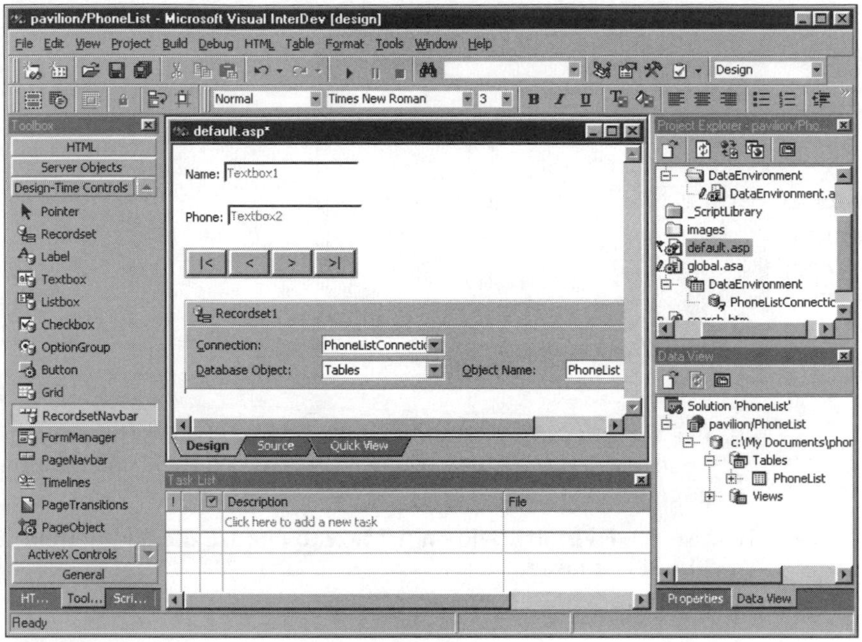

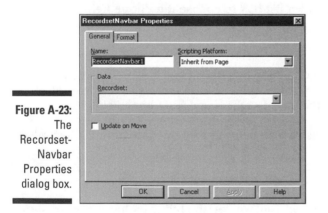

Figure A-22:
Recordset-
Navbar on
the page.

2. **Right-click on the RecordsetNavbar and choose Properties from the pop-up menu. The RecordsetNavbar Properties window appears (see Figure A-23).**

Figure A-23:
The
Recordset-
Navbar
Properties
dialog box.

3. **Use the Recordset drop-down list box to again choose the only option — Recordset1.**

4. **Select the Update on Move radio button.**

Update on Move is a handy little navigation bar that makes it easy to move to the first, previous, next, and last records retrieved.

5. **Click OK.**

Running Your Active PhoneList with Visual InterDev

After you've completed all you need to do to create the PhoneList application, all that's left to do is run it and test it.

1. **Right-click on the** `default.asp` **file in the Project Explorer window.**

2. **Select** `Set As Start Page` **from the pop-up menu.**

3. **Click the Start button on the button bar (it looks like the little right-facing triangle used with CD players to indicate *play*).**

4. **The window changes configuration and a browser window appears.**

Your labels and textboxes appear along with the navigation bar. You won't see the Recordset control, but you *will* see data in the textboxes! (See Figure A-24).

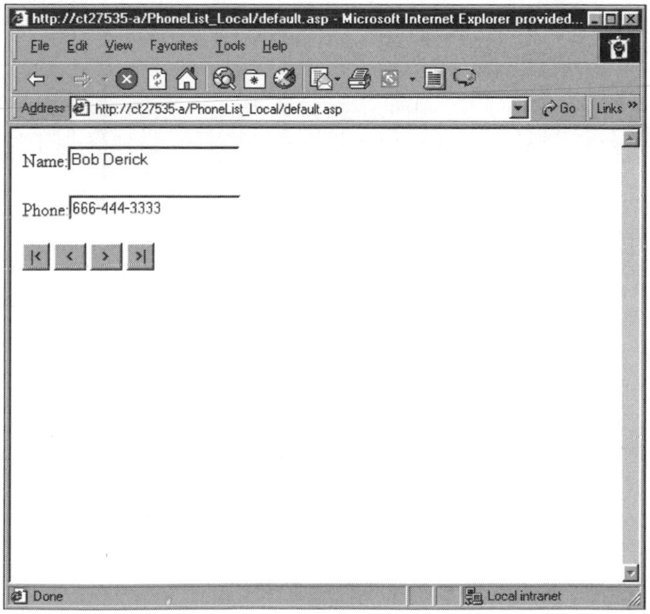

Figure A-24:
The
PhoneList
up and
running.

5. **Click the navigation bar controls to move around and see different records.**

   You may notice that your page makes a round trip to the server every time it displays a new record.

6. **Try changing one of the names — click forward and then click back.**

   Is the name still changed? It should be! Any changes you make are stored in the database. Try changing a phone number and you see it works the same way.

Appendix B

A Crash Course in Database Basics

In This Appendix

▶ Surveying databases, tables, columns, and rows

▶ Understanding primary keys and surrogate keys

▶ Creating relationships between tables

▶ Deciphering the SQL `SELECT` statement

*I*f you have worked with Access, Oracle, or other types of databases in the past, you probably already know what databases, tables, rows, columns, and `SELECT` statements are.

But, if you haven't worked with a database before and you don't recognize these terms, read on — this appendix brings you up to speed quickly on basic database concepts.

What's a DBMS? What's a Database?

A *database* is simply a place where you can store data. Although you use variables and arrays to store data in computer programs, that storage is only temporary. When you turn the computer off, all that data goes away. So you need someplace to store your data permanently. The first place computer programmers began storing information they needed to keep was in simple text files. I use a text file to store information entered for a Guest Book in Chapter 8 by using the `FileSystemObject` and `TextStream` scripting objects.

Text files are simple and straightforward. But when you start to get more data and the data becomes more complex, text files become cumbersome to work with and keep track of. And they slow your program down a lot, too.

So, programmers created a more structured way of storing data — the database. But in order to make this structure easy to use, databases usually come with a *Database Management System (DBMS)*. A DBMS is simply a piece of software that acts as a go-between. Your application asks for the data, the DBMS hears the request, goes out to the database, gets the data, and returns it to your program.

You can think of a DBMS as a full-service library. You go to the librarian and tell him or her what book you're looking for. The librarian goes out, looks through the shelves, finds the book you want, and brings it back to you. The librarian is the DBMS. The shelves and the structured system for storing books on the shelves are the database. The book is the piece of data you want. Without the librarian, you'd have to learn a lot about how the books are stored and where all the different shelves are located. With the librarian, all you have to do is ask for the book. DBMSs make life easy.

I draw this analogy so that you can see the difference between a *database* and a *DBMS*. Lots of people use the terms interchangeably, and this can get confusing sometimes.

DBMSs, like their associated databases, come in all sizes, shapes, and colors. They all support a basic set of features. Most of them support extended features (but these features work differently on each one). And then some features are supported by only one or two DBMSs. And, of course, they are all mostly incompatible with each other.

Because of this incompatibility, most people buy a DBMS from one vendor and stick with it. A variety of DBMSs are on the market:

- ✔ Microsoft Access
- ✔ Microsoft SQL Server
- ✔ Oracle
- ✔ Sybase SQL Server
- ✔ Sybase SQL Anywhere
- ✔ DB/2
- ✔ Informix

And many, many others are available, too.

The information I discuss in this appendix is true for all *relational* DBMSs. Older types of DBMSs (called *hierarchical* and *network* DBMSs) that work differently are out there, but they are old technology, and you don't have to worry about them. Relational databases are used for almost all new development today. And all the DBMSs I mention are *relational* DBMSs.

Tables, Rows, and Columns

A relational DBMS stores data in *tables*. You can think of a table as a grid with rows and columns like you may find in a spreadsheet such as Lotus 1-2-3 or Microsoft Excel. (Although a spreadsheet isn't the same thing as a database, the grids that spreadsheets use are a good way to picture tables.)

The *columns,* also called *fields,* represent different pieces of information that you want to store. For example, an Employee table may have columns like Name, Address, Phone, Position, Department, and so on.

The *rows*, also called *records*, represent one item in the table — a single employee, for instance, in the Employee table. A row has a value for each column. Here's what an Employee table with three employees in it looks like:

Name	*Address*	*Phone*	*Position*	*Department*
Simon	101 Main	334-2323	Manager	Marketing
Kelly	2222 W. 103rd	662-3233	Representative	Marketing
Fred	1411 E. 21st	443-2323	Editor	Acquisitions

The first row isn't really a part of the table. It's just there to tell you the name of each column. As you can see, each row holds the information about one employee and each column describes one aspect of an employee.

Primary Keys and Surrogate Keys

In every table you create, you always need to identify a *primary key*. A primary key is a column (or set of columns) that points out what is unique about each row. For instance, in the table in the last section, you could make Name the primary key. The only problem with making Name the primary key is that if you tried to enter a new employee's record, who also happened to be named Fred, you would get an error. You can't have two records that have the exact same value in their primary key. The computer needs to know how to identify each row individually.

Perhaps Phone or Address would be a better primary key for this table. But then what if you have both a husband and wife working for you? Those identifiers wouldn't work either. Of course, you can say that the primary key is the Name *and* the Phone or the Name, Phone *and* Address, but that begins to get cumbersome.

One solution to the problem of finding a good key is just to make one up. In this case, you can call the new column EmployeeID. It would just be a meaningless number that uniquely identifies each row.

Employee ID	Name	Address	Phone	Position	Department
1000	Simon	101 Main	334-2323	Manager	Marketing
1001	Kelly	2222 W. 103rd	662-3233	Representative	Marketing
1002	Fred	1411 E. 21st	443-2323	Editor	Acquisitions

The meaningless number created just so you can have a unique key is often called a *surrogate key*. And just like a surrogate mother, this key *stands in for* or *substitutes for* the more cumbersome key. This situation happens so often that many DBMSs have the ability to generate surrogate keys automatically for you. It just starts with a number and adds one for each new record you enter. For example, Microsoft Access calls it *AutoNumber* — and you just choose that data type for your field when you create a table.

Relationships between Tables

When you are putting together an application, you may have a number of different tables to hold your data. Take a look at these two tables, for instance.

The Book Table

Title	Author	Publisher
Macs For Dummies	Pogue	IDG
PCs For Dummies	Gookin	IDG
The Internet For Dummies	Levine	IDG

The Author Table

Name	E-mail	Phone
Pogue	pogue@beet.com	342-555-3222
Gookin	gookin@fleet.com	432-555-3399
Levine	levine@meet.com	883-555-0322

Now suppose that you want to present data from these two tables at the same time. Suppose you want to see all the books, authors, and author e-mail addresses in one report. (By the way, the authors' e-mail and phone numbers are imaginary here — but the books are real!) How do you do it? By *joining* the two tables. Joining doesn't mean physically putting the two tables together. It just means taking a column that they both have in common and using that to present the right data from both tables.

In this case, the column these two tables have in common is the author's name. The final report would look like this:

Macs For Dummies	Pogue	pogue@aol.com
PCs For Dummies	Gookin	gookin@fleet.com
The Internet For Dummies	Levine	levine@meet.com

Speaking Database-ese: SQL

Almost all DBMSs allow you to communicate with them using a common language called the Structured Query Language (SQL, often pronounced *sequel*). SQL is a very simple language, and I only introduce you to one of its commands. The only command you really need to know is SELECT.

SELECT allows you to retrieve data from tables in a database. A typical SELECT statement may look like this:

```
SELECT Name, Phone
FROM Employee
WHERE Department = "Marketing"
ORDER BY Name
```

The SELECT statement has four parts:

- The SELECT clause identifies all the columns that will be retrieved from the database.
- The FROM clause tells the DBMS the tables where it can find those columns.
- The WHERE clause sets some condition, usually to narrow the search so that you don't get all the records sent back to you.
- The ORDER BY clause sorts the rows returned by the column specified. You can specify more than one column, if you want.

If the preceding SELECT statement were executed against the Employee table presented in the section "Tables, Rows, and Columns" earlier in this chapter, the result would look like this:

Simon   334-2323

Kelly   662-3233

There are only two names because Simon and Kelly were the only ones in the Marketing department.

You can also use the SELECT statement to get information from more than one table by joining them, as I discuss in the last section of this appendix. Look back at the two tables, "Book" and "Author," described in the last section. Which SELECT statement do I have to use to join those two tables and get the result I did there?

```
SELECT Title, Author, Email
FROM Book, Author
WHERE Author = Name
```

Two things are different here. First, I left off the ORDER BY clause. No big deal — that just means the data won't be sorted. Next, you notice that the WHERE clause is the place where I actually *joined* the tables. Author is the column in the Book table and Name is the column in the Author table. Where they match, the data goes together.

Creating Databases and Tables in Microsoft Access

• •

In This Appendix

▶ Surveying databases, tables, columns, and rows

▶ Creating a database and a table

▶ Entering records of data into a table

▶ Creating an ODBC data source

• •

*M*icrosoft Access is the inexpensive database application development tool of Microsoft that is easy to learn and easy to use. ASP integrates with Access very easily, and for small Internet and intranet sites, it works well. For these reasons I use Microsoft Access in several of the examples throughout this book.

In this appendix, I provide detailed, step-by-step directions showing you how to create a new database, how to create a table, and how to put a few rows of data in that table using Microsoft Access. Even if you've never used Microsoft Access before, you can follow along and discover the basics of using Access.

Creating the Database

To create a new database in Access:

1. **Launch Microsoft Access.**

These instructions are Y2K compliant

The instructions here work for either Access 97 or Access 2000. In Access 2000, the windows look a little different but they work in basically the same way.

---

2. **You see a dialog box asking if you want to create a new database or open an existing one (see Figure C-1).**

3. **Select the radio button labeled Blank Access database and click OK to create a new, blank database.**

4. **The File New Database dialog box appears to find out where you want to save the new database and what you want to name it. You can create a new folder for it, if you want.**

5. **After you find a spot, name the new database. Click the Create button.**

6. **The database window appears with** dbname : Database **in the title bar, where** dbname **is the name you just gave to the database (see Figure C-2). The window has a number of options, including Tables, Queries, Forms, Reports, and so on.**

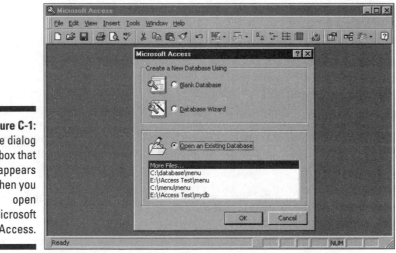

Figure C-1:
The dialog
box that
appears
when you
open
Microsoft
Access.

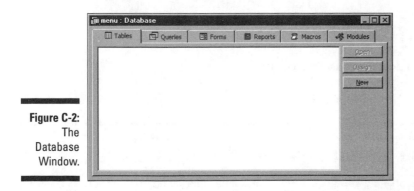

Figure C-2:
The
Database
Window.

Creating a New Table

To create a new table in Access:

1. **Display the database window by either creating a new database (as I discuss in the preceding section) or opening an existing database.**

2. **Choose the Tables option.**

3. **Click the New button.**

    The New Table dialog box appears (see Figure C-3).

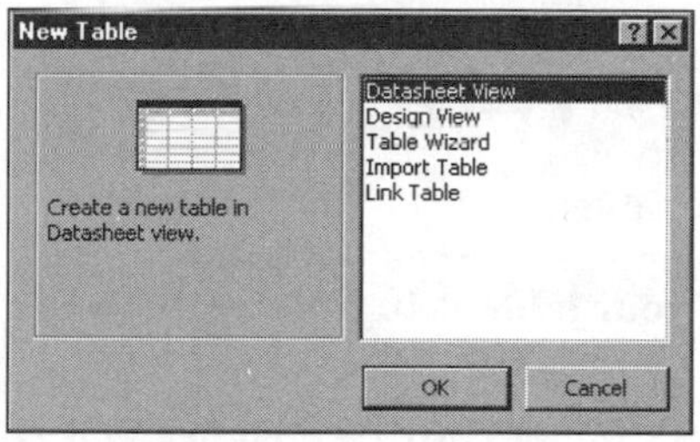

Figure C-3:
The New
Table
dialog box.

4. **Click the Design View item in the list box and click OK.**

5. **The Table window appears (see Figure C-4).**

    You use this window to list the columns you want to be displayed across the top of your table. Although you are entering them as rows here, they appear as columns in the grid when you are ready to enter data, which you do in the next section.

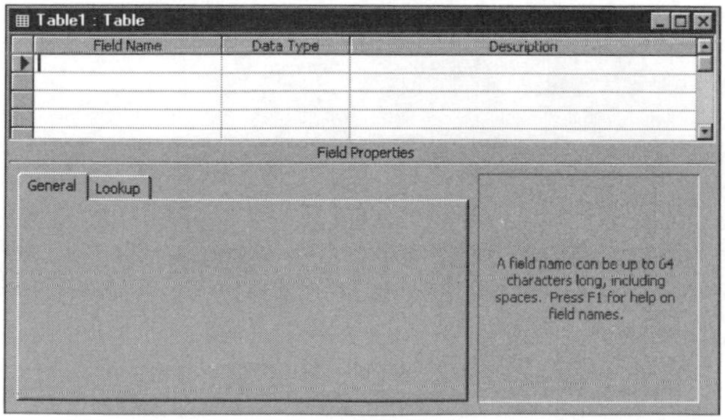

Figure C-4:
The Table
window.

6. **Type the name, data type, and description for each column you want to be included in the table.**

To designate one of the columns as the primary key:

1. **Right-click anywhere in the row where the primary key field is.**
2. **Choose Primary Key from the pop-up menu.**

To save the newly created table:

1. **Choose File⇨Save. A Save As dialog box is displayed.**
2. **Type the table name. Click OK.**

    The table is saved.

Entering Data into the New Table

To enter new rows of data in the table:

1. **After you create and save your table using Design View (as I describe in the preceding section), choose View⇨Datasheet View.**
2. **The Table window changes dramatically (see Figure C-5). The columns are listed along the top, as they should be, and a blank line appears for you to begin entering data.**
3. **Enter as many rows of data as you like.**
4. **Choose File⇨Save.**
5. **Close Microsoft Access.**

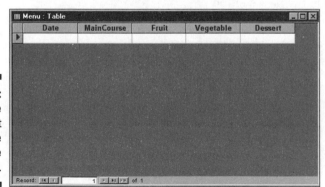

Figure C-5:
The
Datasheet
view of the
Table
window.

Appendix D

Troubleshooting Your ASP Projects

● ●

*A*ctive Server Pages (or ASP) is a very exciting technology. But it can also be very frustrating. You can encounter many pitfalls along the way. In this chapter, I try to help you with some of the common problems and to show you how to fix them or at least work around them.

Getting Set Up

First things first — before you can use ASP, you must have a few basics in place. First, you need a web server that supports ASP. Here is a list of common operating systems and the server that's available for them.

- **Windows 2000 Professional** — Personal Web Services. Comes with the operating system.

- **Windows 2000 Server and above** — Internet Information Server 5.0. Comes with the operating system and fully supports ASP.

- **Windows 95/98** — Personal Web Server (PWS). Available as a download or minimal cost CD-ROM from Microsoft as a part of the NT Option Pack. When you install the NT Option Pack on your machine, it anticipates that you're running Windows 95/98 and installs Personal Web Server.

- **Windows NT Workstation** — Personal Web Services (also PWS). Comes with NT Workstation as the NT Option Pack.

- **Windows NT Server** — Internet Information Server (IIS). Comes with NT Server as the NT Option Pack. If you are using IIS 3.0, you must download and install ASP.EXE from the Microsoft Web site (see the next section for the exact Web address where you can find this file). IIS 3.0 didn't initially come with support for ASP. This module adds that support. IIS 4.0 does come with support for ASP.

But the Server Still Won't Do ASP!

One of the most common complaints after people get started using ASP is that they can't get their server to recognize and execute the ASP code. This problem can come in a variety of ways.

- ✔ "After I go to an ASP page, the browser asks me if I want to download it."

- ✔ "After I go to an ASP page, FrontPage (or Visual InterDev) are automatically launched and bring up the page."

- ✔ "After I go to an ASP page, the page appears in my browser, but when I view source, all the ASP code is still there — it hasn't been stripped out or executed."

All of these problems point to the same issue: The server isn't recognizing and executing the ASP code for some reason. Here are some things to check if you have this problem.

- ✔ Be sure the server is running and that you are receiving the page from the server. You can't simply open an ASP page in the browser and expect it to work. You have to request it from the server and have the server send it to you. This gives the server the chance to execute and extract the ASP script. See "Creating and Testing Your ASP Pages" in Chapter 2 for a suggested setup to easily create, modify and test your pages.

- ✔ Verify the version of your web server. If you are running IIS 3.0 or PWS 1.0, you will need to install ASP.EXE. These web servers didn't initially come with support for ASP. This ASP.EXE file adds that support. You can download ASP.EXE from the Microsoft Web site at:

```
www.microsoft.com/msdownload/iis3/download.asp
```

IIS 4.0 and above, as well as PWS 4.0 and above, come with support for ASP.

- ✔ Be sure that your page is in a virtual directory on the server that allows script execution. To verify this with PWS 4.0 for Windows 95/98, go to the Advanced window, right-click on the folder where your ASP page is, and then choose Properties. Be sure the Read and Scripts checkboxes are checked.

  To verify this with IIS or PWS for Windows 2000 Professional/NT Workstation, open the Internet Service Manager, expand the Default Web Site, right-click on the folder that contains your ASP page, and choose Properties. Under the Virtual Directory tab, verify that the Permissions radio button is on either Script or Execute. You also have ways to set the script execution status directly from FrontPage and Visual InterDev. See the documentation for those tools to find out how.

ASP Executes But I Still Get Errors

In this section, I show you a couple of the problems I've run into and how they're solved. This is, of course, nothing close to an exhaustive list, or even a list of the most common problems. But they are problems I've run into and can help you with.

PROBLEM: After I try to run an ASP application, I get this error (or one like it):

```
Active Server Pages error 'ASP 0134'
Invalid ProgID attribute
/gb/global.asa, line 3
The object has an invalid ProgID of 'MSWC.Counters'
```

SOLUTION: The standard global.asa file, by default, automatically creates several objects for you. This is a convenience designed to make these objects easier to access. Because they are automatically created for you, you can use them as if they were built-in.

However, sometimes these objects cause more trouble than they're worth. In certain applications, these objects cause errors such as the one above. If you simply remove all the lines from the global.asa file, the application will run correctly. This seems to be a bug in how session-level objects are handled.

PROBLEM: I'm trying to create an object and assign it to an application-level variable such as this.

```
Set Application("appdict") =
    Server.CreateObject("Scripting.Dictionary")
```

However, after I run the application, I get this error:

```
Application object error 'ASP 0197 : 80004005'
Disallowed object use /app/default.asp, line 29
Cannot add object with apartment model behavior to
the application intrinsic object.
```

SOLUTION: Without getting into too much detail, objects are usually created with one of two threading models: *apartment threaded* or *both threaded*. These models determine how the objects will run on the server if several people are accessing them at once.

If an object is apartment threaded (like the Dictionary object), you *cannot* use Server.CreateObject to create an *application-level* variable. What you can do is to use the HTML OBJECT tag in the global.asa file to create the application-level object there.

But the HTML OBJECT tag in the global.asa file solution works only if you're running the page on Windows 2000 or Windows NT. If your server is running on Windows 95/98, you'll get errors using this method, too. I know of no good way of creating application-level objects that are apartment threaded with Windows 95/98.

If You're Still Having Problems . . .

I can't possibly cover even a fraction of the problems in this chapter that you may run into. So if you've looked through this chapter and are still having trouble, here are some places you can go for help:

- ✔ The *Active Server Pages For Dummies*, 2nd Edition, Web site Q&A page. I've created this page as an ongoing troubleshooting document. As people e-mail me with problems and solutions that they discover, I post them here to help others. The page is at:

  ```
  www.edgequest.com/VIDFD/QnA.htm
  ```

- ✔ Check out the Microsoft Web site. Microsoft has a particularly good article titled "ASP Troubleshooting Tips and Techniques" at:

  ```
  msdn.microsoft.com/workshop/server/bugzap/tshoot.asp
  ```

- ✔ Another good article on the Microsoft site is called "Ask Tom: Server Q & A" at:

  ```
  msdn.microsoft.com/workshop/server/feature/morqa.asp
  ```

- ✔ Finally, you also want to check out "15 ASP Tips to Improve Performance and Style" at:

  ```
  msdn.microsoft.com/workshop/server/asp/ASPtips.asp
  ```

  Microsoft often changes their site around so by the time you try to get to these pages, they may have moved. If so, just do a search on the site for the article name.

- ✔ Check the other ASP Web sites for articles on the problem that you have. I've listed some of the best in Chapter 15, "The Ten Coolest Web Sites for ASP Developers."

- ✔ Look through all the sources listed in Chapter 14, "The Ten Best Places to Look When You Have a Question."

Appendix E

About the CD

· ·

*H*ere's some of what you can find on the *Active Server Pages For Dummies* CD-ROM:

- ✔ Internet Explorer 5.0, the latest Microsoft Web browser.
- ✔ All the source code from the book, including several ready-to-go applications.
- ✔ Chili!Soft ASP, version 3.0 by ChiliSoft. This add-on allows non-Microsoft Web servers to use Active Server Pages technology.
- ✔ Several interesting third-party server components.

System Requirements

Make sure that your computer meets the minimum system requirements. If your computer doesn't match up to most of these requirements, you may have problems in using the contents of the CD. You must have:

- ✔ A PC with a 486 or faster processor.
- ✔ Microsoft Windows 95 (or later) or Windows NT 4.0 (or later).
- ✔ At least 16MB of total RAM installed on your computer.
- ✔ At least 40MB of hard drive space available to install all the software from this CD. (You'll need less space if you don't install every program.)
- ✔ A CD-ROM drive — double-speed (2x) or faster.
- ✔ A monitor capable of displaying at least 256 colors or grayscale.
- ✔ A modem with a speed of at least 14,400 bps.

If you need more information on the basics, check out *PCs For Dummies,* 5th Edition, by Dan Gookin; *Windows 95 For Dummies,* by Andy Rathbone; or *Windows NT 4 For Dummies,* by Andy Rathbone and Sharon Crawford (all published by IDG Books Worldwide, Inc.).

How to Use the CD

To use this CD-ROM:

1. **Insert the CD into your computer's CD-ROM drive.**

2. **When the light on your CD-ROM drive goes out, double-click the My Computer icon, which is probably in the top-left corner of your desktop.**

3. **Double-click the icon for your CD-ROM drive.**

   Another window opens, showing you all the folders and files on the CD.

Installing the CD software

To install the CD software so that you can use it for your own ASP pages:

1. **Double-click the file called** License.txt.

   This file contains the end-user license that you agree to by using the CD.

2. **Double-click the file called** Readme.txt.

   This file contains instructions about installing the software from this CD.

3. **Double-click the** Default.HTM **file for more information about installing the software.**

   Note: If your browser doesn't support the software installation, follow the steps below:

   - **Double-click the folder for the software you are interested in.**

     The folders are named for the software manufacturers. Be sure to read the descriptions of the programs in this appendix (much of this information also shows up in the Readme file). These descriptions give you more precise information about the programs' folder names and about finding and running the installer program.

   - **Find the file called** Setup.exe, **or** Install.exe, **or something similar, and double-click that file.**

The program's installer walks you through the process of setting up your new software.

What You'll Find on the CD

The software on this CD-ROM comes in two flavors. You can find:

- The source code from the application created in the book
- A set of applications, utilities, and components to help you create your own ASP applications

Source code from the book

Not only are the applications described in this section on the CD-ROM, they're *also* included in the text of the book. Use the CD and the text together and you'll have a great foundation for your ASP pages.

The Guest Book

The Guest Book is a simple guest book application that allows a user to enter his name, age, e-mail address, and so forth. Then the application appends the new entry to a text file that holds information on all the visitors. Another page allows you to list those visitors. **Created:** Chapter 8, "A Guest Book: Creating and Responding to Forms"

A Radio Music to Surf by

This application allows the users who visit your site to select their own favorite style of music to listen to. **Created:** Chapter 8, "A Radio: Music to Surf by"

A Personalized Welcome Page with Cookies

When people sign your Guest Book, why not reward them with a little personal attention? In this application, I build on the Guest Book application created in Chapter 7 and add a Welcome screen that makes use of the information gathered. **Created:** Chapter 8, "A Personalized Welcome Page with Cookies"

Customizing a Page Based on the Date

If you want to attract new people to your Web site and keep them coming back often, you absolutely must keep your site updated on a regular basis. On the other hand, when you're the person who has to keep a site constantly updated, it can be quite a task, especially with a big site. In this application, I write a script that identifies whether the user has visited before and (if so) when. This page also presents one of three different messages depending on whether a certain date is in the future, is today, or is in the past. **Created:** Chapter 8, "Customizing a Page Based on the Date"

Web Site Roulette with Redirect

You may have seen Web site roulette pages before. They allow you to "spin the wheel" and end up at a random Web site. Often the sites you end up at are silly, but sometimes this is a good way to begin browsing and finding sites on topics you never thought to search for. Using ASP pages, a Web Roulette page is easy. First, you need a page to present to users with a link to begin their journey. Then use the Response object's Redirect method to send them on their way. **Created:** Chapter 8, "Web Site Roulette with Redirect"

Menu

This application retrieves information in a database that describes what the cafeteria is planning to serve each day. Several pages are provided, each allowing you to view the information in different ways. I describe the menu application in Chapter 10.

NextLink

These pages demonstrate the NextLink server component that is described in "Linking Your Content" in Chapter 9. They create an online newsletter with a table of contents and easy navigation among the pages.

Listings

This folder contains example listings from several chapters throughout the book. I include them purely to save your fingers from the strain of typing.

The Café

The Café is a complete, real-time chat room. Users sign in and choose a nickname to identify themselves in the room. Then on the main window, the nicknames of all the users appear on a list down the right side of the window. At the top of the window is an edit where users can enter anything they'd like to say and a button to send the text off so that others can see it. Finally, the bottom part of the window shows the running flow of the conversation. **Created:** Chapter 12

Classy Classifieds

A complete solution for offering classified ads on your site. Users can place their own ads in any category they choose. And later, if they need to, they can update or delete the ad. Users can also browse the ads by category or search for specific ads that they are interested in. Then they can respond to an ad via e-mail. **Created:** Chapter 13

Demos, Shareware, and Freeware

The software described in this section is a collection of applications, utilities, and components to create ASP applications. Some of them are complete and free. Others are limited, either in functionality or in usage time and you must pay for the full, commercial release.

Chili!Reports Enterprise Edition by Chili!Soft (trial version)

Chili!Reports helps you design and deliver reports from any ODBC data source through an Internet or intranet Web page. Includes Visual InterDev design-time controls. For more information, go to www.chilisoft.net

Chili!Soft ASP by Chili!Soft (trial version)

This exciting add-on allows non-Microsoft Web servers to use Active Server Pages technology. Available for Netscape's FastTrack and Enterprise, O'Reilly's WebSite, Lotus GO, and others. For more information, go to www.chilisoft.net/ChiliASP/default.htm.

AuthentiX by Flicks Software (trial version)

AuthentiX protects premium content by requiring a user ID and password. This software doesn't use a Windows NT password database; instead, user information is stored in an ODBC database. For more information, see www.flicks.com/flicks/authx.htm

Internet Explorer 5.0 by Microsoft (commercial product)

This is the latest and greatest version of Microsoft's browser. Important for testing to see how your pages will look to the masses! For more information, go to www.microsoft.com.

xSMTP 2.0 and xPop3 2.02 by LightCom Solutions (shareware)

xPop3 enables you to check and retrieve e-mail and xSMTP makes it possible to send new e-mail messages — all from your ASP scripts. For more information, see www.algonet.se/~jekman/components.htm

xBrowser 2.1 by LightCom Solutions (shareware)

xBrowser is a minimal Web browser built as a server component. You can create content on your pages by using the content of pages you access through this browser. For more information, go to www.algonet.se/~jekman/components.htm#xBrowser

Perl for Win32 and PerlScript (GNU software)

If you have experience using the Perl scripting language for doing CGI applications on your Active Server Pages, use these utilities to make your transition a lot smoother. Plug them in to Microsoft's ASP language engine and you can use Perl for all your ASP scripting needs. The use of this program is subject to the terms of the GNU General Public License contained on the CD. For more information, check out www.activestate.com/software/default.htm.

SA-FileUp by Software Artisans, Inc. (evaluation version)

Use of SA-FileUp's easy form allows users to quickly upload files to a web server from their browsers. Follows RFC 1876. Good documentation. Supports Secure Sockets Layer. Seamless integration with Visual InterDev. For more information, see `www.softartisans.com/softaartisans/saf.html`

A$P Charge for Windows NT by BlueSquirrel (trial version)

A$P Charge accepts credit card information for a service (like iBill, CyberCash, and so on) or acts as an interface to ICVerify, which is the software that allows you to accept credit cards yourself (in which case you must have a merchant account with each credit card you accept). Check out `www.bluesquirrel.com/products/asp/asp.html`

PCAuthorize by Tellan Software, Inc. (demo)

With PCAuthorize you can authorize credit transactions. This software supports all major credit card types and does batch transactions, detailed reporting and more. For information, go to `www.tellan.com`

Chart FX Internet Edition 3.5 by Software FX, Inc. (demo)

Chart FX creates fully interactive charts using both client and server-side component technology. Retrieves information using ADO from any ODBC-compliant database to automated data population. For more information, see `www.softwarefx.com/cfxie/default.asp`. See CD for User ID and Password.

If You've Got Problems (Of the CD Kind)

The two likeliest problems are that you don't have enough memory (RAM) for the programs you want to use, or you have other programs running that are affecting installation or running of a program. If you get error messages like `Not enough memory` or `Setup cannot continue`, try one or more of these methods and then try using the software again:

- ✔ Turn off any anti-virus software that you have on your computer. Installers sometimes mimic virus activity and may make your computer incorrectly believe that it is being infected by a virus.

- ✔ Close all running programs. The more programs you're running, the less memory is available to other programs.

- ✔ Have your local computer store add more RAM to your computer. This is, admittedly, a drastic and somewhat expensive step.

If you still have trouble with installing the items from the CD, please call the IDG Books Worldwide Customer Service phone number: 800-762-2974 (outside the U.S.: 317-572-3993).

Index

(continued)

IDG Books Worldwide, Inc., End-User License Agreement

READ THIS. You should carefully read these terms and conditions before opening the software packet(s) included with this book ("Book"). This is a license agreement ("Agreement") between you and IDG Books Worldwide, Inc. ("IDGB"). By opening the accompanying software packet(s), you acknowledge that you have read and accept the following terms and conditions. If you do not agree and do not want to be bound by such terms and conditions, promptly return the Book and the unopened software packet(s) to the place you obtained them for a full refund. This agreement does not apply to every program on the CD. Please consult the About the CD appendix for details.

1. **License Grant.** IDGB grants to you (either an individual or entity) a nonexclusive license to use one copy of the enclosed software program(s) (collectively, the "Software") solely for your own personal or business purposes on a single computer (whether a standard computer or a workstation component of a multiuser network). The Software is in use on a computer when it is loaded into temporary memory (RAM) or installed into permanent memory (hard disk, CD-ROM, or other storage device). IDGB reserves all rights not expressly granted herein.

2. **Ownership.** IDGB is the owner of all right, title, and interest, including copyright, in and to the compilation of the Software recorded on the disk(s) or CD-ROM ("Software Media"). Copyright to the individual programs recorded on the Software Media is owned by the author or other authorized copyright owner of each program. Ownership of the Software and all proprietary rights relating thereto remain with IDGB and its licensers.

3. **Restrictions on Use and Transfer.**

   (a) You may only (i) make one copy of the Software for backup or archival purposes, or (ii) transfer the Software to a single hard disk, provided that you keep the original for backup or archival purposes. You may not (i) rent or lease the Software, (ii) copy or reproduce the Software through a LAN or other network system or through any computer subscriber system or bulletin-board system, or (iii) modify, adapt, or create derivative works based on the Software.

   (b) You may not reverse engineer, decompile, or disassemble the Software. You may transfer the Software and user documentation on a permanent basis, provided that the transferee agrees to accept the terms and conditions of this Agreement and you retain no copies. If the Software is an update or has been updated, any transfer must include the most recent update and all prior versions.

4. **Restrictions on Use of Individual Programs.** You must follow the individual requirements and restrictions detailed for each individual program in Appendix E of this Book. These limitations are also contained in the individual license agreements recorded on the Software Media. These limitations may include a requirement that after using the program for a specified period of time, the user must pay a registration fee or discontinue use. By opening the Software packet(s), you will be agreeing to abide by the licenses and restrictions for these individual programs that are detailed in Appendix E and on the Software Media. None of the material on this Software Media or listed in this Book may ever be redistributed, in original or modified form, for commercial purposes.

5. **Limited Warranty.**

   (a) IDGB warrants that the Software and Software Media are free from defects in materials and workmanship under normal use for a period of sixty (60) days from the date of purchase of this Book. If IDGB receives notification within the warranty period of defects in materials or workmanship, IDGB will replace the defective Software Media.

   (b) **IDGB AND THE AUTHOR OF THE BOOK DISCLAIM ALL OTHER WARRANTIES, EXPRESS OR IMPLIED, INCLUDING WITHOUT LIMITATION IMPLIED WARRANTIES OF MERCHANTABILITY AND FITNESS FOR A PARTICULAR PURPOSE, WITH RESPECT TO THE SOFTWARE, THE PROGRAMS, THE SOURCE CODE CONTAINED THEREIN, AND/OR THE TECHNIQUES DESCRIBED IN THIS BOOK. IDGB DOES NOT WARRANT THAT THE FUNCTIONS CONTAINED IN THE SOFTWARE WILL MEET YOUR REQUIREMENTS OR THAT THE OPERATION OF THE SOFTWARE WILL BE ERROR FREE.**

   (c) This limited warranty gives you specific legal rights, and you may have other rights that vary from jurisdiction to jurisdiction.

6. **Remedies.**

   (a) IDGB's entire liability and your exclusive remedy for defects in materials and workmanship shall be limited to replacement of the Software Media, which may be returned to IDGB with a copy of your receipt at the following address: Software Media Fulfillment Department, Attn.: *Active Server Pages For Dummies,* 2nd Edition IDG Books Worldwide, Inc., 10475 Crosspoint Blvd, Indianapolis, IN 46256, or call 800-762-2974. Please allow three to four weeks for delivery. This Limited Warranty is void if failure of the Software Media has resulted from accident, abuse, or misapplication. Any replacement Software Media will be warranted for the remainder of the original warranty period or thirty (30) days, whichever is longer.

   (b) In no event shall IDGB or the author be liable for any damages whatsoever (including without limitation damages for loss of business profits, business interruption, loss of business information, or any other pecuniary loss) arising from the use of or inability to use the Book or the Software, even if IDGB has been advised of the possibility of such damages.

   (c) Because some jurisdictions do not allow the exclusion or limitation of liability for consequential or incidental damages, the above limitation or exclusion may not apply to you.

7. **U.S. Government Restricted Rights.** Use, duplication, or disclosure of the Software by the U.S. Government is subject to restrictions stated in paragraph (c)(1)(ii) of the Rights in Technical Data and Computer Software clause of DFARS 252.227-7013, and in subparagraphs (a) through (d) of the Commercial Computer–Restricted Rights clause at FAR 52.227-19, and in similar clauses in the NASA FAR supplement, when applicable.

8. **General.** This Agreement constitutes the entire understanding of the parties and revokes and supersedes all prior agreements, oral or written, between them and may not be modified or amended except in a writing signed by both parties hereto that specifically refers to this Agreement. This Agreement shall take precedence over any other documents that may be in conflict herewith. If any one or more provisions contained in this Agreement are held by any court or tribunal to be invalid, illegal, or otherwise unenforceable, each and every other provision shall remain in full force and effect.